AF396479

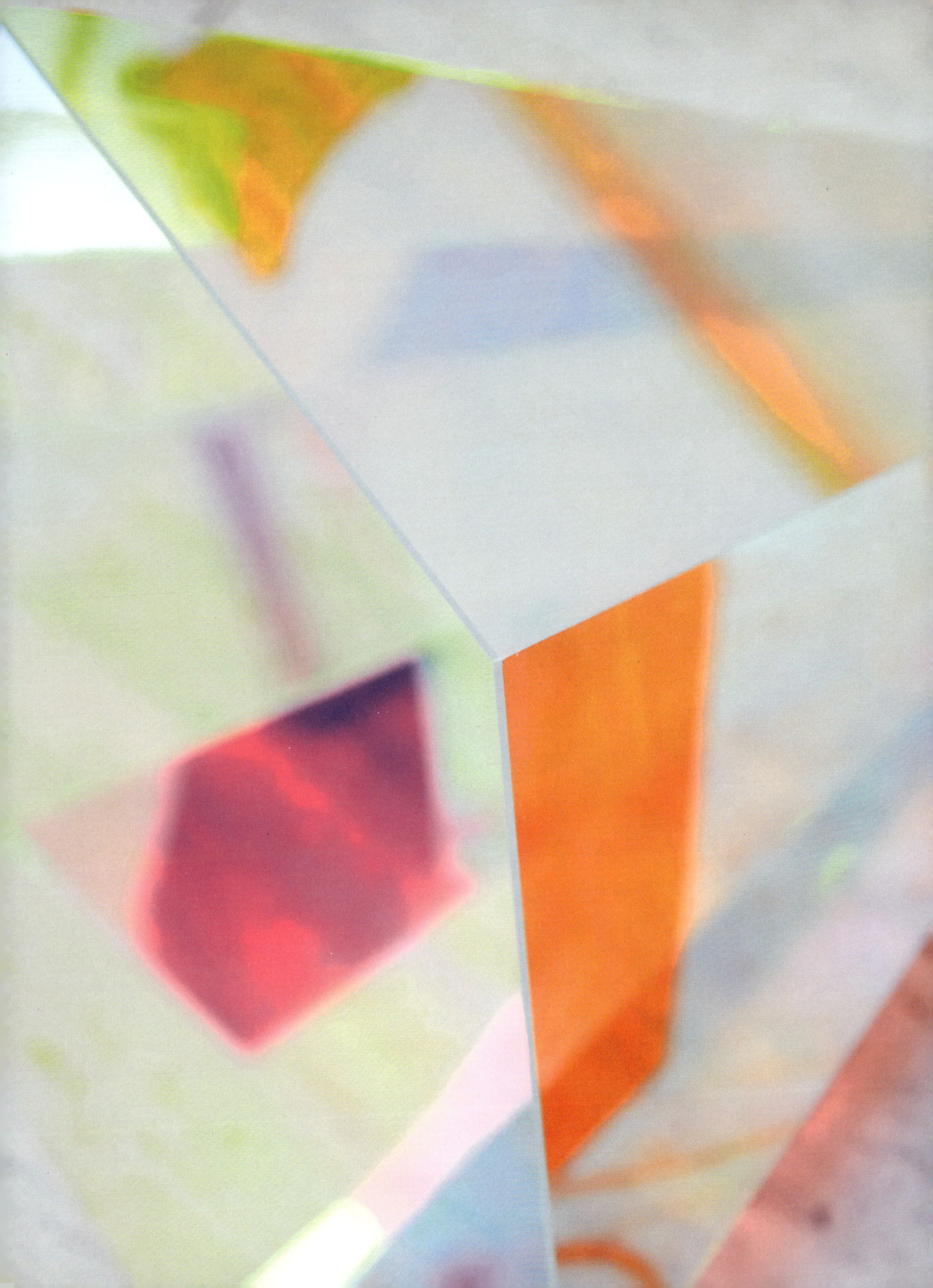

Mikala Dwyer

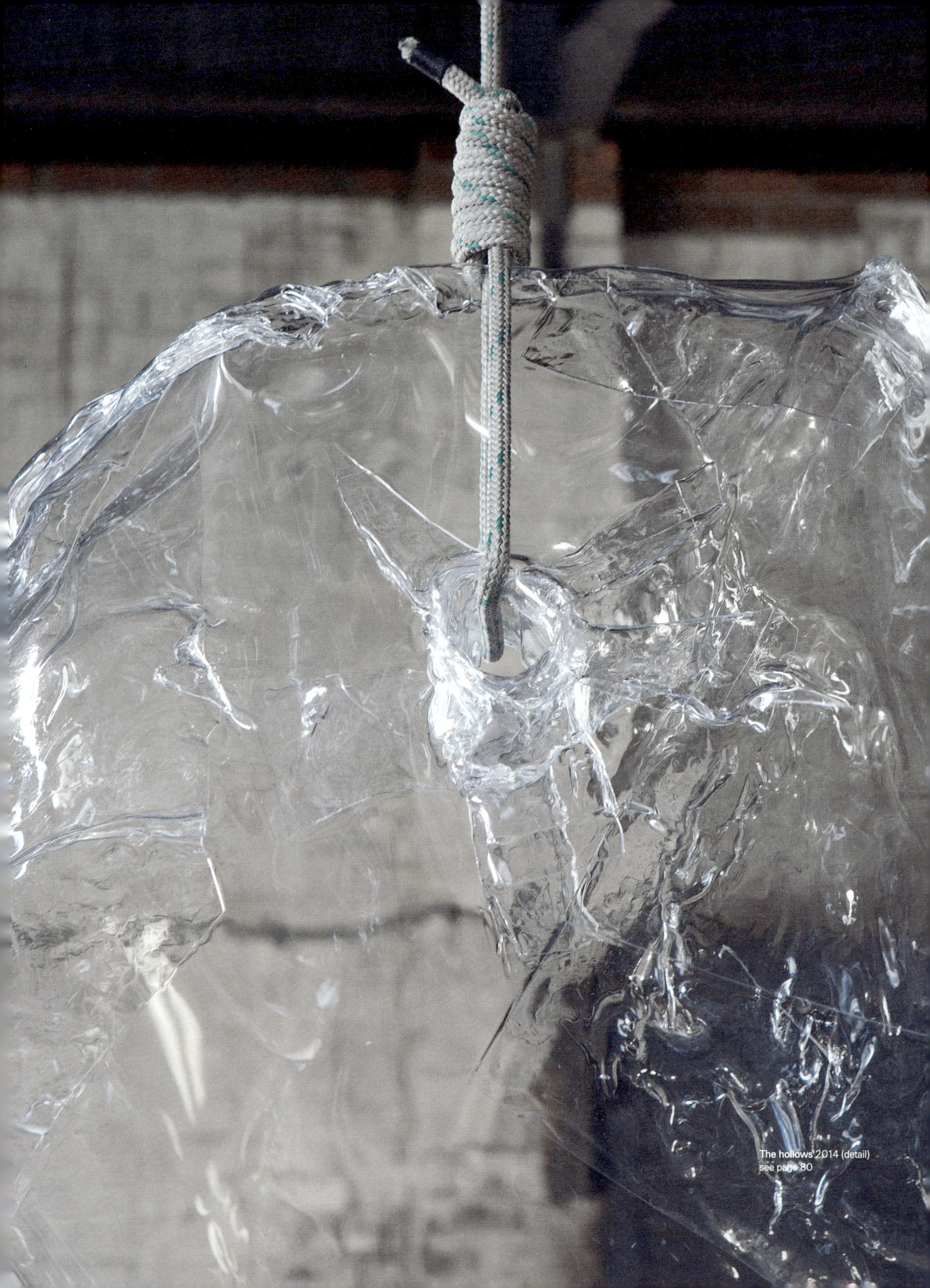

The hollows 2014 (detail)
see page 80

Mikala Dwyer

A shape of thought

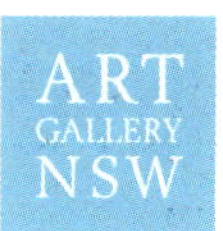

Wayne Tunnicliffe
with Susan Best and Helen Hughes

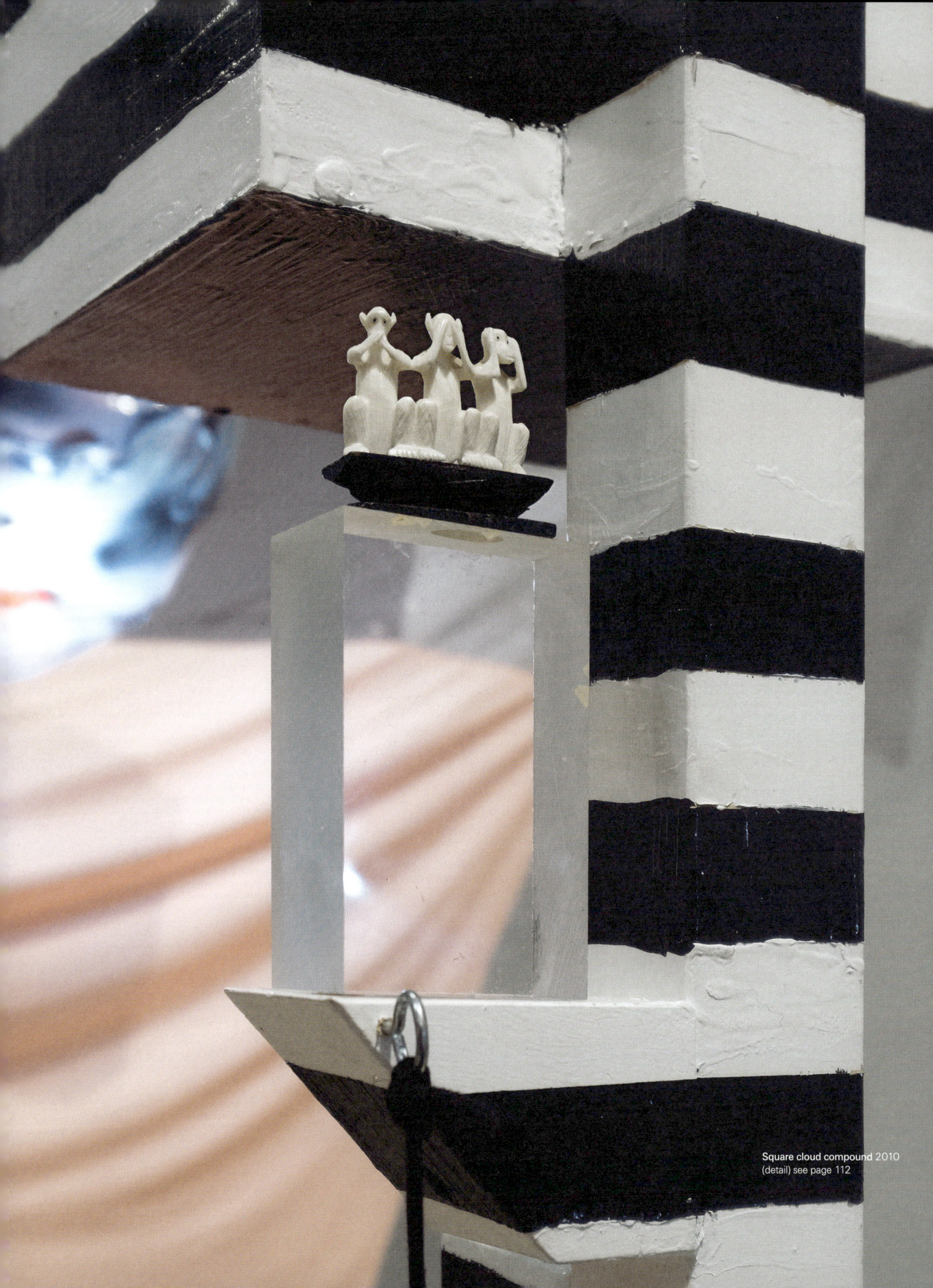

Square cloud compound 2010
(detail) see page 112

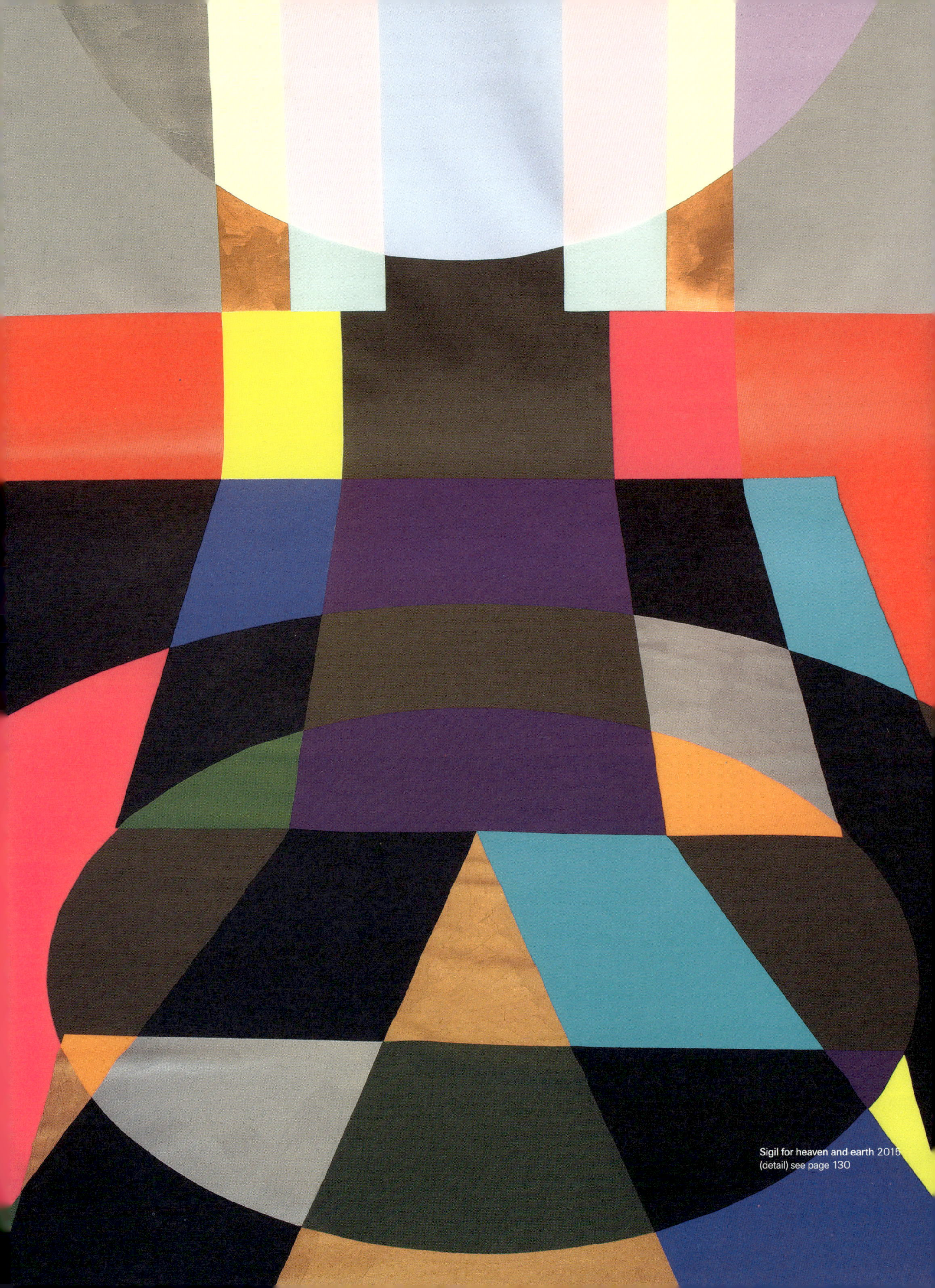

Sigil for heaven and earth 2015
(detail) see page 130

Mikala Dwyer: a shape of thought is the first in a new series of books by the Art Gallery of New South Wales on contemporary Australian artists. I believe it is an essential part of our role as a public art museum to support living artists and their art by making their work available to the widest possible audience through collecting, exhibiting, researching and publishing – as we have done since we were founded in 1871 and our first art acquisitions were made soon after from living Australian artists.

Mikala Dwyer first exhibited at the Gallery as part of **Australian perspecta** 1993 when her work memorably dressed the vestibule columns in gaudy sequin fabric and covered the floor in rubber bath mats. Since then, Dwyer has developed an exceptional sculptural practice which is always unexpected and mind-expanding. Her highly original visual language explores ideas about shelter, childhood play, modernist design and the relationship between people and objects. There is an underlying feminist perspective woven through her choice of materials and forms; her work cannot help but alter our experience of the everyday world around us.

As we approach twenty-five years since Dwyer first exhibited at the Art Gallery of New South Wales, it is entirely fitting that we mark her contribution to art in Australia with both a new exhibition and a new publication. This book is conceived as a survey of Dwyer's practice since she came to prominence in the early 1990s. Wayne Tunnicliffe, our head curator of Australian art, has written an essay exploring the development of Dwyer's practice over this time and with a focus on her ambitious recent work. Dr Helen Hughes, research curator at the Monash University Museum of Art, has written on the impact of Dwyer's parents on her art, particularly Dorothy Dwyer's work as a modernist silversmith and jeweller. Dr Susan Best, professor of art theory and deputy director at the Queensland College of Art, Griffith University, writes on Dwyer's recent engagement with Christian religious iconography, which is also a return to Dwyer's formative years. Mikala Dwyer's own words in an extensive interview are particularly enlightening about her motivations and methodologies, as well as recounting how she came to be an artist in the 1980s.

Mikala Dwyer continues an anti-classical trajectory in art that can be aligned with such diverse movements as dada, surrealism and anti-form art. Her objects and installations are exuberant, playful and provocative, re-imagining familiar materials and what they say to us about the world in which we live. Beguiling in their colour and profusion, they haunt us long after we encounter them as the ideas they embody unfold over time. This book is an illuminating journey through the art and life of one of Australia's most richly inventive artists, and, as such, is a significant contribution by the Gallery to research and publishing on Australian art.

Michael Brand
Director
Art Gallery of New South Wales

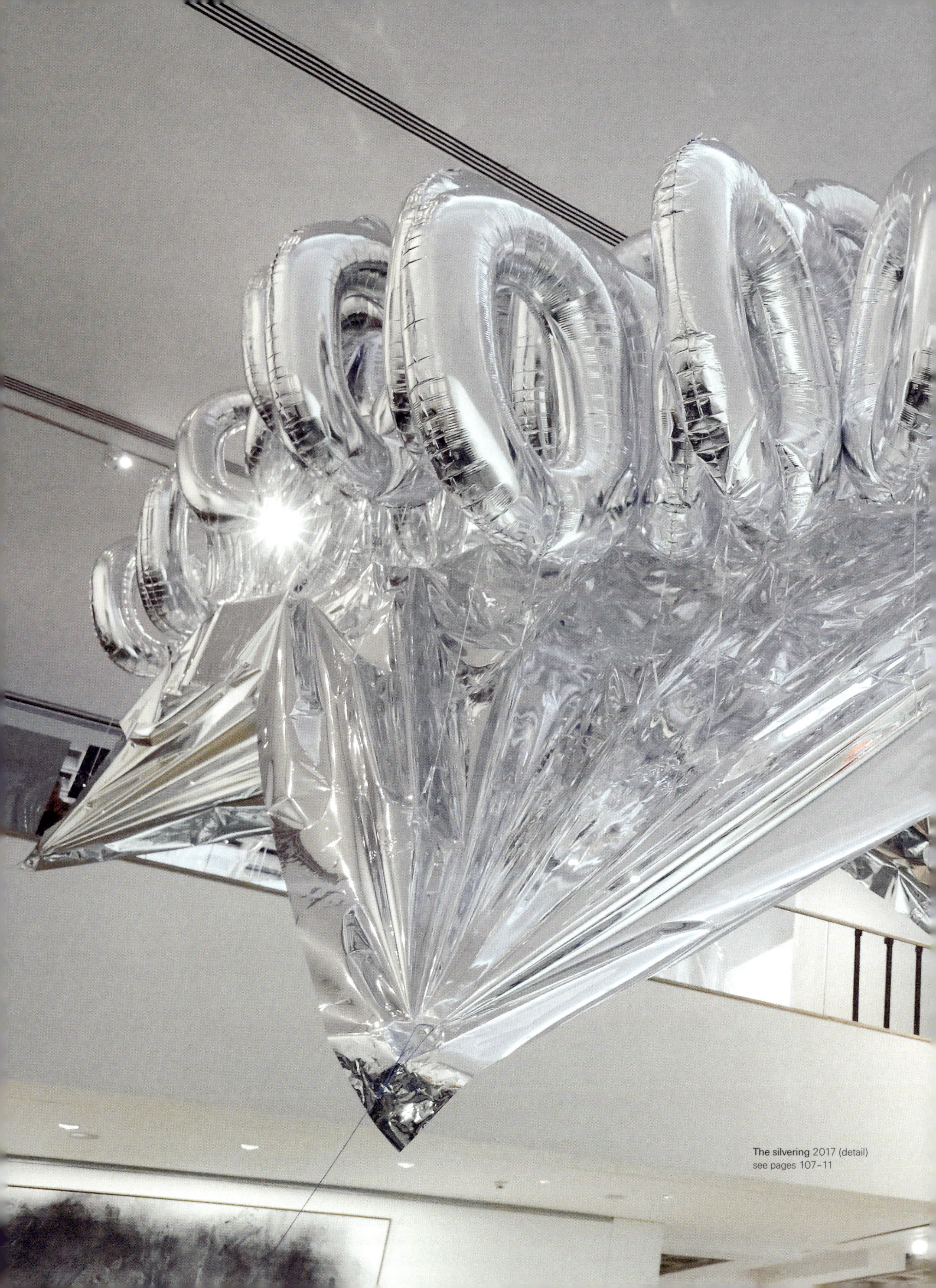

The silvering 2017 (detail)
see pages 107–11

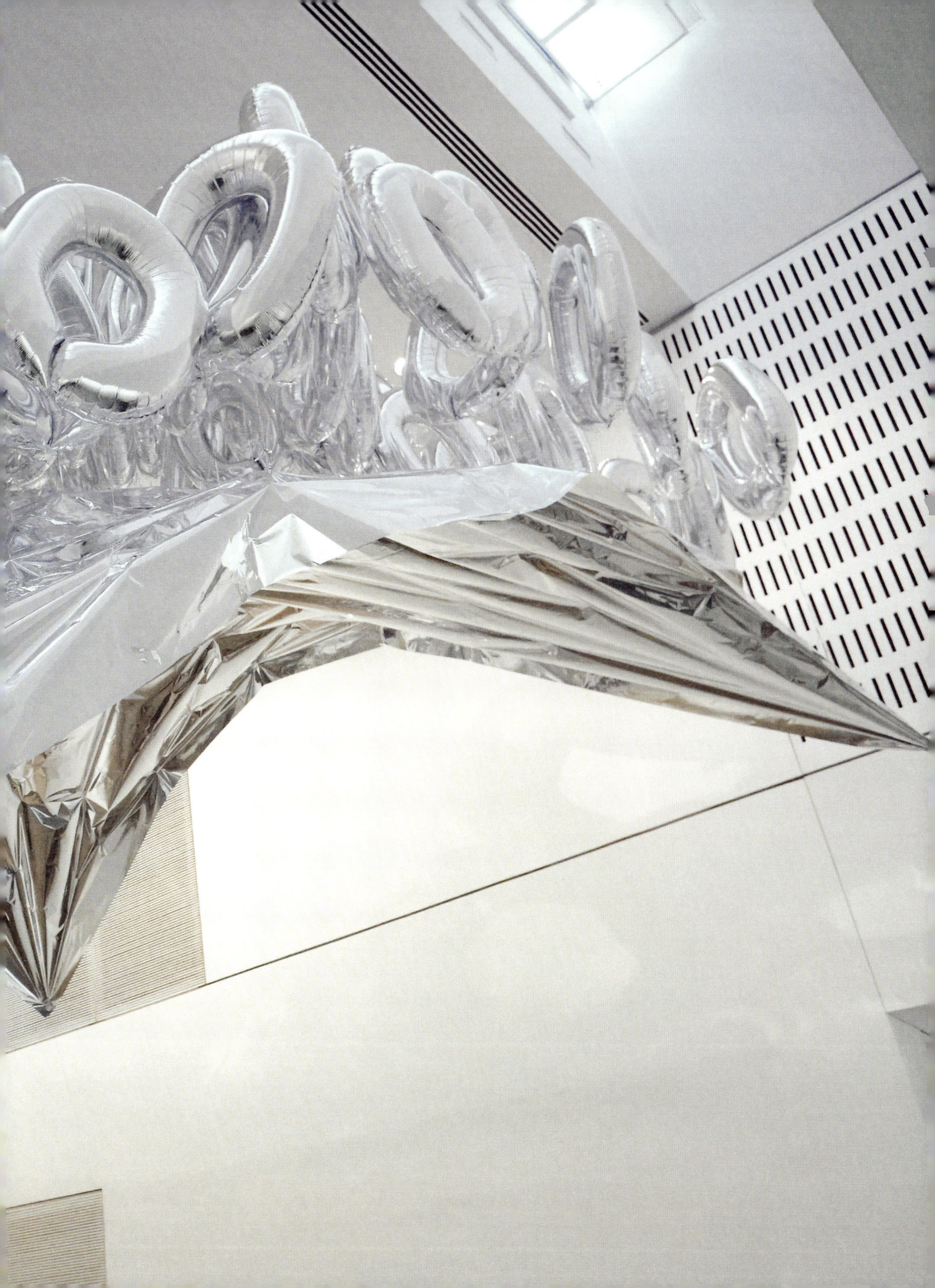

Mikala Dwyer

Wayne
Tunnicliffe

A shape
of thought

Mikala Dwyer's richly inventive sculptural practice is marked by a receptiveness to the physical properties of materials and the matrix of meanings that gather around them. Dwyer has written of the importance to her of the 'consciousness and liveliness of matter, and the animation of matter and objects', and an attentive response to the substance of our world has driven her practice for more than thirty years.[1] Her work is expansive, engaging and even excessive as it embodies ideas in a panoply of forms and the spaces these forms occupy. Dwyer's agency in making is paired with a cultural medium's capacity to channel unexpected meanings from everyday objects, and her works almost always combine the found with the made. She is deeply attuned to how materials affect us both overtly and at a subconscious level and her art haunts our imagination and our psyche long after we encounter it. Dwyer's adventurous exploration of the relationship between objects, and between objects and us, means she has also not resiled from engaging with the irrational and the suppressed, with animism and even the occult, thereby continuing an anti-classical trajectory in art that can be aligned with such diverse movements as gothic, dada, surrealism and anti-form, as well as more recent aberrant practices.

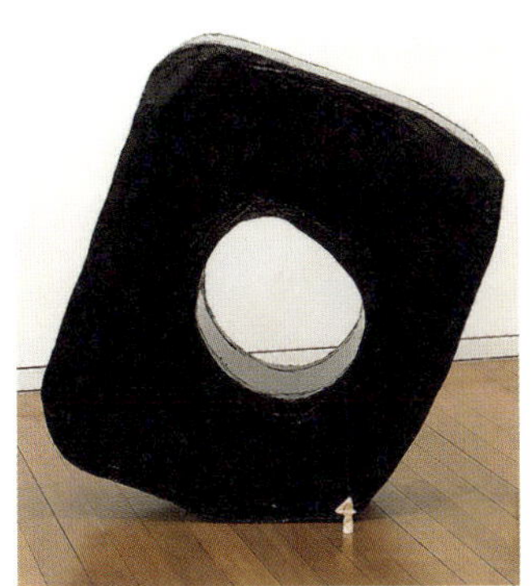

Dwyer makes her artworks for the locations they inhabit, and the interplay of object, space and architecture is vital to the experience of her work. The relationship between these elements is often porous, with boundaries blurring and distinctions between audience and art becoming unclear as her exuberant works spill over into what we may think of as our space. This lack of restraint is another characteristic of Dwyer's practice, which is the opposite of the kind of formal good taste defined by careful balance, distilled shapes and harmonious colours. Further clues to the relationship between object and subject in her work, and the fact that she never just presents form for form's sake, can be found in Dwyer's consideration of things as ideas:

> I look at all things in the world as kind of 'cooled ideas', as 'thinking' that has slowed down or cooled into forms: whether it be a building, or a chair, a road, or a plan of a city, a toy or a playground. Or fashion. It's all an idea or thinking at some point. That's where the materiality comes from.[2]

Dwyer's use of 'cooled ideas' to think through matter and meaning has resulted in an art practice that is cumulative and iterative, and that includes its own history as a generative tool. Previous works are recycled into new works as they evolve into new spaces and new exhibitions, and entirely new works may be made while retaining titles and key forms from the past. The distinctive elements of Dwyer's sculptural practice were apparent from when she began exhibiting after graduating from Sydney College of the Arts in 1983, including in artist-run spaces in London where she lived for a short time before returning to Sydney in 1987. From 1989 onwards her work was curated into group exhibitions in the more experimental public art galleries in Sydney and Canberra. In the early 1990s her use of everyday and even trashy materials that carry a freight of meaning – cigarette butts and bandaids, cheap sequin fabric, nail polish and stockings – and her transformation of exhibition spaces with everything from small gestures to whole-room installations, was quickly picked up in institutional exhibitions. Dwyer's free-flowing, inventive and hard-to-pin-down work connected with a post-recession zeitgeist for the provisional, disruptive and unexpected.[3]

In the early 1990s Dwyer's work was notably curated into two institutional surveys of new Australian art in Sydney: the inaugural **Primavera** exhibition at the recently opened Museum of Contemporary Art in 1992 and the high-profile **Australian perspecta** 1993 at the Art Gallery of New South Wales. For **Primavera**, Dwyer stencilled Beatrix Potter-inspired bunnies on painted walls in a room environment filled with a plethora of objects as diverse as satellite dishes and planks of wood wrapped and bound in blankets, bandaids and other materials. The verticals in the room were often swaddled as if ready to lie down for sleep or even burial, while the horizontal

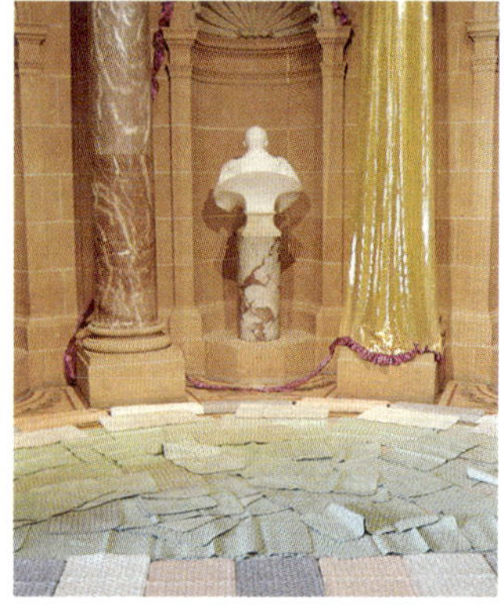

elements were provided with props and supports which meant they 'were stood up to attention' in this somewhat sinister version of a child's nursery.[4] For **Perspecta**, Dwyer transformed the Art Gallery of New South Wales's grand neo-classical vestibule through another form of swaddling: wrapping the marble columns in glitzy sequin fabric; covering the dark leather seating in purple, orange and yellow material; and strewing the floor in rubber non-stick bath mats. It was both camp and domestic, a make-do local drag reprise of international artist Christo's high-profile white monochrome wrap of the vestibule in 1990.[5] Both projects sought to highlight the latent ideologies of institutional spaces through this act of veiling, although Christo's more high-minded approach was counterpoised by Dwyer's creation of a 'kind of hybrid space by introducing signifiers of other rooms, for example: the bathroom, disco and gym – sweat, shit and sex'.[6]

Dwyer's inclusion in these prominent survey exhibitions brought considerable curatorial and critical attention to her work, and to that of a cluster of her Sydney contemporaries who were being grouped together at the time by curators and critics. This new wave of artists was associated with the artist-run Firstdraft Gallery and the CBD Gallery (directed by David Thomas) and included Hany Armanious, Adam Cullen, Tony Schwensen and Justene Williams. All were using modest everyday materials to make provisional artworks that avoided the more grandiose manifestations of postmodern art from the previous decade and were shown in exhibitions with titles such as **Rad scunge**, **Shirthead** and **Monster field**.[7] In an article in *Art + Text* magazine in 1993 Jeff Gibson described their work as 'avant-grunge' and drew connections between it and Seattle-based indie rock music and the idea of generational disenfranchisement embodied in Douglas Coupland's 1991 book *Generation X: tales for an accelerated culture*.[8] 'Avant-grunge' was a catchy name for their practices, but most of the artists grouped under this rubric were opposed to the label as it was inevitably reductive in framing their work and ignored their formal and conceptual differences as well as their often quite specific local cultural references.

opposite:
woops 1994 (detail)
see page 39

Vestibule (for Jed) 1993 (detail)
see page 36

opposite:
The silvering 2017
see pages 107–11

Although Dwyer's work and that of her contemporaries marked a strong break with the more theory-dependent practices associated with postmodernism, their immediate precursors in Australia included the unfiltered household materials used by some artists in the 1980s, such as Jenny Watson's paintings on hessian with collaged elements, and the 'junk 'n' funk' aesthetic of the Annandale Imitation Realists who worked with found urban detritus in the early

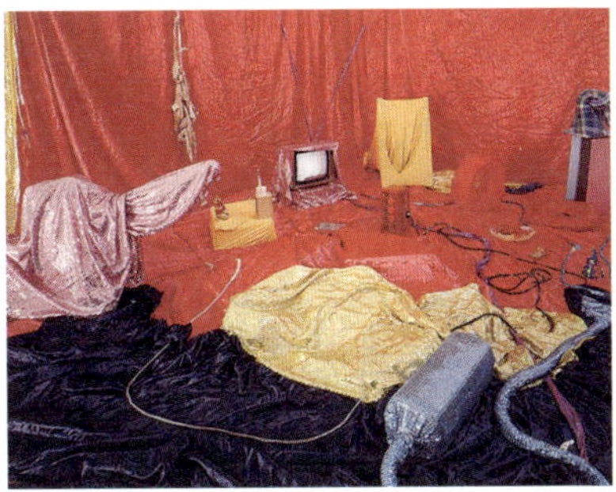

1960s.[9] Their international antecedents include arte povera (literally 'poor art'), some aspects of pop art such as Claes Oldenburg's food sculptures, and the more eccentric sculptural practices that arose concurrently with industrial minimalism in the 1960s in the work of artists such as Robert Morris. Dwyer's use of fabric, nail varnish and pantyhose was also associated with a feminist materiality, one that referenced an absent body and a latent rather than overt politics, and with Eva Hesse and Louise Bourgeois among other highly individual practitioners.[10] Robert Morris's 1968 definition of anti-form in art remains relevant to Dwyer's work in its emphasis on gravity as being as important as space in constituting the art object, and in its acceptance of chance and indeterminacy as part of the process of making art.[11] However, Dwyer's approach is more wilful than Morris's: empathy, chance and gravity play a part in her working process, alongside the considered manipulation of materials.

Since these first major exhibitions in the early 1990s, Dwyer's practice has been characterised by remarkable invention. While her work often takes on new forms, her aesthetic parameters have been consistent and she has expanded on earlier elements and antecedents as her knowledge of both has deepened. Gravity and artistic precursors come together in works such as **The silvering** 2010–17, whose levitating silver mylar forms recall Andy

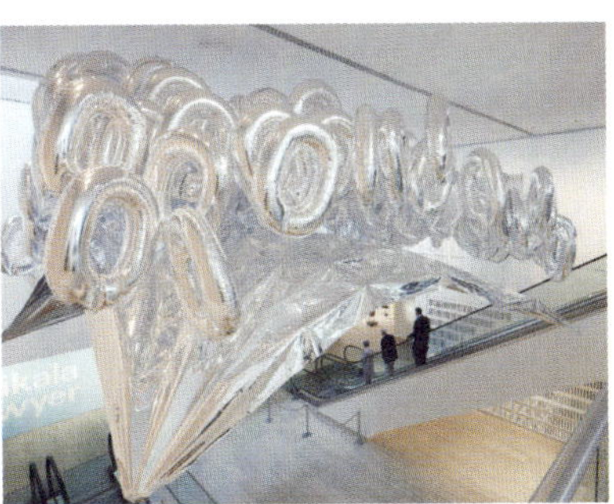

Warhol's floating **Silver clouds** 1966 as well as the shiny space-age aesthetic of 1960s fashion and film design.[12] **The silvering** was first shown in Berlin in 2010 and has subsequently been remade in Melbourne, Brisbane, Dublin, Berlin (again), Paris and now in Sydney. In its second showing in Berlin in 2013 its connection to pop was made evident when it was installed in a room at the Hamburger Bahnhof containing major Warhol paintings from the 1960s and 1970s.[13] Each presentation of the work is a new iteration owing to the short lifespan of its materials and because it is adapted to the specific dimensions of the space in which it is displayed.

The silver 'O' forms that comprise **The silvering** connect with Dwyer's use of circular forms since the early 1990s and her exploration of the space they describe as inside and outside – with all the psychological connotations of insider and outsider, belonging and not belonging. Dwyer has progressed in that time from including circular objects in larger installations to the installations themselves assuming a circular form. Circles have appeared in many of her works: in the blanket-swaddled satellite dishes of her **Untitled** 1992 **Primavera** work; the sequin-fabric-wrapped forms in **woops** 1994; the 'O' in the **I.O.U.** works of 1996 onwards, with their suggestion of a one-sided cultural pact between the artwork and audience; the circular cut-out in the hovering magic carpet platform in **Recent old work** 1996, which echoed elements of the gallery space in which it was installed; the essentially circular arrangement of **Olloodoo** 1998, a collaboration between the artist and her

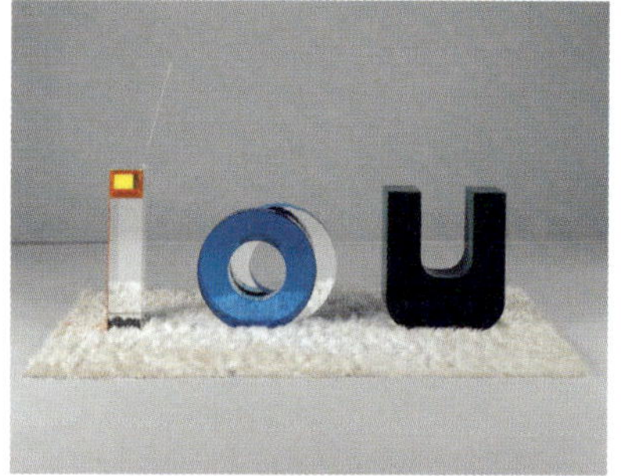

daughter Olive; in the cylindrical PVC pipes that form the brightly coloured contingent townscape in **Iffytown** 1999; in the ocular- and target-like inclusions on the baggy vinyl **Hanging eyes** works of 1999 and 2000; and in the circular gatherings of disparate sculptural elements in what is known as **The additions and the subtractions** series begun in 2007.[14]

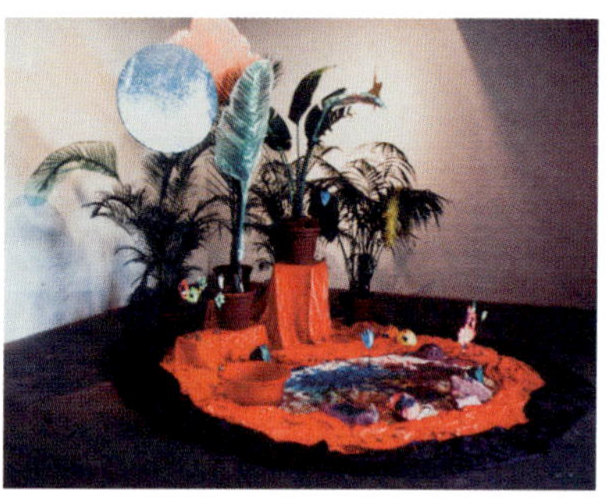

Hovering and rustling, crinkling and shimmering, bumping together in the gentle eddies of the air-conditioned room, Dwyer's levitating silver balloons are leashed to a silver sheet that is in turn tethered to both the gallery's architecture and to handcrafted clay base anchors to prevent them drifting off into other artworks or escaping out the gallery's front door. The 'O's are quite a gathering; in fact, there were more than 150 balloons in the work's latest manifestation, of the type that usually spell out names or numbers for birthday parties or special anniversaries. Their shiny reflective surfaces suggest a party modality or event status, although displaced from their usual context they are more than a little poignant: have we missed the party or has it not yet begun? Either way, in occupying the gallery air space (usually untouched by art) and reflecting us in their rustling forms, the balloons make us aware of the gravitational pull of our own bodies; evoke the childhood pleasure and pain involved in the conflict of holding onto a balloon or letting it float away (or, worst of all, accidentally popping it); and suggest the ultimate endgame that is the zero that awaits us all at the end of our lives.[15] This latter meaning is particularly relevant for Dwyer as she is interested in materialising the immaterial and the zeros that comprise this work suggest the 'void' – a concept of emptiness or nothingness at the heart of our universe that has preoccupied many philosophers and artists. In using helium, Dwyer calls on its nature as a key constitutive component of the universe, as well as using its levitational abilities to set her sculpture temporarily free from the bounds of gravity that govern us all.

A tussle with gravity is also a constitutive part of **Square cloud compound** 2010, one of Dwyer's most significant works of recent years and which again riffs on forms that have appeared previously in her practice.[16] While **The silvering** levitates in the gallery's air space, **Square cloud compound** combats gravity by being stretched taut and lashed to the structure of the gallery itself. This exuberant arrangement of colourful cubic shapes is held aloft by stockings tied to the walls and ceiling, and anchored by a series of

opposite:
Hanging eyes 2 2000
vinyl, plastic, synthetic polymer paint on canvas, synthetic fur, felt, steel eyelets
National Gallery of Victoria, Melbourne, purchased through the NGV Foundation with the assistance of the Rudy Komon Fund, Governor, 2001

I.O.U. 1997–98
transparent and opaque synthetic polymer resin, synthetic fur, mirror, television
National Gallery of Victoria, Melbourne, presented through the NGV Foundation by Peter Fay, Fellow, 2002

Olloodoo 1998
collaboration with Olive Corben Dwyer
palm trees, rocks, fabric, paint, paper, wood, polystyrene
installed in *Beauty 2000*, 2 July – 1 August 1998, Institute of Modern Art, Brisbane

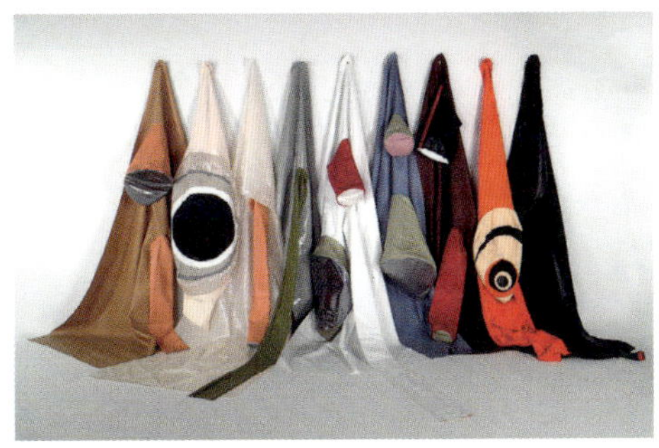

lamps that demarcate the perimeter of the space. The fabric cubes have a lineage in Dwyer's work, from her soft renditions of formalist sculpture and painting, such as her two drooping vinyl works with protruding American mid-century abstraction-like targets, **Hanging eyes** 1999 and **Hanging eyes 2** 2000, and her minimal fabric wall-work **Untitled** 1995.[17] **Untitled** is one of a small group of works made from shimmering organza fabric sewn and pinned into the shape of the fundamental structuring forms of geometry and sculpture: cubes, cones and triangular prisms. Pinned to the gallery wall, they are glamorous, transparent and beguiling – characteristics not usually associated with the aesthetic of minimalist sculpture. Dwyer subjects hard-edge and geometric precursors to softness, drooping, colour and – quite literally – frayed edges. These works have been discussed as a feminising of masculine hard-edge formalism, although this leaves the gendered association of hard/male and soft/female intact, while Dwyer has spoken of them as questioning the logic of geometry and, by extension, logic itself: '[formal geometry]. It's a given. Everything's built on those premises and it's the shape of logic. I started questioning: whose logic? What does logic look like? What's the shape of my logic? And trying to understand why everything's built on those kind of things.'[18]

Dwyer has scaled up this alternative fabric geometry in **Square cloud compound**, with some forms more successfully taut and squarish than others, which sag down into the overall space of the work. The distinctive stocking tethers have been present in Dwyer's practice since the early 1990s in works such as **Untitled** 1993 (exhibited in **Shirthead**), and in two of Dwyer's impressive solo exhibitions at Sarah Cottier Gallery's first incarnation in Sydney's Newtown, **woops** 1994 and **Hollow-ware & a few solids** 1995.[19] In both exhibitions the stockings had an anchoring function; stretched taut with legs pulled from crotches in different directions, they had a resourceful fit-for-purpose capability as sculptural components while as gendered clothing items they were quite fetishistic. The deviant sexuality of the splayed legs was undercut by the humour of seeing stockings put into sculptural service like this. The absent body inferred by the stockings is echoed in the sentinel-like lampposts that surround **Square cloud compound**, which also have a sense of being human stand-ins, guarding as well as demarcating the perimeter of the installation. The addition of right-angled armatures to these totems gives them an air of being jolly sets of gallows, reinforced by the prison stripes with which some of them are painted. They are self-contained sculptural ecosystems, for as well as carrying light fittings that help illuminate the sculpture, they support miniature cubbyhouse-like nest boxes, are adorned by suspended mobiles and other objects, and are inhabited by china and glass ornaments like so many offerings to the square cloud spirits.

Square cloud compound developed from a residency Dwyer undertook on Cockatoo Island in Sydney Harbour in 2010 and responds to the specific sites and histories of this evocative location. Cockatoo Island figures large in Sydney's colonial past. The site was initially used as a convict prison surrounded by a shark-inhabited harbour, and then as a reform school for young 'wayward' women and, concurrently, one of Australia's most important shipyards. While Dwyer produced works that connected closely to the history of Cockatoo Island, **Square cloud compound** takes a more lateral approach to this place.[20] The delightful absurdist title of the work suggests both containment (compound) and dreams of escape (clouds as a metaphor for reverie and freedom) – although the impossibility of square clouds anchors it to the realm of thwarted desires (the imprisoned). While Dwyer's work has often been discussed in the context of provisional children's play structures, such as cubbyhouses, the analogy of the architecture of **Square cloud compound** can be extended to the artist's studio itself. In re-creating the work each time it is exhibited, the artist turns the gallery into a form of studio, a zone both safe and confronting as making and creating unfold with all their triumphs and anxieties. Dwyer's installation offers escape and containment, comfort and confrontation, as its wonderful excess spills over into our space and engages our desire to inhabit its beguiling dream-encouraging shelter while its sentinel lampposts and the gallery's guards balance this through monitoring our interaction.

The improbable title, **Square cloud compound**, is testament to irrationalism as a working methodology in Dwyer's practice, particularly her interest in the occult, supernatural and paranormal. These 'others' to the scientific and philosophical enlightenment erupted into the popular imagination in the nineteenth century when seances, ouija boards, ectoplasm, ghostly manifestations and fairies at the bottom of the garden vied for attention and for pseudo-scientific proof of existence. Combined with a dadaist interest in absurdism evident in the accumulations and excesses of **Square cloud compound** and its related performance videos, a genealogy of cultural otherness and outsider art informs Dwyer's practice, including her interest

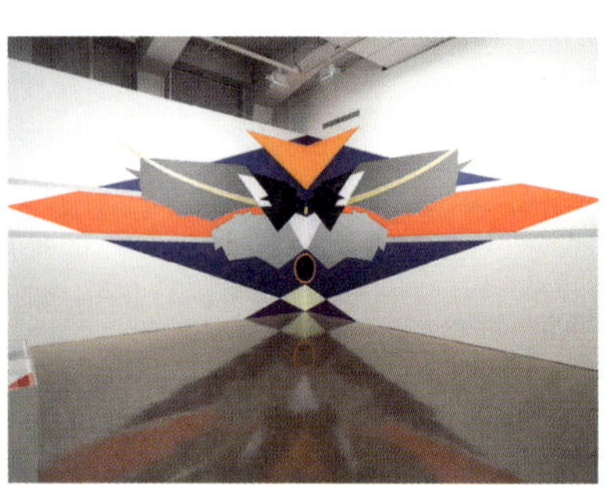

in some of the more obscure spiritualist underpinnings of early modernism as well as her occasional practice of consulting a clairvoyant for advice on how to resolve particularly tricky artworks. Dwyer's empathy with the outsider is apparent in the gatherings of disparate and unlikely objects, and elements both found and made, that are arranged in ritualistic circles in her series **The additions and the subtractions**, a major example of which – **An apparition of a subtraction** 2010 – Dwyer made on Cockatoo Island following her residency. Gravity anchors these objects to the gallery floor, while the circles magically unify elements which could be otherwise difficult to associate. Assembled together in this way, they allow comparisons to be made and highlight certain formal sculptural qualities – scale, mass, density, transparency, colour and balance – in objects where we may not expect to find them.

While circles have been an essential part of Dwyer's practice from the beginning, it was only about a decade ago that they emerged as an organising principle. The circular gatherings began small in **Black sun, blue moon** 2007 and **Monoclinic** 2008, gathered force in **Outfield** 2009, and reached peak

opposite:
The divisions and subtractions 2017
(detail, figure by Andre Bremer)
see pages 124–29

Spell for a corner (Aleister and Rosaleen 2017 (detail), in *Occulture: the dark arts*, City Art Gallery | Te Whare Toi, Wellington, New Zealand, 2017 clustering in such major works as an **An apparition of a subtraction**, **Panto collapsar** 2012 and **The additions and the subtractions** 2012.[21] The lampposts in **Square cloud compound** also trace out a circular form that contrasts with the less contained fabric superstructure. The circle has proved to be endlessly inventive for Dwyer, enabling each work to develop a distinctive identity through the choice of component parts, some of which reappear in subsequent works as their aesthetic energy is needed. The most recent example, **The divisions and subtractions** 2017, works in the same way as all these gatherings, establishing an object circle which demarcates an inside and an outside, with a threshold that tests the viewer's resolve in remaining an observer outside the ring or becoming the focus of the sculpture's attention by passing into the inner circle. As Dwyer has said of these works: '[they are] a tight form of geometry, a completely closed system – a psychic fortress that can hold together disparate thoughts and objects.'[22]

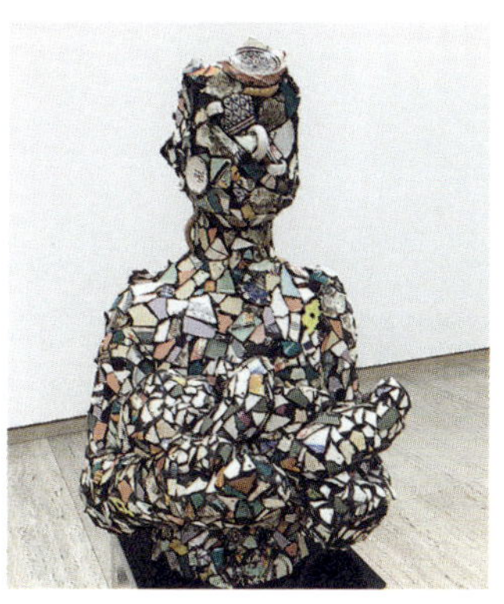

The divisions and subtractions brought together a community of artists who worked with Dwyer on the work's individual components as well as more broadly in conceiving it, the former including Hany Armanious and Nick Dorey, and the latter Adriane Boag, Andre Bremer, Stevie Fieldsend and Matthys Gerber. The resulting work presents disparate gifts to the sculptural gods, to the gallery and to the viewer, invoking a childlike sense of wonder in discovering the remarkable in the everyday and overlooked. Dwyer has an interest in pedagogy and theories of education and has herself been an influential art teacher in Sydney for many years, so these gatherings could also be a circle of pupils.[23] A further childlike sense of object-magic is suggested by Dwyer's oft-cited interest in the theories of Friedrich Fröbel, an early nineteenth-century German educator who recognised that children have unique educational needs. Fröbel developed his theories in the 1830s and coined the word 'kindergarten' (meaning 'children's garden') as a name for his institute for young children that advocated for play and games as ways of learning – theories controversial at the time. He designed a set of educational toys known as 'Fröbel gifts' – coloured balls, wooden spheres, cubes, cylinders and triangles – intended for children to explore and develop object relations at successive stages of development.[24] Dwyer's works invite us to reconsider our own object–subject relations and to see things with fresh eyes, which also recalls a modernist preoccupation with reinvention through emulating children's vision, a form of local rather than exotic primitivism that coincided with the traumas of war and other devastating events during the twentieth century. As children are also capable of great cruelty, being in the centre of Dwyer's circular works can give the sense that the sculpture's gaze may be judging us and finding us wanting.

The anthropomorphism present in Dwyer's art strays into an animist spirit at times, as is evident in the **The additions and the subtractions** series with its sense of a ritualistic gathering of objects for ceremonial purposes. This can appear pagan, emphasised by Dwyer's inclusion in her installations of hooded costumes – also worn for performance events in galleries and outside in woodland glades – as well as the circular forms that recall ancient stone

circles. Animism, the attribution of a spiritual essence to all things living
or inanimate, which also allows for all material phenomena to have agency,
is another organising principle that can be considered in relation to Dwyer's
work. As one of the world's most ancient belief systems, common across
many cultures and still surviving in some, animism is another way of thinking
and believing that can suggest alternatives to the consideration of ourselves
as apart from the natural world and the belief that things are governed
only by their inherent physical properties. This is not to suggest that Dwyer
is a New Age spiritualist, but rather that 'listening' to her materials and
seeking to understand their place in the world can be creatively rewarding and enable thinking outside the rationalist systems that continue to entrench power in economic elites.

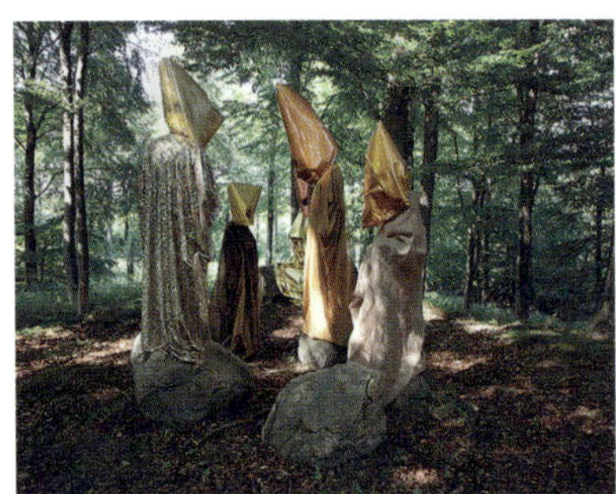

Dwyer's sculptures often suggest an absent body – implied by her materials, such as stockings; her making of den and cubbyhouse structures; and her addition of eyes and other facial features to inanimate objects – but the human body itself has also been very present in her performance works. The performance accompanying the 2013 exhibition **Goldene bend'er** at the Australian Centre for Contemporary Art in Melbourne brought Dwyer's circular forms, ritualistic gatherings and the human body together

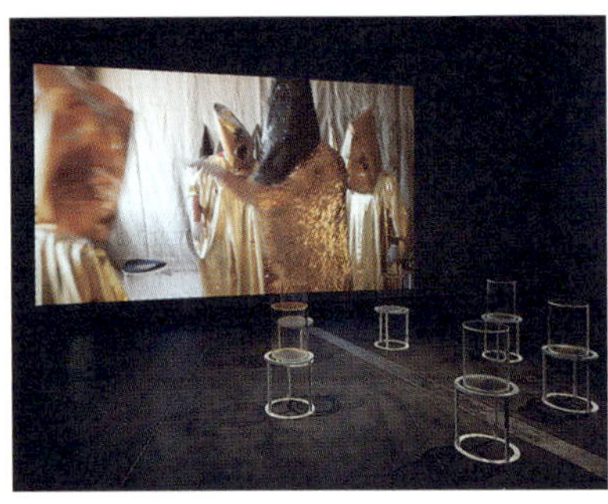

in perhaps their most fundamental way.[25] Dancers dressed in elaborate gold
costumes circled a series of cylindrical seats in a solemn rhythm before sitting
on them. The participants occupied these thrones in still rectitude as they
focused on their bodies and bodily functions and, over a period of time,
passed faeces and urine with greater and lesser success into transparent
cylindrical containers under the seats. Dwyer's earlier interest in the abject,
in the porous and liminal zones of the body and what is injected and ejected,
was here made manifest in the gallery space as she enacted a reverse
alchemy of turning gold into shit. Viewing these natural everyday acts in an
unnatural ritualistic setting was somewhat voyeuristic, with its sadomasochistic
undertones, but it also brought into the public realm the normally private and
most basic of bodily functions. The circularity expressed in this work is one
of the core organising principles of life itself: what goes into the body must
come out. That such an indisputable fact remains taboo in public discourse
was evident from the outcry this work invoked from the right-wing cultural
commentariat.[26]

In looking across Dwyer's own art history as she is now entering her fourth
decade of practice, a clarity of purpose can be discerned in her alchemical
transformation of everyday materials and objects into cultural gold in an
iterative and evolving practice. Her work comes from a long-term engagement
with materials and methodologies led by her deeply curious mind, but in
which material empathy and intuition also play an important part. As Dwyer
has explained:

Agebbo skoven 2013
see pages 76–77

Goldene bend'er 2013 (detail)
see pages 76–77

> I think all matter is conscious to some degree. Everything has a frequency. Sometimes, it takes a while for material to warm up to you so you can actually sense it. You have to be in an attentive state. I try to get to a point where things can speak for themselves rather than having me impose my voice upon them.[27]

The idea of intuition in art practice has been discredited as art historians have sought more concrete analytical terms to quantify art and its role in society, but if intuition can be thought of as the unconscious sum of life experience, dedicated practice, engagement with the world, personality, ability, intellect and insight, then perhaps it is the closest term for describing how Dwyer approaches making her works, in tandem with the deep thinking required to find the shape of their final form and understanding its place in the world. For Dwyer, there is always pleasure and playfulness in this process, which we experience in our encounter with her work.

Inheritance

Jewellery and the sculpture of Mikala Dwyer

Helen
Hughes

Mikala Dwyer believes that certain of her aesthetic predilections are hardwired – a continuation of the practices of both her father, industrial chemist Peter Dwyer, and mother, modernist jeweller Dorothy Dwyer (nee Ellen Dorothy Bjorn).[1] In conversation with the curator Robert Leonard in 2014 she stated her belief that: 'Knowledge gets passed down in your DNA. Whether you know it or not, you are often just riffing off your parents.'[2] Where her father's work involved melting and forming plastics and polyurethane, Dwyer has used hot-air guns to craft hollow sculptural objects from sheets of transparent plastic.[3] These forms either hang weightlessly from the ceiling like mobiles (as in **The hollows** for the 2014 Biennale of Sydney), or prop up other objects like ashtrays, chairs and houseplants as if they were being cradled by invisible poltergeists (as in the **Smoking and drinking** sculptures from 2006). And where her mother's work involved mixing, casting, filing and hammering metals to create necklaces, earrings and bracelets to adorn the body, Dwyer frequently works with metals and has produced massively scaled-up 'earrings for ceilings' (mobiles – such as **Diviner** 2012) and 'wall necklaces' (such as **Wall necklace** 2012) to adorn the architecture of art galleries and museums.[4]

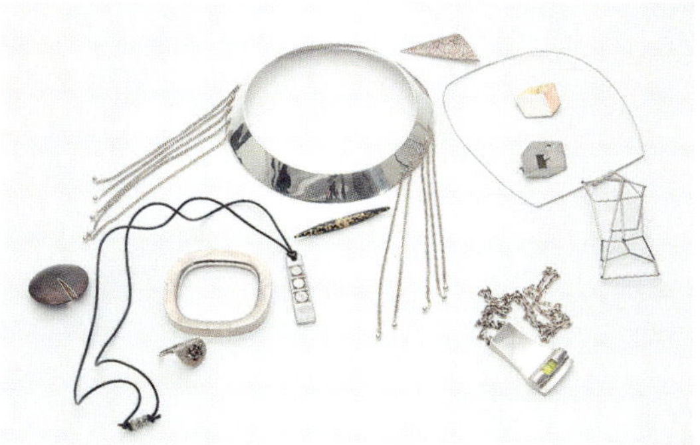

Jewellery by Dorothy Dwyer from the mid to late 1900s

In an earlier, pre-industrial era intergenerational family craft practices were commonplace, but today, under the signs of neoliberalism (with its cult of the individual) and globalisation (with its mass-production of consumer goods), such formal relationships are fast becoming rare. Parental influences instead sneak into Dwyer's practice – and they often do so subconsciously, rather than as the result of direct instruction or intention. Intergenerational and, more specifically, matrilineal relationships can be traced between Dwyer's works that reference her mother's practice, as well as collaborations with her own daughter Olive (such as **Olloodoo** 1998). By considering the nature of these parental influences we can gain new insights into Dwyer's work and her methodology as an artist. For instance, thinking through Dwyer's assertion that she has 'inherited' forms and processes from her father's work as an industrial chemist and her mother's jewellery practice helps Dwyer to consciously build a picture of herself as an artist-as-medium, as opposed to artist-as-author. Put another way, this genealogical determination of artistic tropes and techniques partially diminishes Dwyer's authorial agency and makes space for the artist to instead channel other voices and processes through her work. The act of channelling rather than creating allows for new and unexpected forms to appear in Dwyer's work, thereby minimising the risk of falling into a stylistic or conceptual groove.[5] To take another example, the paradigm of jewellery (which is the focus of the remainder of this essay) presents us with a useful framework for understanding important aspects of Dwyer's work and its relationship to the body, which is frequently discussed in terms of its absent or spectral presence in her sculptures and installations.[6] In many cultures jewellery developed as a means of portraying status – whether via the use of precious metals and gemstones, or codified ornaments. Indeed, at different moments and in different places throughout history, sumptuary laws have been introduced to regulate the wearing of jewellery and to reinforce its symbolic social function (perhaps most forcefully in medieval Europe). However, as the modernist project unfurled throughout

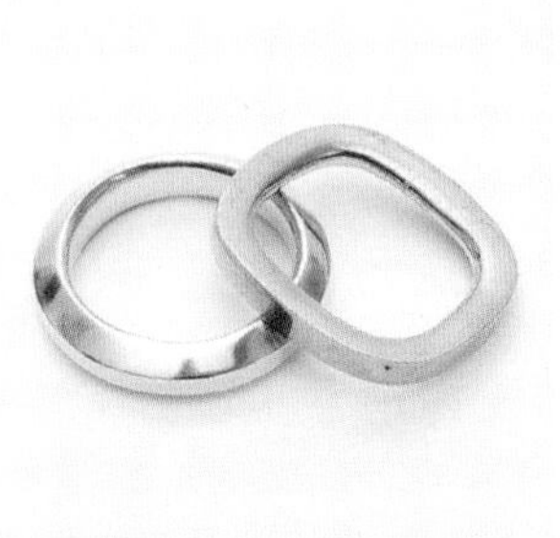
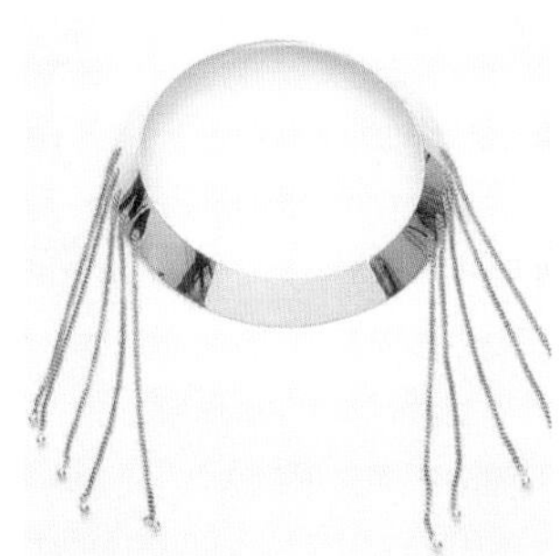

the western world, and against jewellery's by now almost complete assimilation into capitalist industry, a strand of avant-garde jewellery became concerned instead with more conceptual modes of self-expression, uncoupling jewellery from expensive materials. In 1927, for instance, the French modernist designer Charlotte Perriand famously designed her ball-bearings necklace, or *collier roulements à billes*, which was a collar of chrome silver balls that imitated a traditional pearl necklace in shape and sheen but instead expressed an affinity with the modernist industrial project.[7] Such avant-garde jewellery practices quickly developed a strong critique of preciousness (rejecting the use of materials such as gold and gemstones in many cases) and embarked on a critical exploration of jewellery's orientation to the body, its time and place.[8]

Dorothy Dwyer fits into these (oversimplified) narratives of avant-garde jewellery as a mode of self-expression, a critique of preciousness, and as a means for exploring the scale and form of the body. Her jewellery was an expression of her Danish heritage (her parents were émigrés from Denmark and, although born in Australia, she lived in Denmark and Sweden between ages four and twenty-seven). Dorothy gravitated towards modernist Scandinavian design tropes in her work, such as simple curved forms and clean surfaces. As well, her jewellery was typically executed in non-precious metals, which she would often mix to form new alloys and patinas like an alchemist. The art historians Damian Skinner and Kevin Murray have argued that modernist jewellery design was introduced to Australia, in large part, by twentieth-century European migrants. Again, this rings true in the case of Dorothy, who studied silver smithing in Sydney in the 1970s under the instruction of the modernist Dutch jeweller Walraven van Heeckeren. Van Heeckeren trained in Rochester in the United States under Hans Christensen, who, in turn, trained in Denmark under the instruction of the renowned modernist Danish jeweller Georg Jensen.[9] As Skinner and Murray explain, van Heeckeren migrated to Sydney in 1968 and quickly remedied the lack of opportunities to train as a jeweller in the city. He started his own workshop, ran a private school in St Leonards (which Dorothy attended in the 1970s), and opened a shop in Argyle Arts Centre (where Dorothy later gave working demonstrations).

Packing up Dorothy's jewellery studio after her death in 2010, Dwyer found numerous objects that caused her to feel like 'we were working on the same forms but at different scales'.[10] The following year, Dwyer incorporated parts of her mother's jewellery into her own artwork for the first time. The

opposite:
Charm for wall 2016
ceramic, wood, modelling clay, moonstone, philosopher's stone, turquoise, Midori, synthetic polymer, brass wire, string, acrylic, glass, chain

resultant work – **Necklace for wall (silver)** 2011, now in the Michael Buxton Collection in Melbourne – was her first wall necklace. It comprises a steel chain more than two metres long with dangling pendants made of moonstone, turquoise, a shell, leather, copper and hand-modelled clay ornaments. It also includes scraps of silver that Dorothy left unfinished in her studio. Nailed to the wall in two places, the centre of the necklace slumps in an inverted arc, recalling the sagging felt wall works of Robert Morris, which Dwyer referenced more explicitly in **Neoprene work** 1995 – a fluorescent yellow rectangular fabric wall hanging with horizontal ribbons cut into its centre, which droop to reveal an orange verso. Pushing a consciously feminine post-minimalist modality even further, **Necklace for wall (silver)** references the jewellery tradition of wearing charms and talismans, with the individual charms functioning to denote significant life events (such as mourning the death of one's mother), and the talismans functioning to bring their wearer good luck or ward off evil.[11]

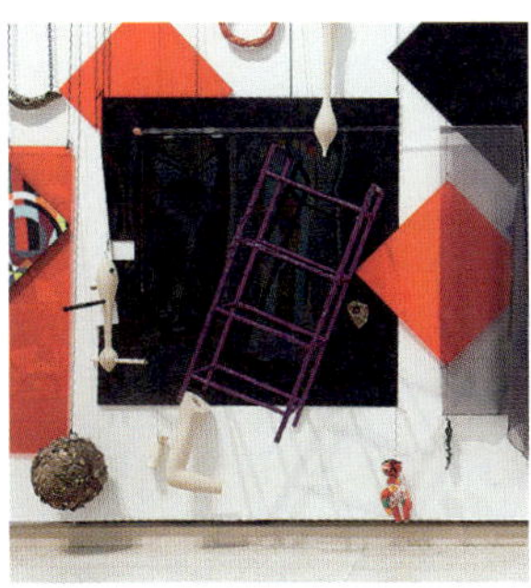
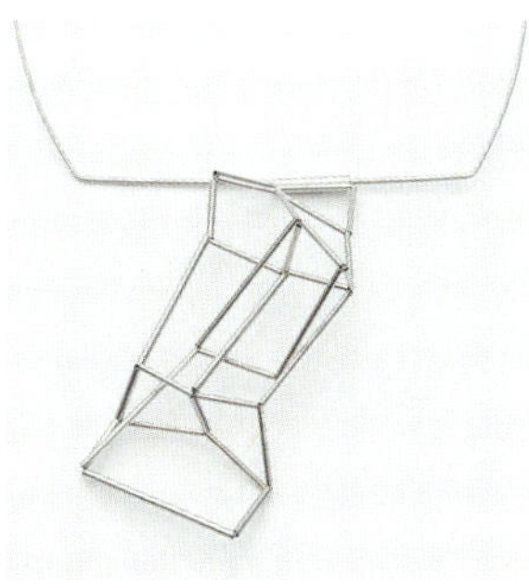

In 2012 Dwyer made another wall necklace titled **Methylated spiritual**. This version contained a bottle of her mother's whisky as one of its oversized charms, as well as a bottle of methylated spirits, a number of large, hand-shaped ring forms, sheets of brightly coloured hanging acrylic and other handcrafted ceramic objects – including one with a rolled-up $100 note stuck through it, like a prayer wedged into the Wailing Wall. The gently shifting acrylic squares reflect different surfaces and angles of the gallery's interior architecture, as well as fragments of the viewer's body, thereby mangling the spatial properties of the gallery space in their reflection. For **Mikala Dwyer: A shape of thought**, Dwyer presents a new wall necklace – **Wall charm** 2017 – this time in significantly enlarged proportions. At nine metres long, its charms have also grown in size to include large-scale readymade objects, such as a chair. The intention of this work is not to animate the building or treat it like a body by adorning it with human ornaments (Dwyer would be much more interested in what she would term 'building consciousness' than in anthropomorphising a wall). Rather, she prefers to confuse and blur the distinction between the two. As the artist explained in a 2004 interview:

> To me, a sculpture, an object, a body, a building, are all quite connected – they're all 'porridge-y'. I try to make it as fluid as possible. So that the edges to things get quite porous. If you're standing in front of one of those sculptures, and if it's doing its job, you'll be getting a bit of an identity crisis with it: you're not quite sure where you begin and it ends.[12]

In this respect, Dwyer not only scales up jewellery from body- to building-size but scales down architecture from building- to body-size too. She has described her hooded costumes, such as those exhibited in her 1999 Sarah Cottier Gallery exhibition **Uniform**, as an architecture of the body – 'a sort of cubbyhouse' that creates an 'elsewhere'.[13]

In addition to making wall necklaces that reference the broad tradition and symbolic function of charm jewellery, Dwyer has re-created specific items of jewellery made by her mother as large-scale sculptures. In 2013, for her major solo exhibition at the Australian Centre for Contemporary Art in Melbourne, **Goldene bend'er**, Dwyer scaled up one of Dorothy's rings (one that she wore regularly) to form a series of three abstract sculptures, titled **Hollowwork (ringing)**, made from Corten steel and polished aluminium. (A small mirror-polished stainless steel version of this work was included in the exhibition **A shape of thought**.) At their newly enlarged scale, presented as discrete and monumental sculptures rather than finger adornments, the **Hollowwork** sculptures and their voids are more reminiscent of the smooth, carved forms of Isamu Noguchi or Barbara Hepworth than the abject or formless sculptures of Eva Hesse and Lynda Benglis, with whose

work commentators more readily compare Dwyer's. Indeed, as the curator Linda Michael has observantly noted, the **Hollowwork** sculptures sit at odds with Dwyer's typically 'grunge' or handmade aesthetic, and instead bear the 'precisely articulated, clean lines of modern design, purged of ornament'.[14] Unlike the wall necklaces, which are inherently slack, tensioned only by gravity and two nails in the wall, these ring forms maintain their structural integrity. Curiously, the necklaces that Dorothy designed typically took the form of solid neck cuffs, which also maintained their shape independently of the body, whereas Dwyer seems to be interested in materials losing their shapes then finding new ones.[15] The channelling of Dorothy's modernist Scandinavian aesthetic in the **Hollowwork (ringing)** sculptures therefore operates as a circuit breaker in Dwyer's installations – or at least as a point of tension.

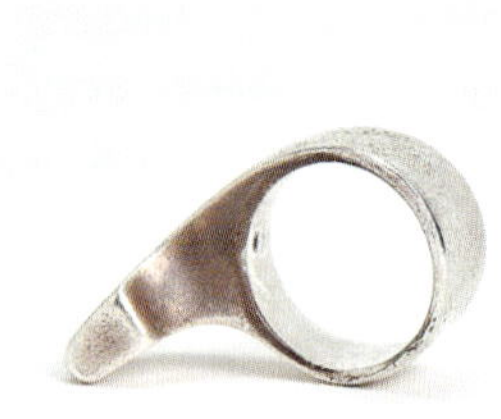

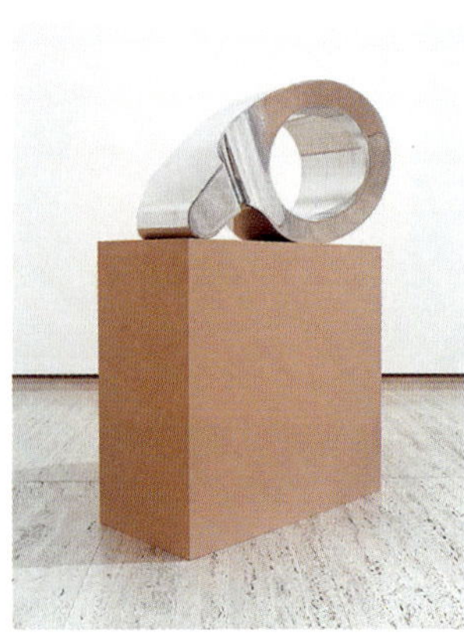

What, finally, is the significance of jewellery for a sculpture practice? Due to its shape, scale and function, jewellery can be understood as a strong index and metonym of the body. A ring implies a finger, a bracelet a wrist. Moreover, an historical or second-hand item of jewellery not only implies the body part on or around which it was once worn, but also the specific person who wore it. Take, for instance, the earrings Peggy Guggenheim wore at the opening of her New York gallery Art of This Century in 1942: on one lobe an earring made by Alexander Calder and on the other an earring by Yves Tanguy, signifying her equal commitment to abstraction and figuration. People often wear the jewellery of a deceased loved one – for example, their grandmother's ring, which they frequently refer to as 'my grandmother's ring' as opposed to 'my ring', thus signifying the importance of their relationship to the deceased person. At other times an engagement or wedding ring, despite its financial value, is buried with its deceased owner as it considered to be an extension of their body – having been worn continuously by them from the moment of their wedding ceremony until

Jewellery by Dorothy Dwyer
from the mid to late 1900s

Ring by Dorothy Dwyer and
Hollowwork (ringing) 2013
see pages 74, 119–23

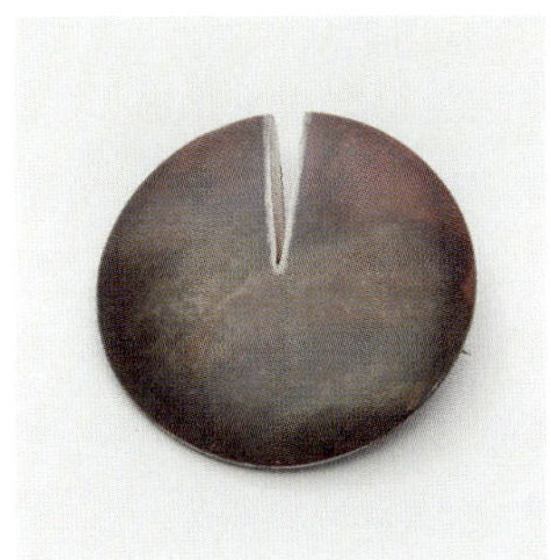 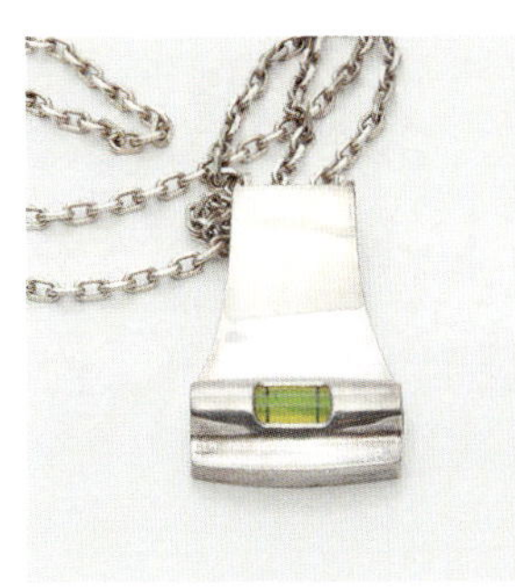

their death. In these ways, jewellery can powerfully evoke the imagination of both a general and a specific body, and come to signify life after death. Dwyer's adaptation of certain jewellery practices into sculptural forms summons and confuses the contours of the body by virtue of the scale of her work and its relation to space. In so doing she creates a distributive consciousness among her sculptures, their environs and viewers. Dwyer's more specific invocation of her mother's jewellery practice creates a distributive authorship among her works, one that – true to the artist's slightly magical form – manages to both time travel and to transcend the distinctions between life and death.

Marys, Lindas and other spirited vessels

Susan
Best

The letterbox Marys. Just the title of Mikala Dwyer's installation makes me chuckle. Marian devotion, roadside shrines and the postal service collide in this marvellous image. It is worthy of the British television comedy series *Father Ted*. The plotline might be that a parishioner gives the parochial household a statue of the Virgin and as the house is already chock-full of Marys they decide she has to go somewhere outside yet highly visible. Closer to home, a letterbox Mary could be the kind of practical accommodation to religious feeling one might find in rural or outback Australia, sort of 'statuary with a purpose'. I can well imagine a Marian devotee deciding no better saint should oversee and safeguard the dwindling supply of delivered mail. As Marina Warner has noted in her book *Alone of all her sex: the myth and cult of the Virgin Mary* (1976), the meagre references to Mary in the Bible have in no way limited the many and varied uses made of her story or, indeed, her body.[1]

In the first installation of **The letterbox Marys** at Roslyn Oxley9 Gallery, Sydney in 2015, two wonderful prototypes for a Mary letterbox were exhibited alongside a range of earthly and metaphysical objects: three large banner-like paintings titled **The angel**, **Possession** and **Sigil for heaven and earth**, two shadow lamps, a wall necklace, uranium glass vessels and a large acrylic puzzle. Foregrounding the Virgin Mary in the title of the work is both a feminist gesture and, of course, a typically Catholic one. Dwyer has previously woven Catholic

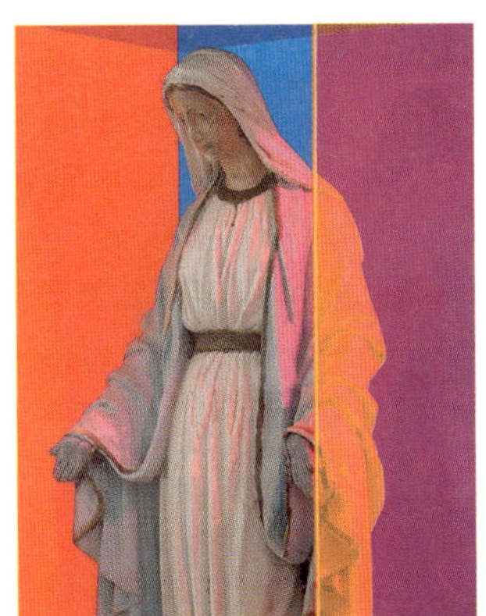

references into her work – it is a spiritual tradition familiar to her from childhood – but in a less direct fashion. In her 2008 installation **Moon garden**, for example, an appliquéd banner listed the placenames given to the lunar surface by the seventeenth-century Jesuit priest Giovanni Battista Riccioli (see pages 60–61). Dwyer observes with characteristic acuity the fabulous range of topics conjured in these names: 'There's success, love, and rot, and there's rainbows, sleep, fear, and forgetfulness – but no sex.'[2] Similarly, in the version of **The additions and the subtractions** exhibited at the Institute of Modern Art in Brisbane in 2012, Catholic kitsch features: a small Jesus on top of a tall plinth performing a puzzling Toyota-type 'oh what a feeling' leap.

In **The letterbox Marys** Dwyer puts Mary on a pedestal of sorts – her traditional location – but also brings her down to earth. Such a location better serves Mary's role as the messenger, conduit or medium that connects the physical and spiritual realms. The so-called pedestals are actually typical minimalist-style gallery plinths but painted a deep grey instead of the customary white; both have apertures suitable for standard-sized letters cut vertically into the fabric, and below the slits are open cubes that could be used for receiving newspapers and other larger items. This section of the sculptures in proportion and design reminds me of the expensive bespoke letterboxes one often sees outside swish architecturally designed houses in Australian cities. On top of these structures are standard-issue religious statues of Mary but in this instance she is turned to appear in profile. In fact, the two Marys face each other; their doubling is somewhat disconcerting given the singularity so often attributed to her – alone of all her sex, et cetera. Surprisingly, it is hard to describe the standard pose she displays; it is puzzling,

not part of normal bodily comportment or movement. The head is slightly
bowed, presumably in modesty rather than shame; the arms are slightly
raised away from the body; and the hands are turned palm-outwards in a
gesture redolent of supplication and possibly welcome. It isn't exactly a
gesture of open arms but it suggests some kind of availability, confirming her
status as an intermediary, more approachable perhaps because she is a mere
mortal and a maternal figure. Hence she intercedes on our behalf. Her pose
is seemingly meant to suggest that task and indeed this particular stylisation
of Mary is usually referred to as Our Lady of Grace; she is invoked as a
go-between to obtain God's grace on our behalf.

In Dwyer's hands the pose is made strange and thus available for close and
curious attention – partly, as I mentioned earlier, because Mary appears in
profile, an unusual orientation for a religious image, but also because the
figure is framed by highly coloured acrylic sheets that throw her form
dramatically into relief. We notice her slightly stooping position and the
elaborate folds of her drapery when our routine ways of seeing – or, more
accurately, not seeing – are disrupted. The sheer beauty of the two pieces,
their perfect proportions and scintillating colour contrasts, disarm or disallow
any suggestion of derision that this radical, almost fluorescent, illumination
provides. The wonderful quirkiness of a psychedelic Mary atop a letterbox
is nonetheless very apparent.

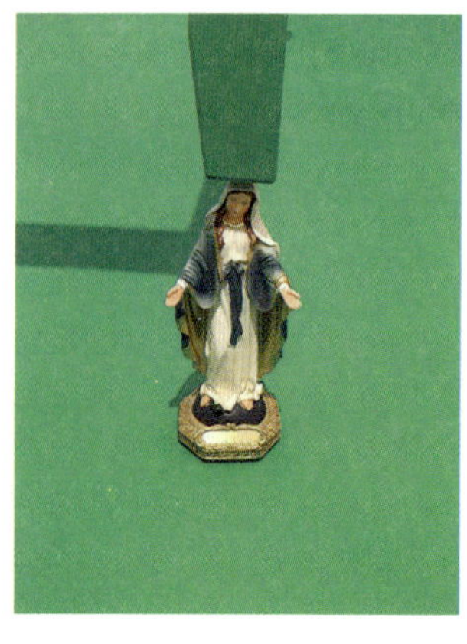

Mary appears in other parts of the installation,
including as a small figure atop one of the
gallows-like structures that support the shadow
lamps. There are two shadow lamps that, as their
name implies, cast shadows instead of emitting
light. These anti-lamps of dark acrylic are shot
through with colour like black opals. The small
Mary on the lampstand has her arms raised to bring
her hands closer to her chest in the gesture typical
of Mary of the Immaculate Heart. Mary also
features as a kind of caryatid for the hind legs of
the bedframe in **Possession**, the most minimal of
the three wall-to-floor paintings. The bed is positioned obliquely across an
abstract painting simply divided into two blocks of colour: blue and green.
Two of the bed legs terminate with small statues of Mary. **Possession** moves
to the darker side of Christianity: demonology. The infamous bed scene from
the film *The exorcist* (1973), where actress Linda Blair projectile vomits at the
attending priest, is conjured by the title of this component of the installation
and the clump of putty-coloured material stuck to the bedframe. Studded with
coins and stones, this abject bulge contrasts with the carefully painted frame.
The hard-edged abstraction of both canvas and painted bedframe lends a
compositional formality and restraint to this component of the installation that
reins in or contains the humorous touches.

Contrasting with the simple geometry of **Possession**, **The angel** is a much
more complex composition. The interlocking shapes of brilliant colour with
their clean contours have a bold, playful quality that reminds me of childhood
delights like Fuzzy-Felt or similar construction sets that utilise colour and shape

opposite:
The angel 2015
see pages 130, 132–33, 135

Mary detail in **Possession** 2015
see page 130

to stimulate the fledgling imagination. The scale of the shapes, well outside the parameters of such games, in no way diminishes the association. It is as though the largeness simply delivers to us a feeling of comparative smallness.

As so many commentators have noted, the playfulness and inventiveness of Dwyer's art is also tempered by its knowing engagement with the dense and complicated history of abstraction. For example, the title of **The angel**,

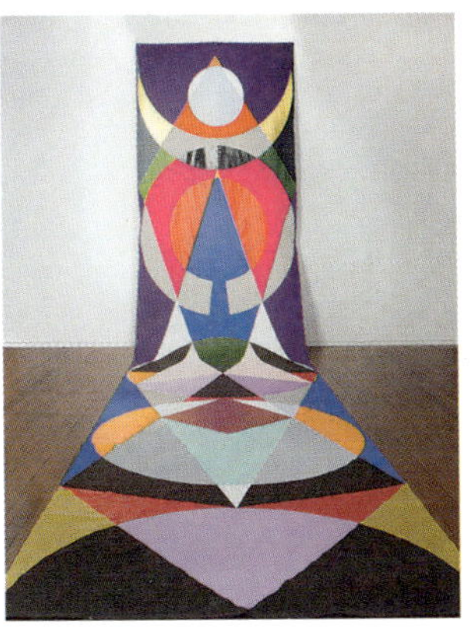

with its clear reference to representational content, reminds us of the figurative underpinning of much early abstraction, particularly in the early work of Wassily Kandinsky, but also the more recently discovered women pioneers of abstract art like Hilma af Klint and Emma Kunz. The mystical and spiritual traditions of abstraction guide Dwyer's practice. She, like the pioneers of abstraction, refers to incorporeal beings, alchemical experiments, number magic, sacred geometry and occult symbolism. The idea that there are dimensions to artmaking and its reception other than the perceptual and the rational is well articulated by Kandinsky. As he put it: '[It is] not an obvious ("geometrical") construction that will be the richest in possibilities, hence the most expressive, but the hidden one, which emerges unnoticed from the picture and hence is destined less for the eye than for the soul.'[3] The unconscious communication suggested here, from picture to psyche bypassing the eye, is perhaps more routine than we suppose. How often do we see, without really seeing images? Art historians' stock in trade is precisely the capacity to make explicit in an image what most others overlook.

That said, Dwyer does not believe images can hasten change in the world by speaking directly to the soul, or that they provide a more perfect model of it – both common theories of early abstraction, Kandinsky and Mondrian respectively. But images are not without effect, albeit that power or capacity is very hard to quantify. Of course, Dwyer is much, much less earnest than the pioneers of abstraction; humour, whimsy and absurdity always bubble away in the background. **The angel**, for example, could be described as almost cartoonish. The shapes that create an angel-like form in the top half of the canvas also recall the simple ciphers of children's drawings: a circle for a head, a triangle for the body, and arms formed by an upturned crescent. The interlocking forms of the whole composition and the complex colour interplays are, of course, all very far from childish. Dwyer's capacity to hold in tension contradictory positions, states or feelings is abundantly evident in this extraordinary amalgam of simplicity and complexity. Just as the painting can slide between abstraction and figuration, the composition can seem entirely abstract; the angel simply disappears if one chooses not to assemble the various shapes into that particular form.

The third wall painting in the installation, **Sigil for heaven and earth**, calls forth the occult side of spiritualism. A sigil is a magical symbol, talisman, action or word. In this case the magic word is a well-known expletive: 'holy shit'. The top half of the painting rendered in delicate pastels spells out 'shit' while the section running along the ground in highly saturated hues spells out 'holy'. Base matter and the ethereal world of the spirit are nicely condensed in this everyday expression. As an expression of surprise, famously associated with the comic superheroes Batman and Robin, it has a camp quality. It is another instance of a Mary-like bridge between the polarised domains of the sacred and the profane. And, of course, it has a comic twist; it is highly irreverent but not in an obvious in-your-face way. Indeed, it takes some time to decipher the superimposed letters that spell out the two words.

All three wall paintings join wall and floor in an intriguing fashion, reminiscent of the sculptures of Eva Hesse, such as her 1968 work **Area**, which similarly climbed the wall and crossed the floor. Often seen as blurring the line between sculpture and painting, Hesse's late works (including **Area** and **Contingent** 1968) are strange shadows that haunt the space of both. With literal surfaces rather than painted ones they seem sculptural, yet their transformation of space into two-dimensional form is entirely painterly. Dwyer's three large paintings, along with her allied series **In the heads of humans** 2016, operate in this same domain between wall and floor, real and illusory, two dimensions and three.

Dwyer's use of vibrant colour is, of course, a substantial departure from the tenets of minimalism and post-minimalism. So while the form of her work retraces minimalist and post-minimalist concerns, the content is aligned with early abstraction, including the embrace of colour, as well as the many and varied references to the spiritual in art. Dwyer thus blends together the languages of early abstraction and the late abstraction of minimalism and post-minimalism.

It is interesting in this regard to consider the rejection of this part of abstraction's history by the minimalist painter Frank Stella. In a 1984 interview he explicitly criticised what he calls the anti-materialist aspect of early abstraction:

> I have no difficulty appreciating (and up to a point understanding) the great abstract painting of modernism's past, the painting of Kandinsky, Malevich and Mondrian, but I do have trouble with their dicta, their pleadings, their defence of abstraction. My feeling is that these reasons, these theoretical underpinnings of theosophy and anti-materialism, have done abstract painting a kind of disservice which has contributed to its present-day plight.[4]

Materialism versus anti-materialism: one can't help but wonder whether these two alternate in some seasonal or cyclical fashion. Each one returning to correct the imbalance caused by the previous bias. In Dwyer's work, however, there is the demand to think of the position of the go-between, the Mary, the conduit between any two positions. Only in that way can we hope to escape the eternal return of successive extremes. And when we laugh at the whole situation, we are truly delivered from such extremism.

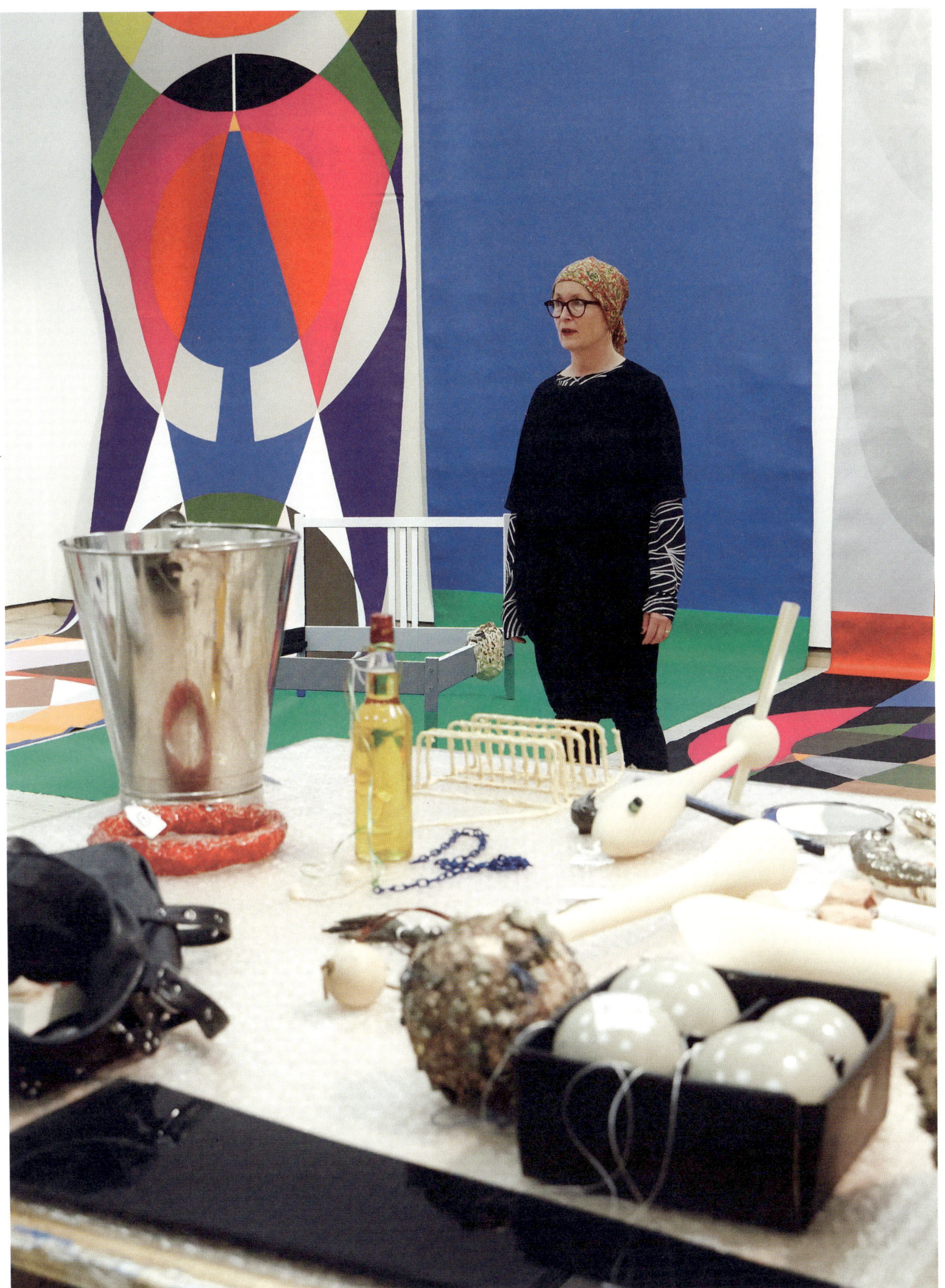

Selected works and exhibitions 1992—2017

2 September — 13 December 1992
Museum of Contemporary Art
Australia, Sydney

—

Untitled 1992
plastic, aluminium satellite dish,
elastoplast bandage, synthetic
polymer paint, glass, jelly, ceramic,
bedding

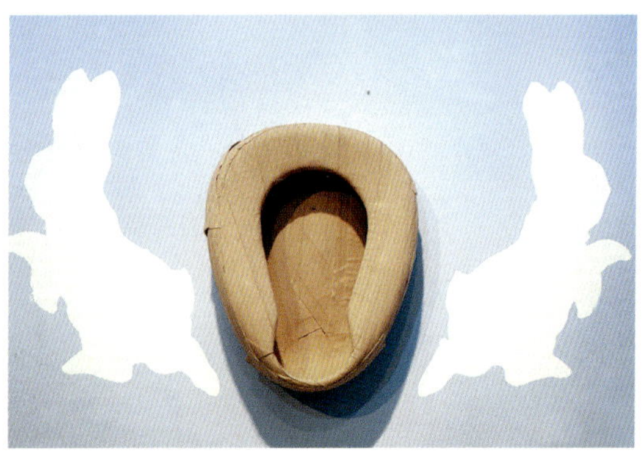

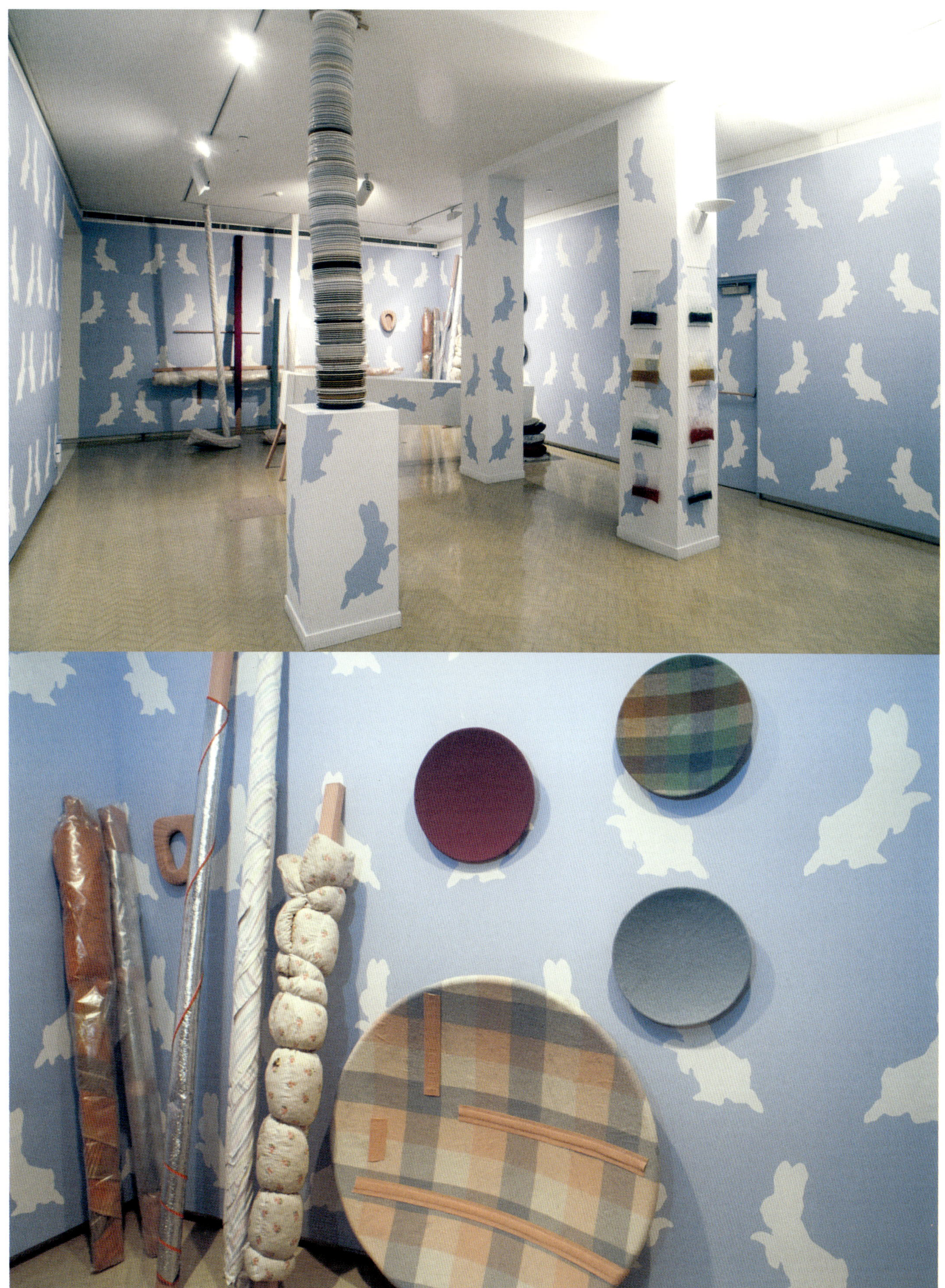

6 October — 28 November 1993
Art Gallery of New South Wales,
Sydney

—

Vestibule (for Jed) 1993
sequin fabric, lycra, toilet seats, soap,
bath mats, feather boas, knitted nylon,
bedpans, plastic, rubber

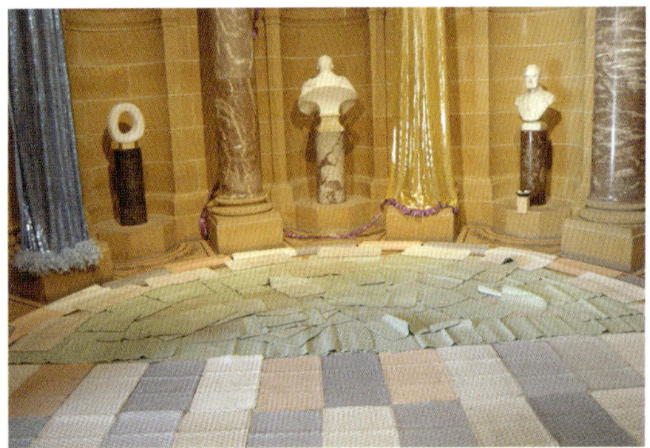

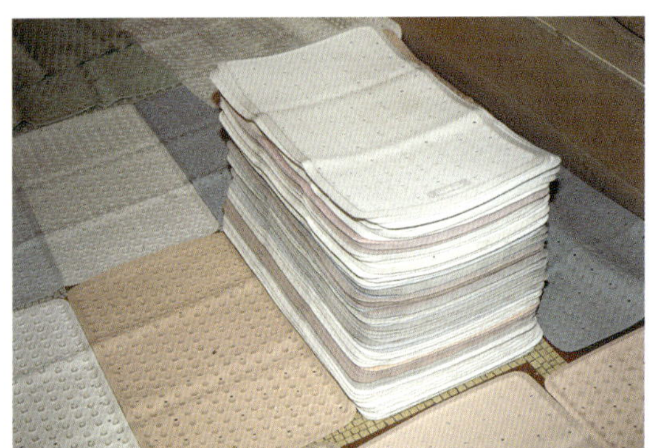

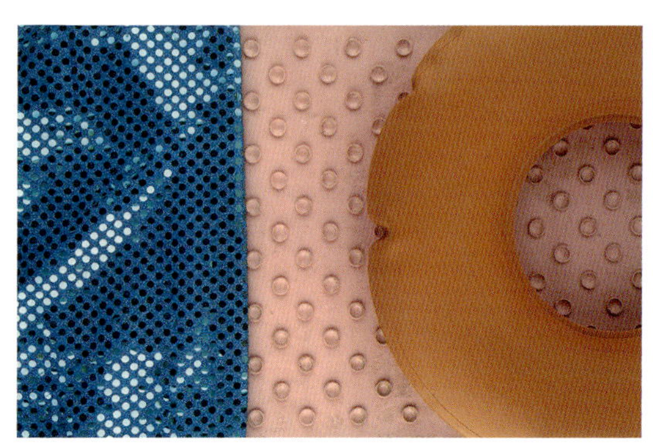

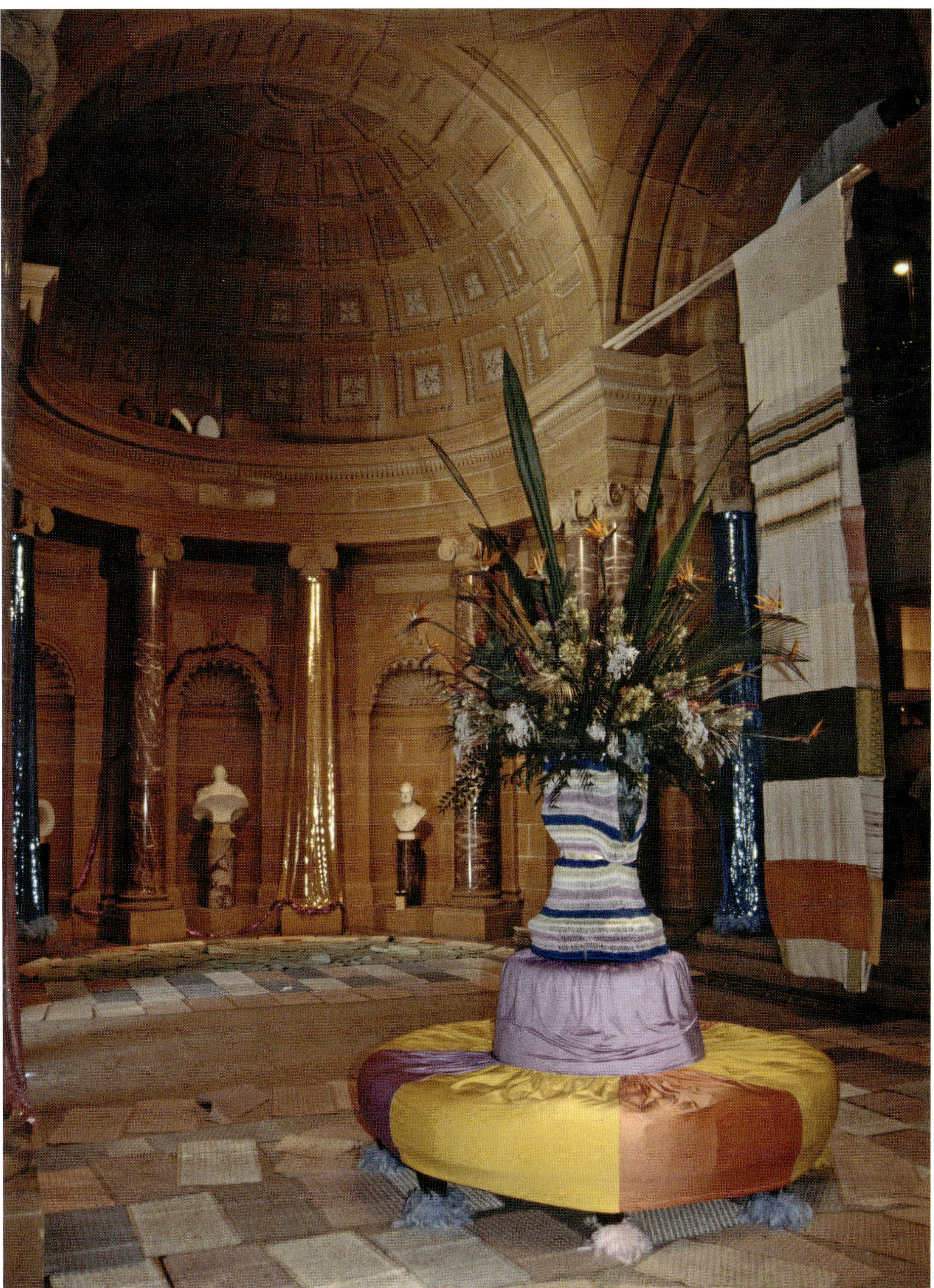

Mikala Dwyer:
woops

8 June — 12 July 1994
Sarah Cottier Gallery, Sydney

—

woops 1994
sequin fabric, satin, nail polish,
canvas, plastic, stockings, perfume,
glue, hair gel, elastoplast bandage,
body bag, underpants, car parts,
vacuum cleaners, TV, radio, lights,
easel, bedpans, trolley, metal detector
and other objects

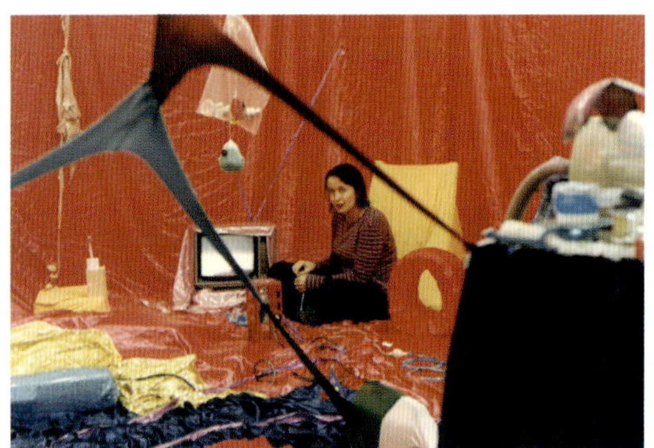

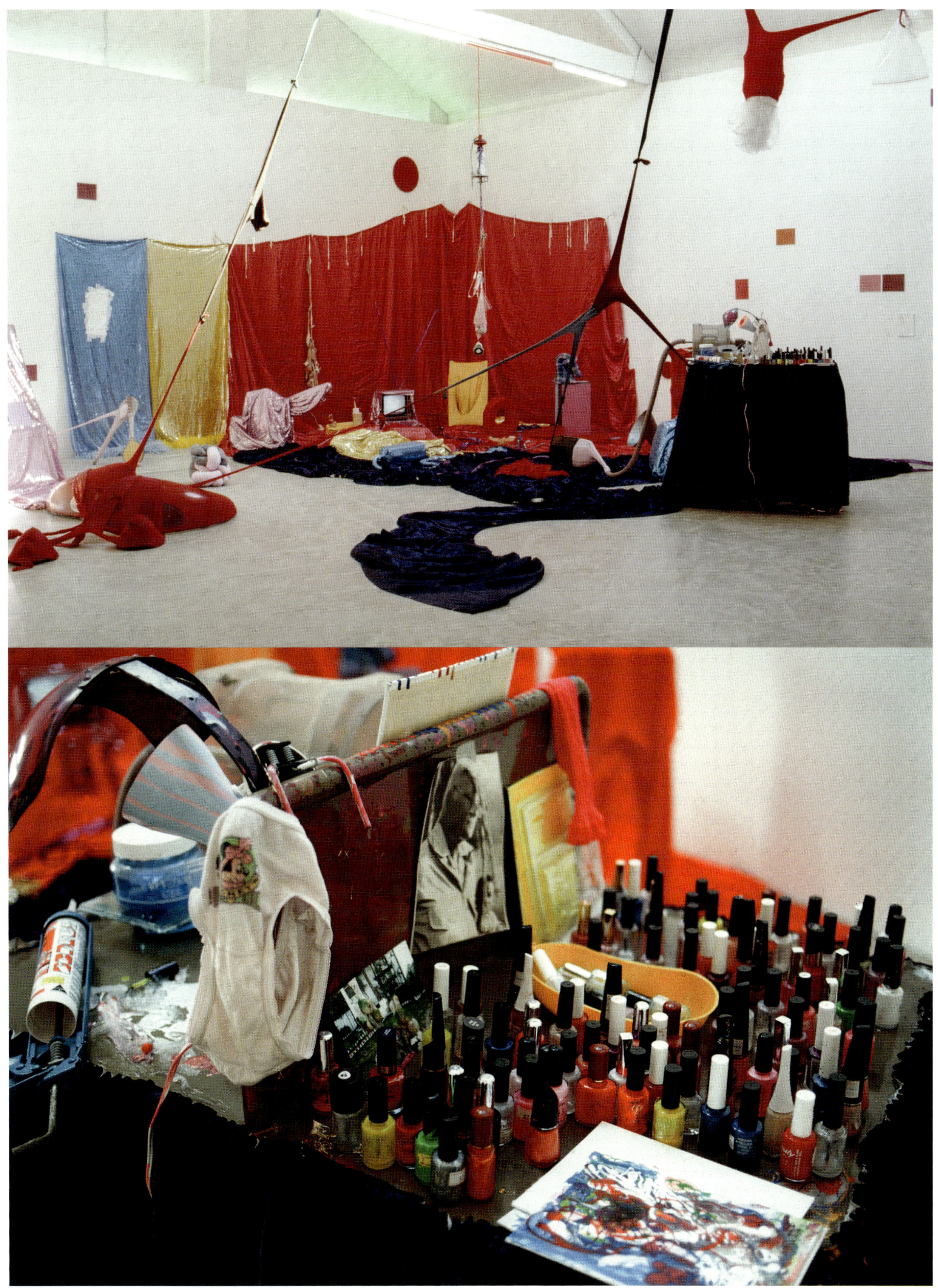

Mikala Dwyer:
Hollow-ware and a few solids

14 October — 18 November 1995
Sarah Cottier Gallery, Sydney

—

Hollow-ware and a few solids
1995
modelling clay, cardboard, plastic,
organza fabric, stockings, neoprene,
cigarette burns and taffeta on canvas,
synthetic polymer paint on canvas,
silicon glue, glass, terracotta pots,
TV aerial, VHS tape, plinths, plasticine,
vinyl, tulle, pins, air-dried clay, acrylic

opposite below:
Untitled 1995
organza fabric, pins

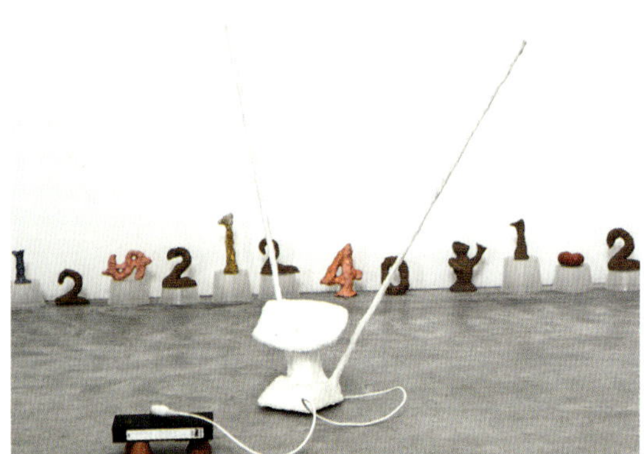

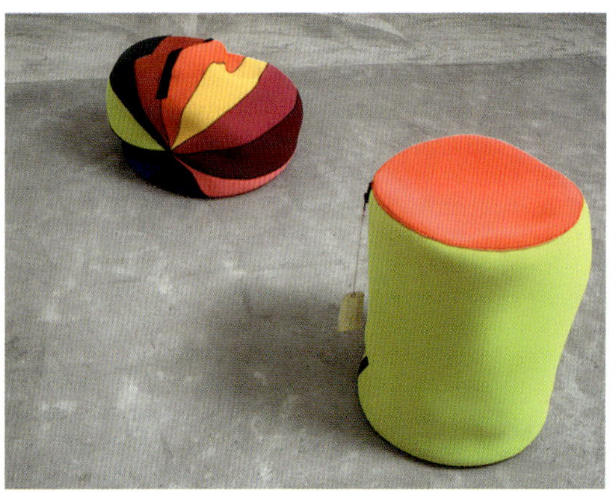

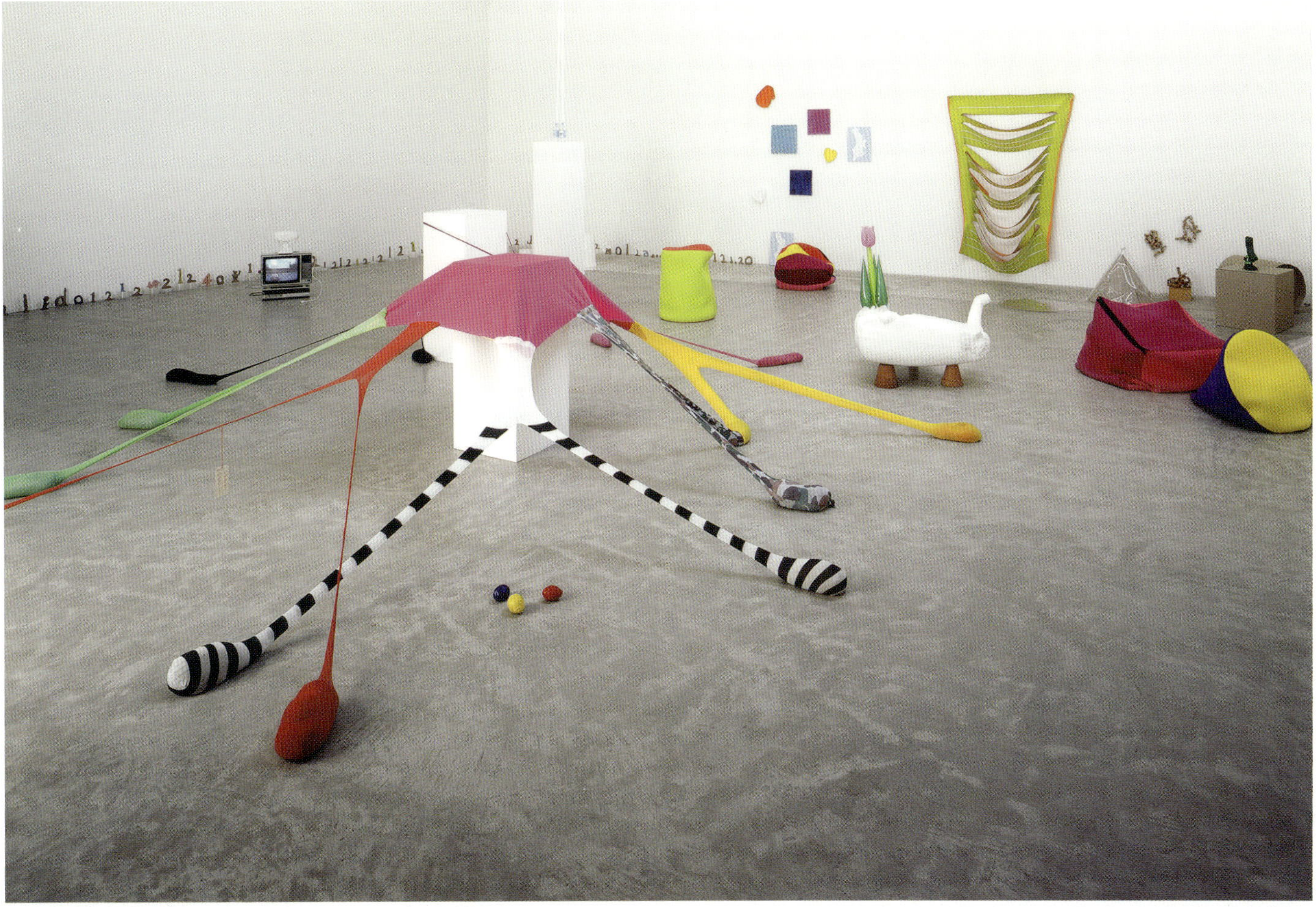

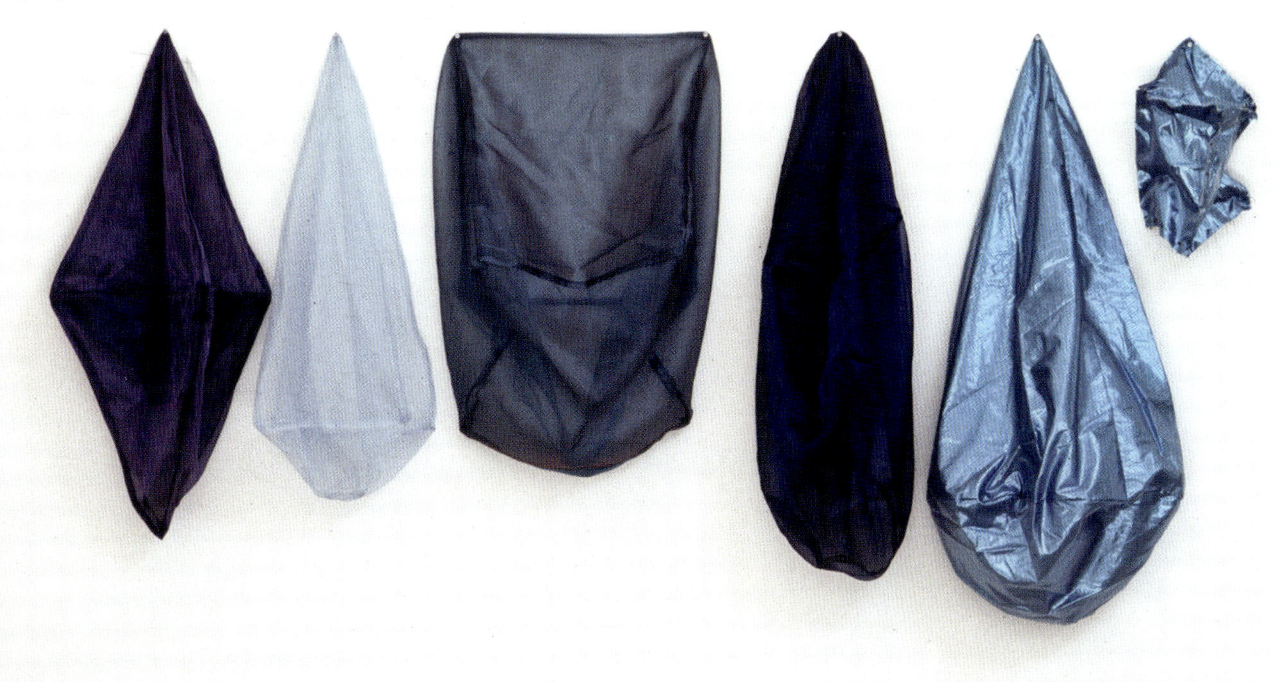

Mikala Dwyer:
Recent old work

30 October — 23 November 1996
Sarah Cottier Gallery, Sydney

—

Recent old work 1996
wood, plasterboard, wool, carpet,
synthetic clay, fabric, baked vinyl,
glass, pins, sand, metal cable and
pulleys

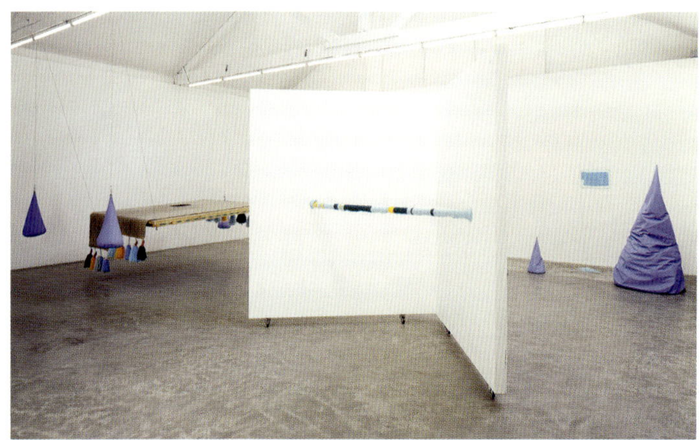

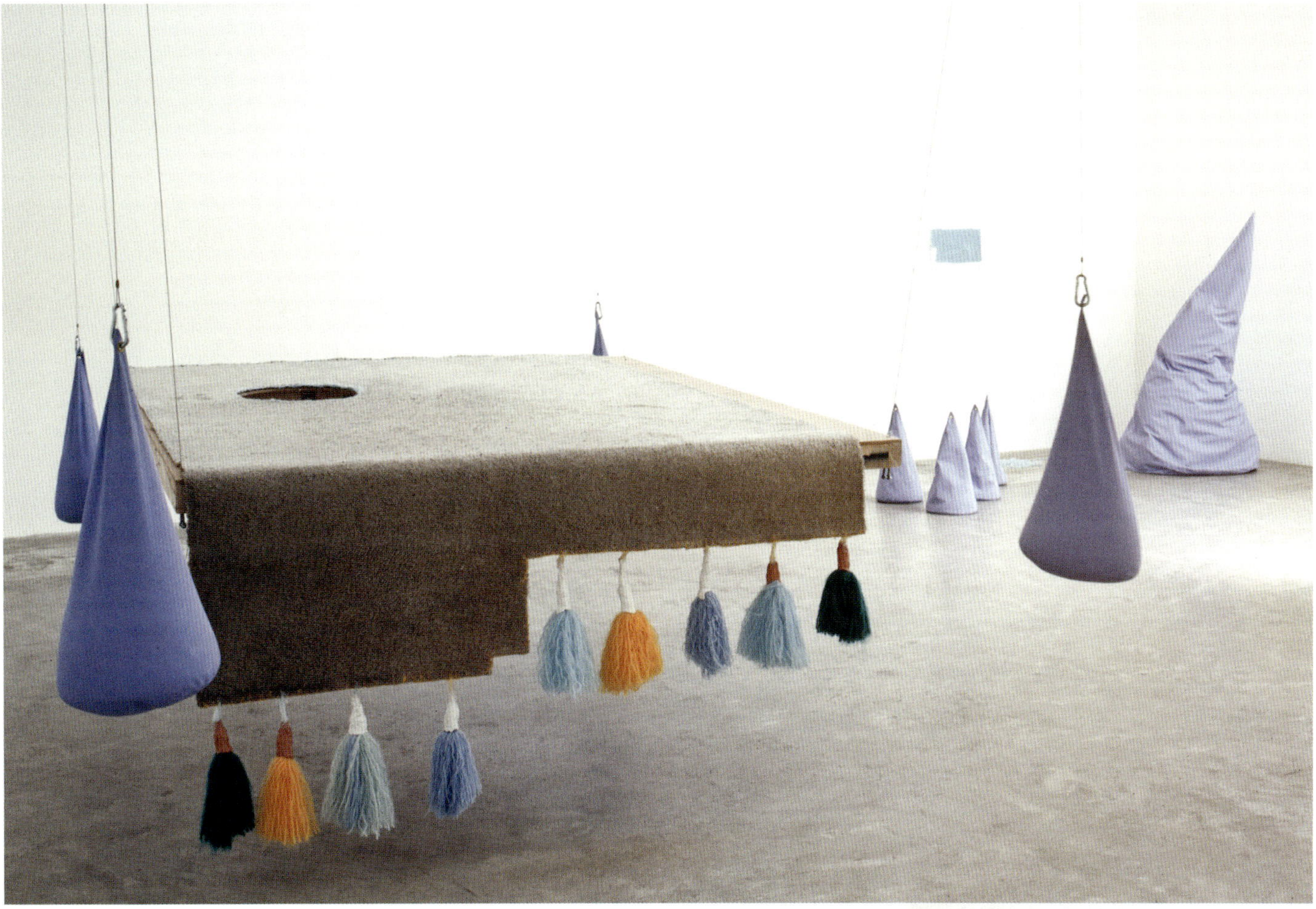

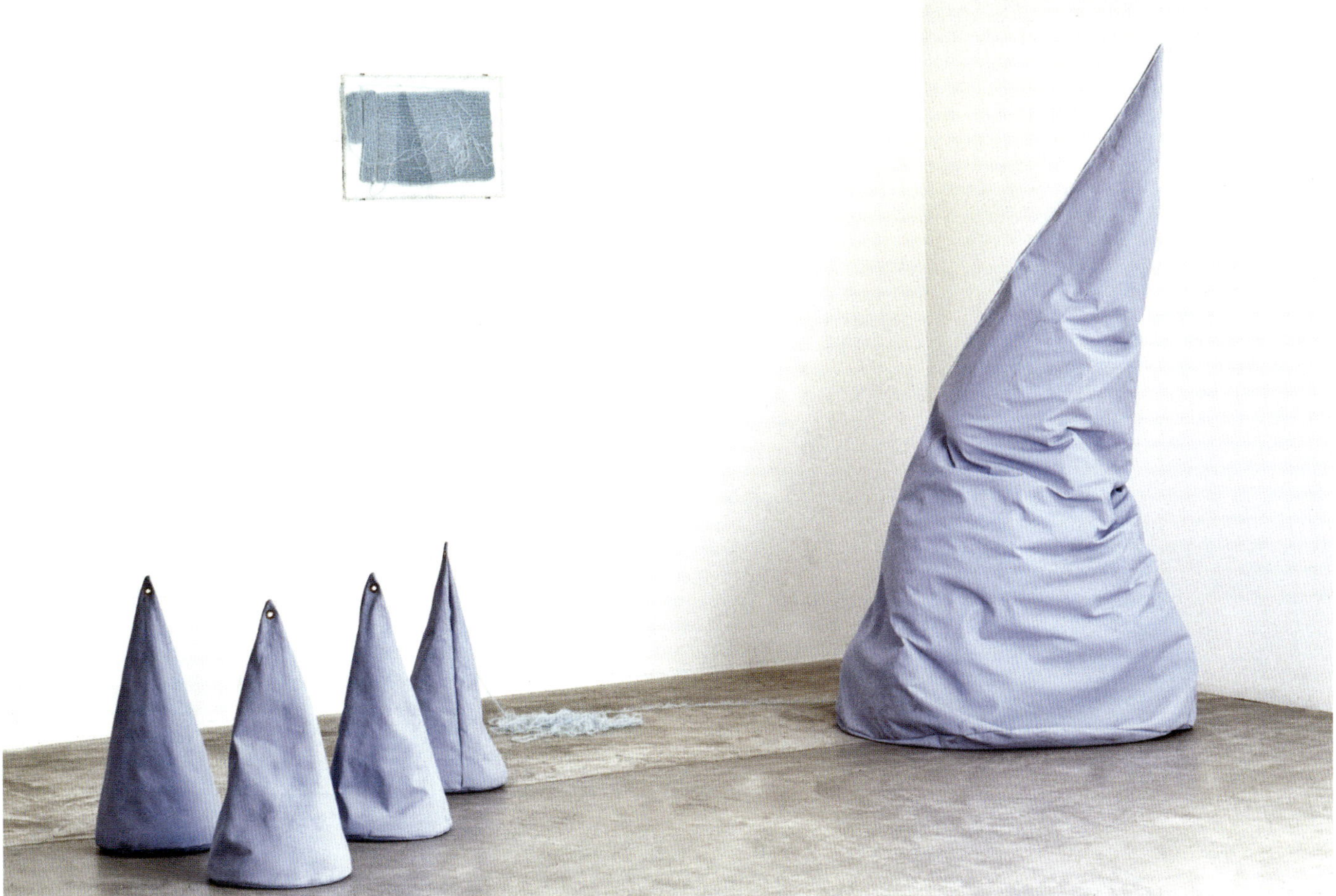

Mikala Dwyer:
Uniform

14 April — 15 May 1999
Sarah Cottier Gallery, Sydney

—

opposite from top:

Iffytown (foreground left) 1999
wood, vinyl, electric light bulb, PVC
pipes, government-issue steel ashtray,
canvas, synthetic polymer paint,
glue, marine varnish, pot plant, TV,
toothbrush, bottled water, blanket,
acrylic

Hanging eyes 1999
vinyl, canvas, synthetic polymer paint

below from left:

I.O.U. 1999
wood, glue, marine varnish, acrylic

Closing eyes 1999
wood, pot plant, TV, toothbrush,
bottled water, blanket

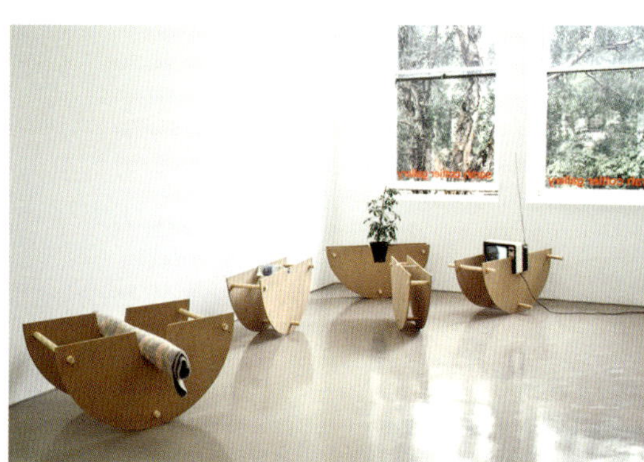

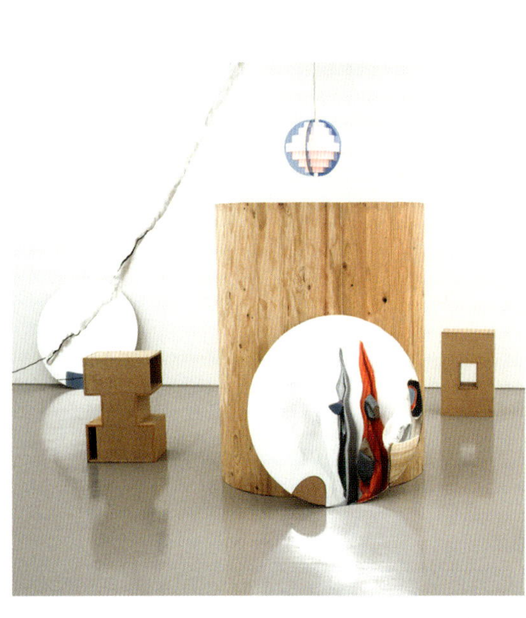

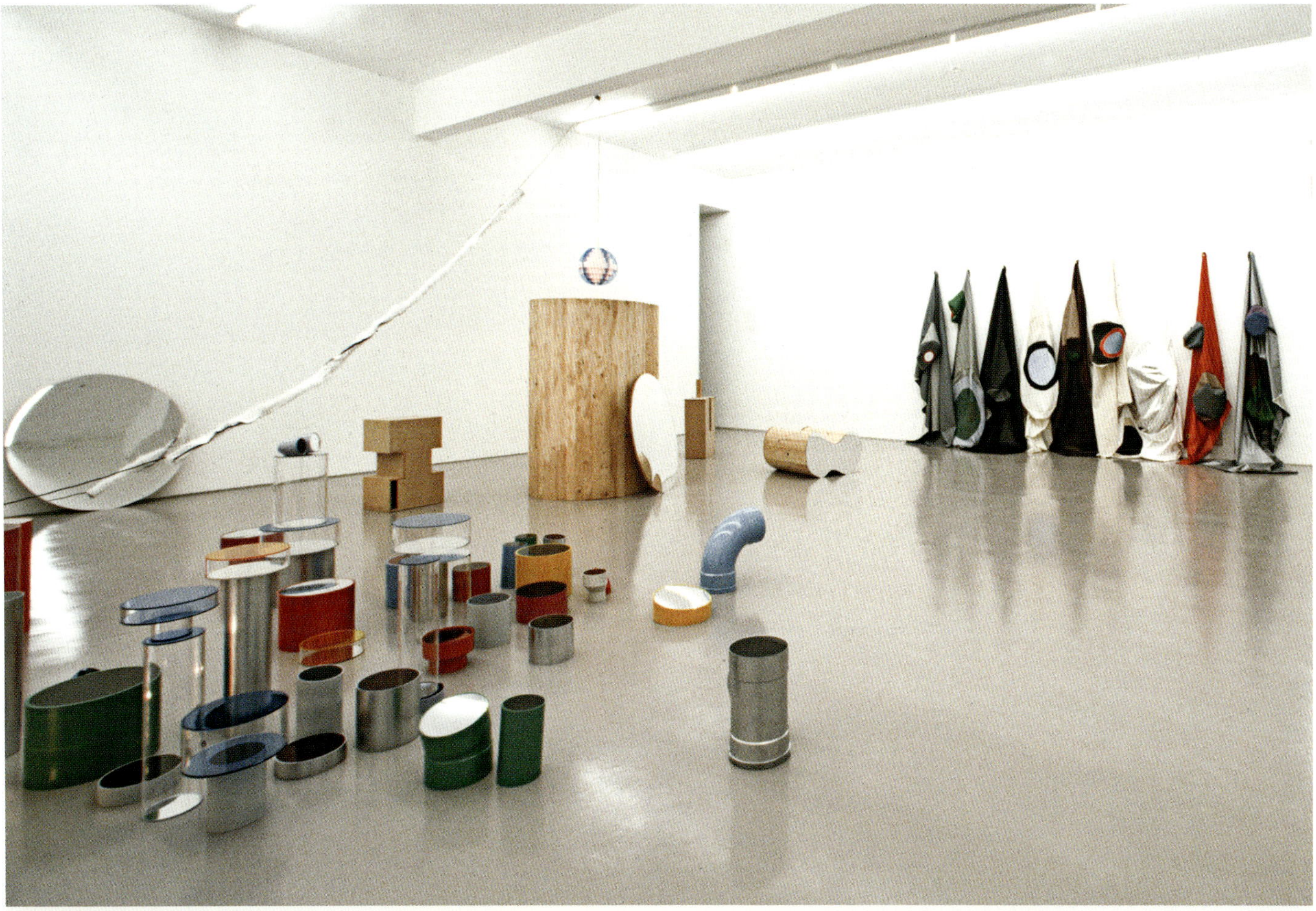

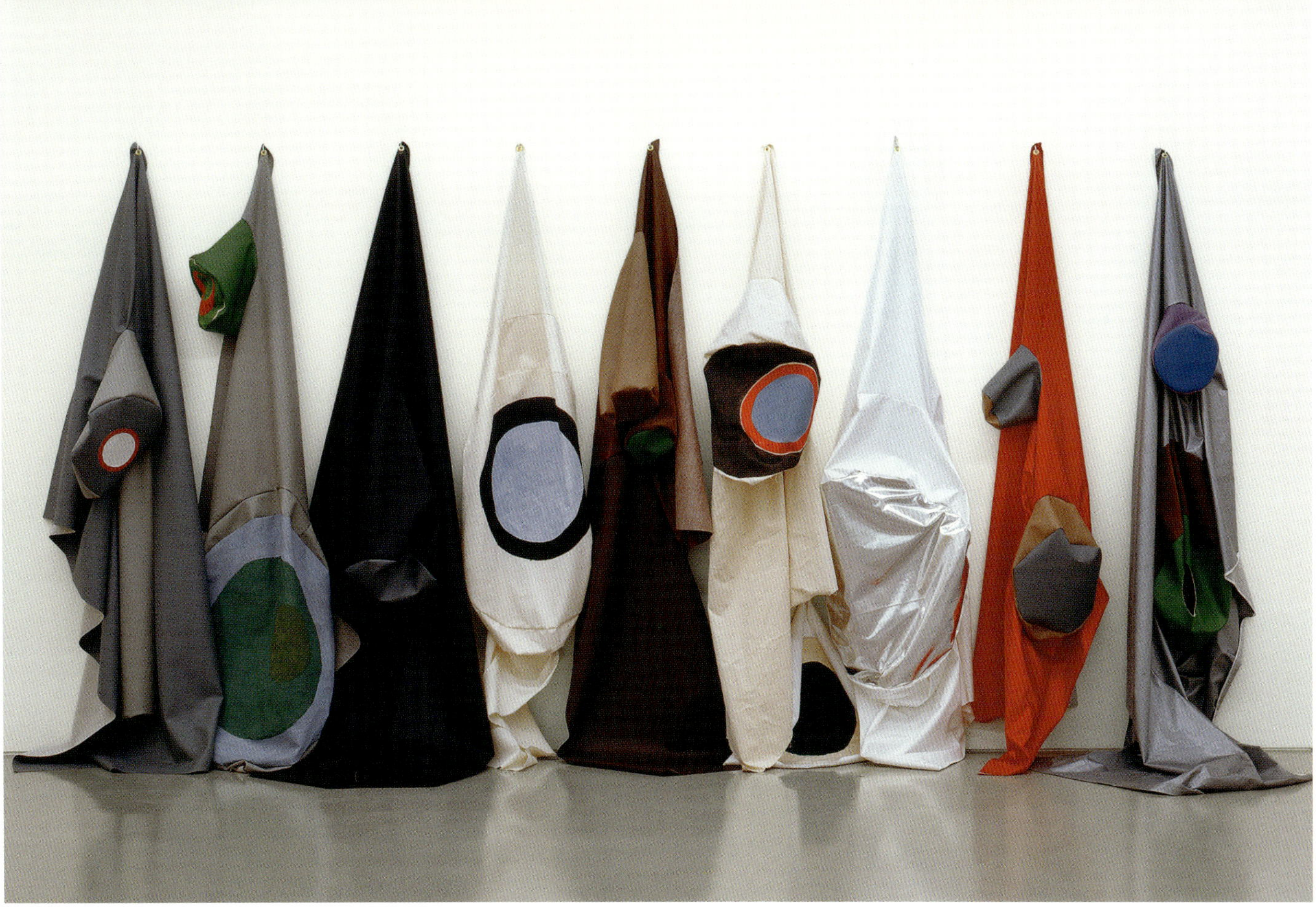

6 December 2000 —
28 January 2001
Museum of Contemporary Art
Australia, Sydney

—

opposite foreground:
Iffytown (extended version)
1999–2000
wood, vinyl, electric light bulb,
acrylic, PVC pipes, government-issue
steel ashtray

opposite background:
un 1999
wood shelf, modelling clay, glass,
acrylic, plasticine, audio tape, fabric,
glue, synthetic polymer paint

below:
exhibition installation details

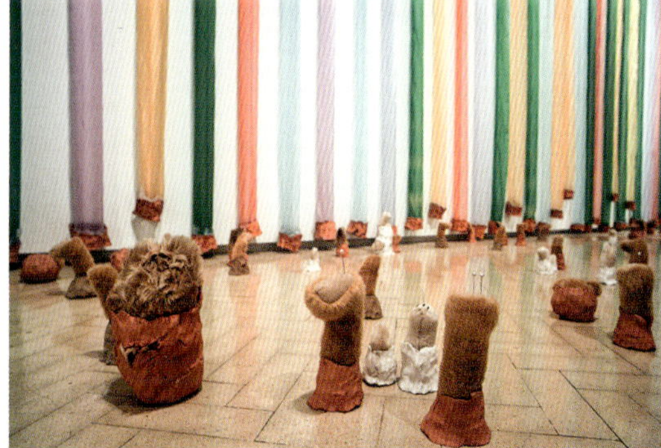

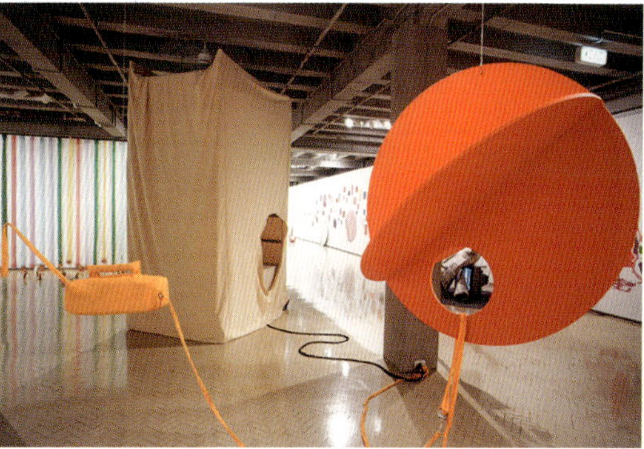

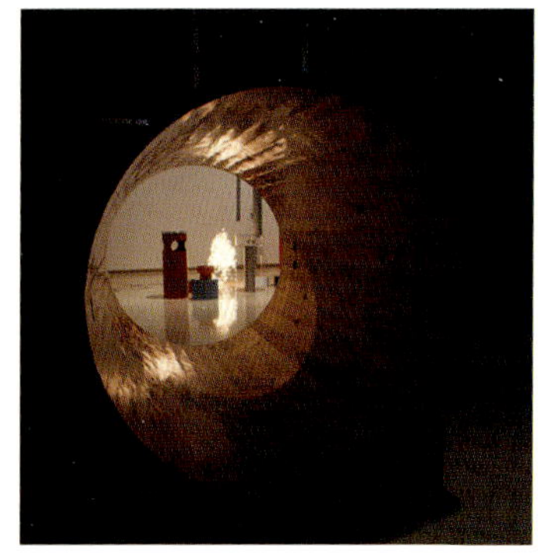

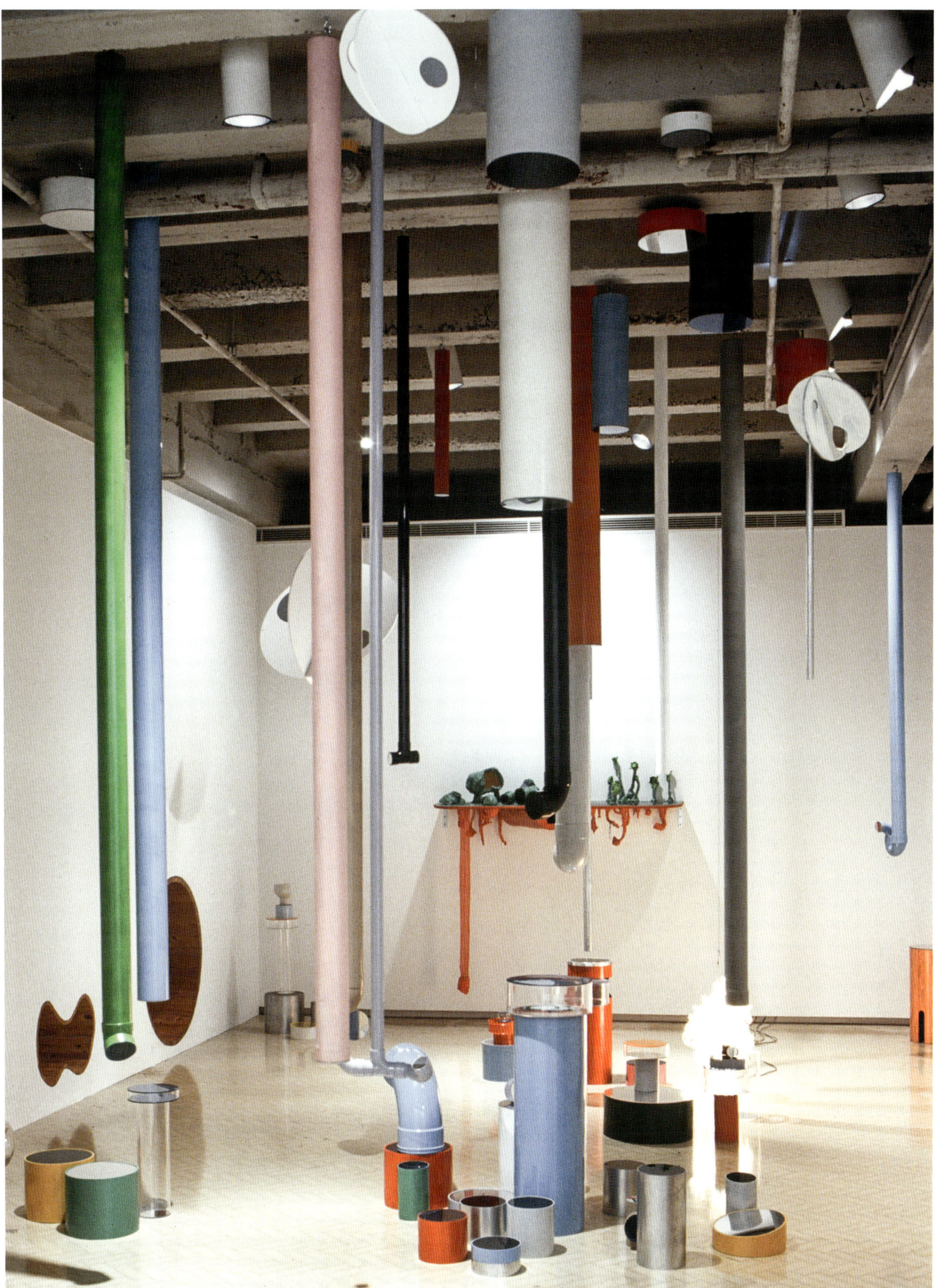

Still life:
the inaugural Balnaves Foundation
sculpture project

6 September — 2 November 2003
Art Gallery of New South Wales,
Sydney

—

Lovesongs for the cannibals 2003
plaster, plastic, wood, mirror styrene,
vinyl, DAS, modelling clay, fabric,
synthetic polymer paint, PVC, acrylic

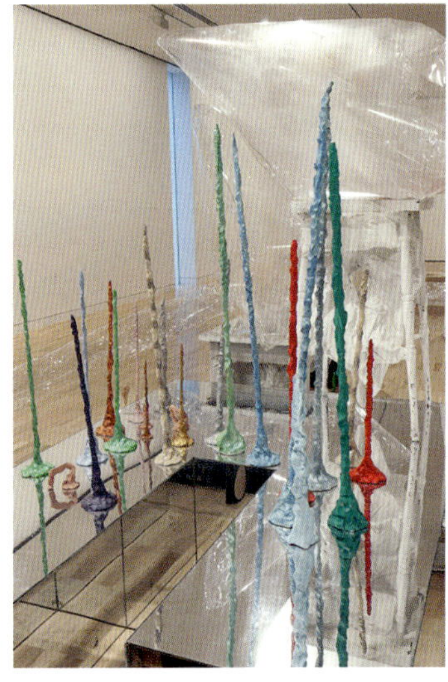

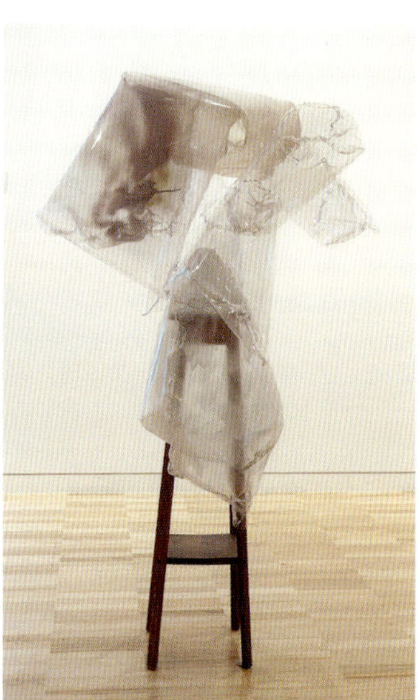

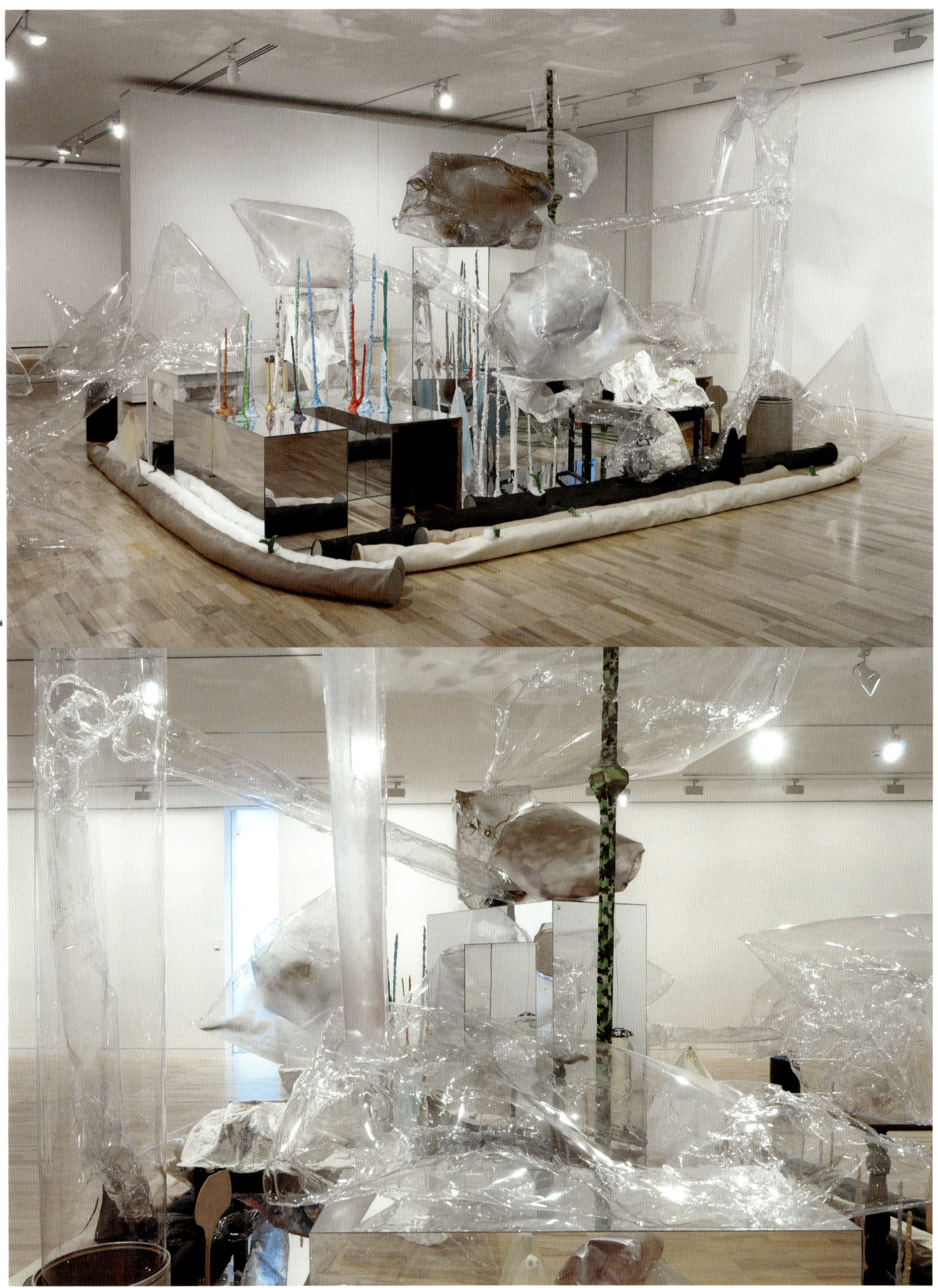

Face up:
contemporary art from Australia

—

We maybe you 2003
plastic, synthetic polymer paint,
wood, foam, fabric, modelling clay,
plaster, vinyl, mirror styrene, furniture

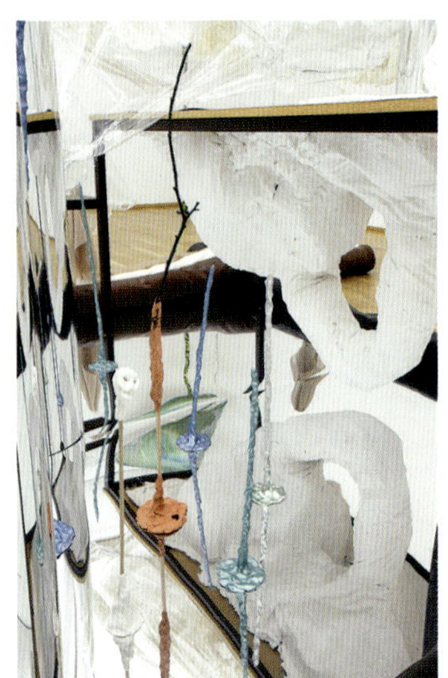

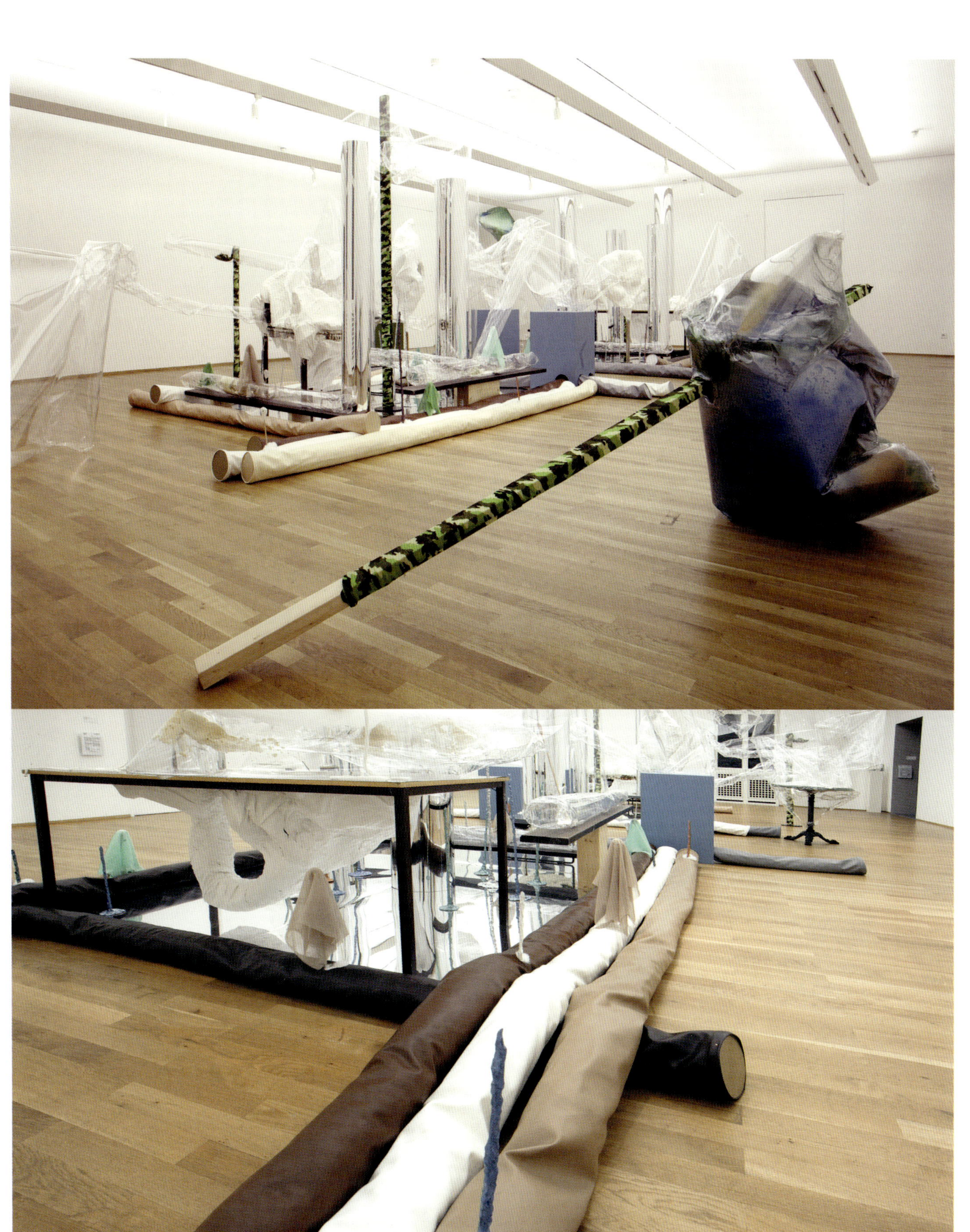

Mikala Dwyer:
Flowers, flies and someone else

11 June — 3 July 2004
Anna Schwartz Gallery, Melbourne

—

Flowers, flies and someone else
2004
plastic, wood, TV, video, plinth,
plants, Hebel stone, concrete render,
synthetic polymer paint, fabric,
acrylic mirror

below:
I maybe we 2004
Hebel stone, concrete render,
synthetic polymer paint

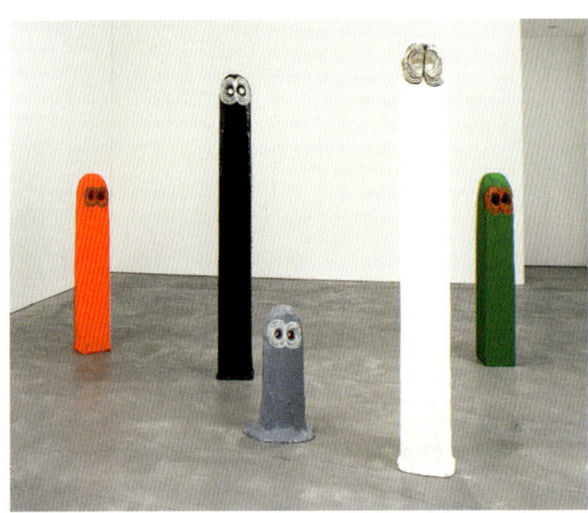

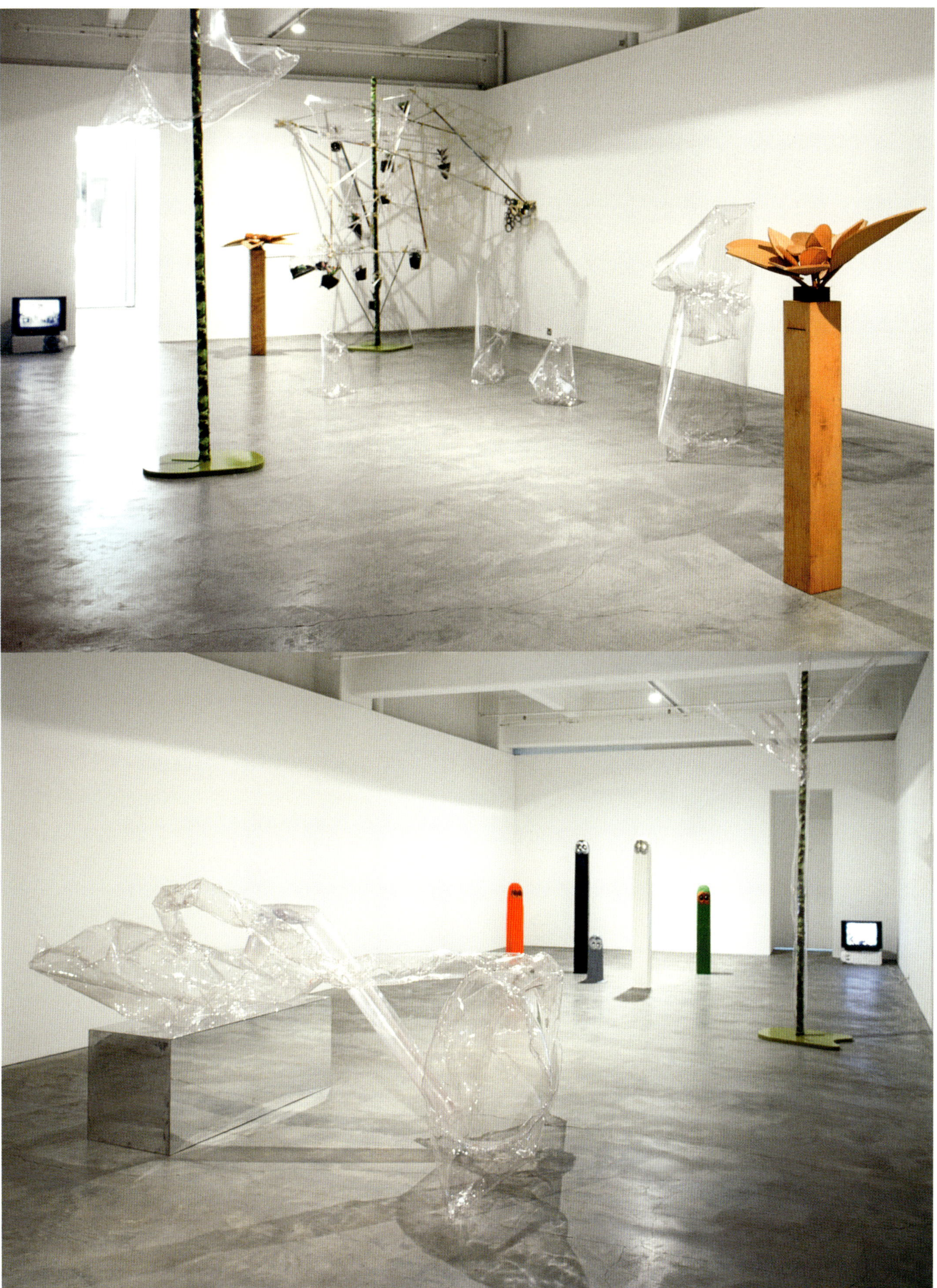

Mikala Dwyer:
Black sun, blue moon

3 February — 3 March 2007
Hamish Morrison Galerie, Berlin

—

opposite from top:

Hanging garden 2007
plastic, soil, plants

**The additions and the
subtractions** 2007
Hebel stone, balsa wood,
modelling clay, found objects

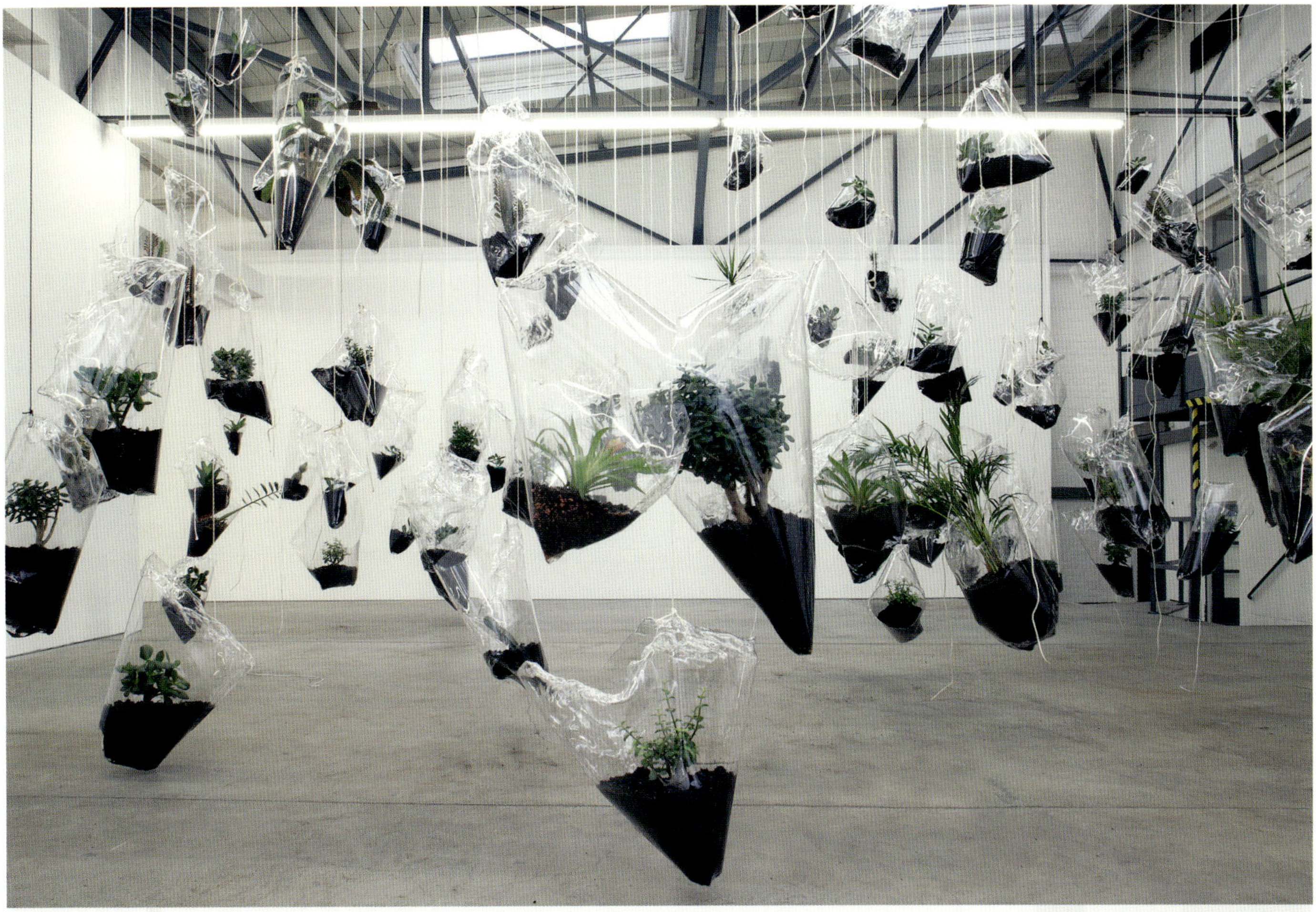

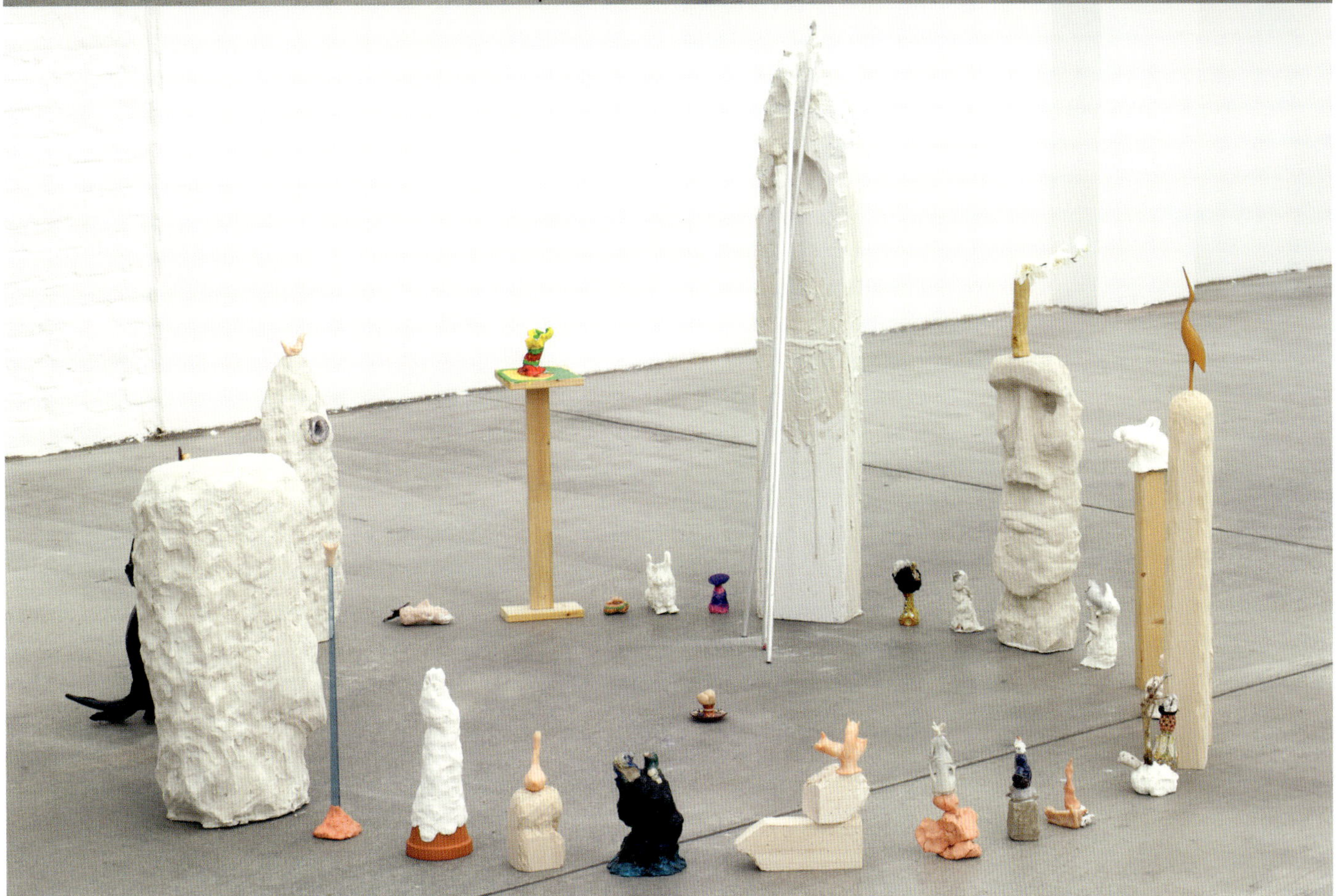

Mikala Dwyer:
Monoclinic

2 February — 2 March 2008
Hamish McKay Gallery, Wellington

—

Monoclinic 2008
clay, glass, plastic, plants, fabric, cardboard, mirror styrene, helium, balloons, sticks, concrete, hessian, felt, found chair and table, mixed media

opposite top:
Opening performance

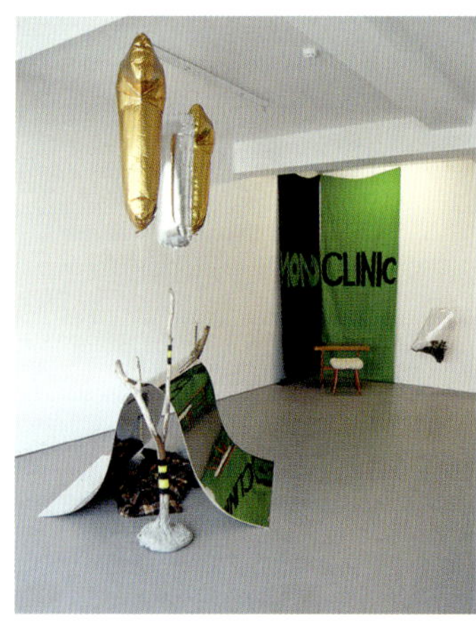

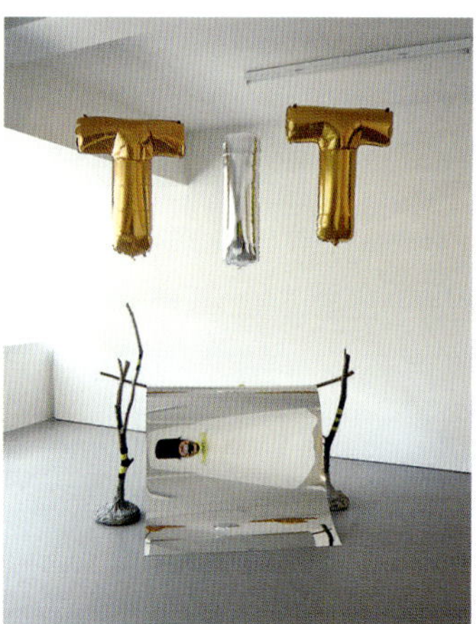

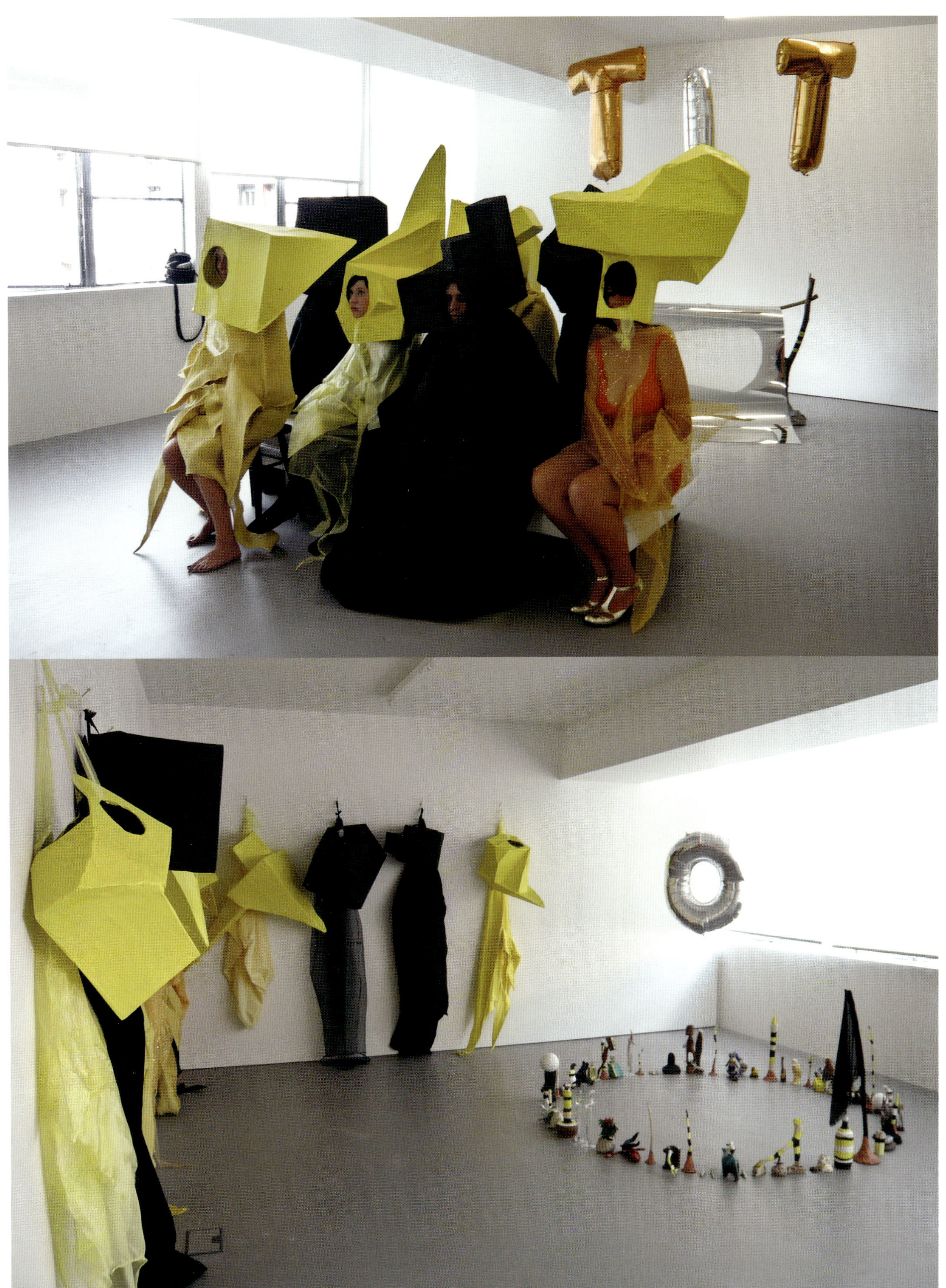

Mikala Dwyer:
Swamp geometry

10 July — 9 August 2008
Anna Schwartz Gallery, Melbourne

—

opposite from top:

Hanging garden 2008
plastic, soil, money plants

**The additions and the
subtractions** 2008
mixed media

below:

Costumes 2008
fabric, cardboard

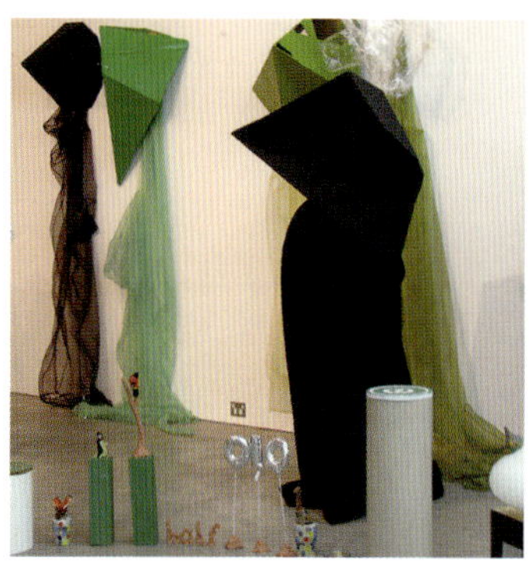

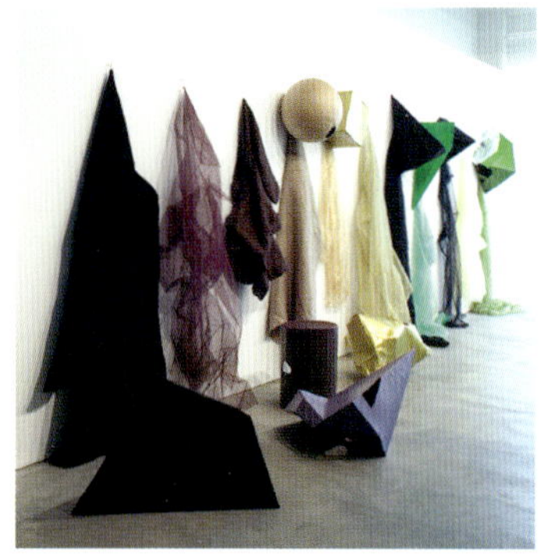

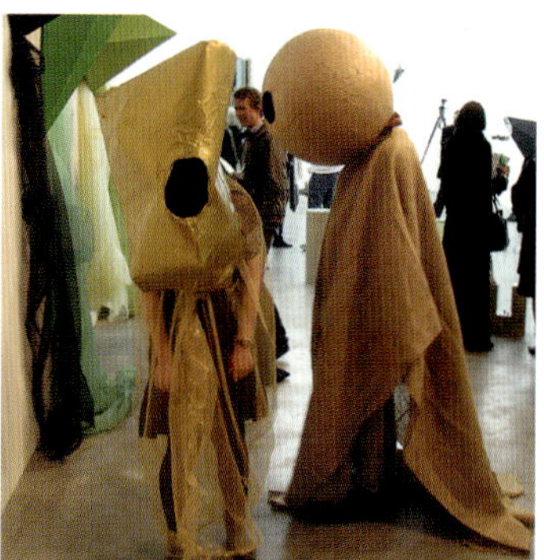

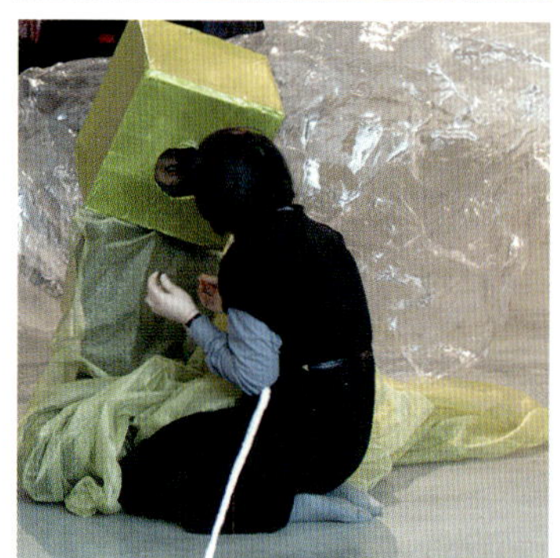

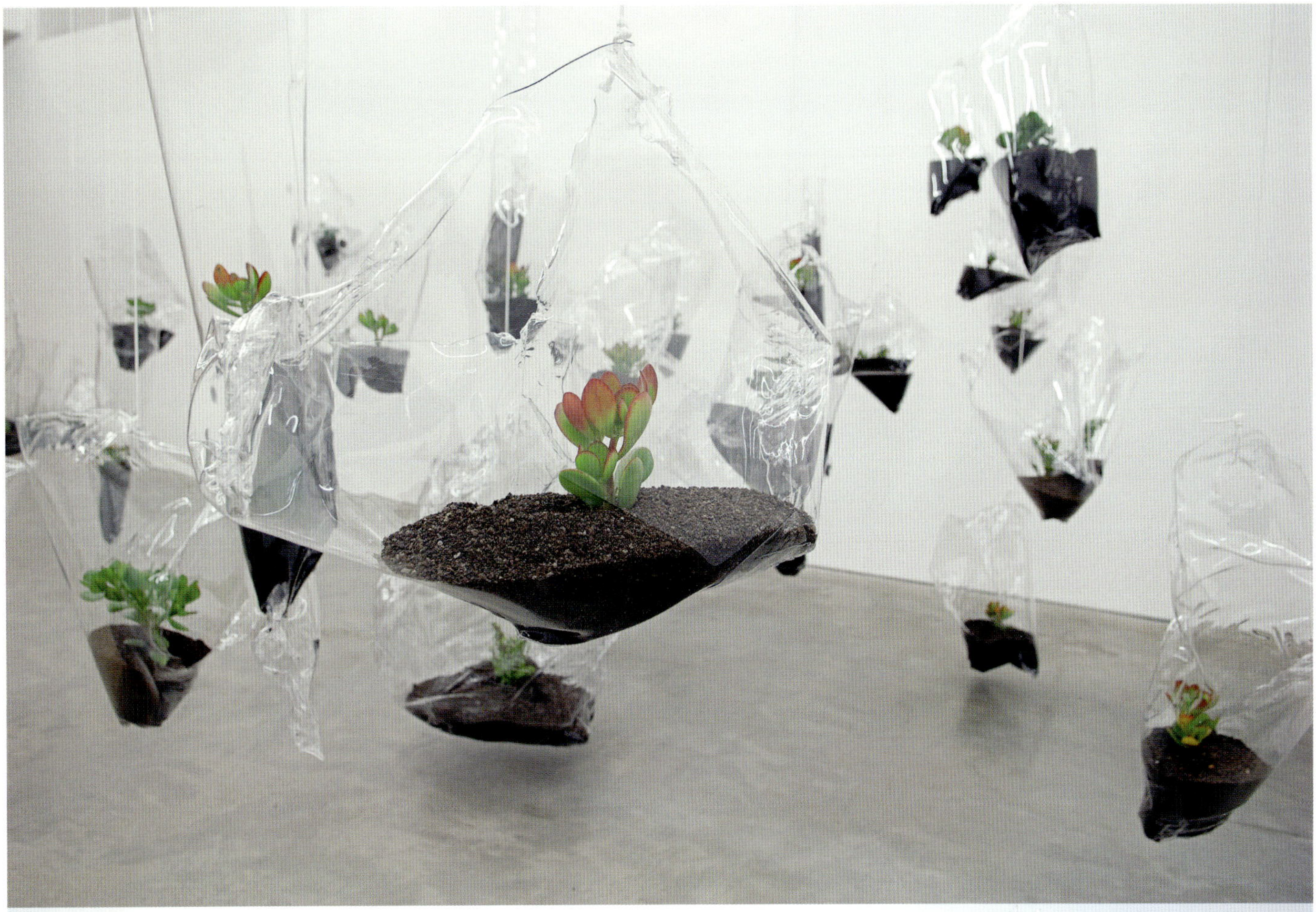

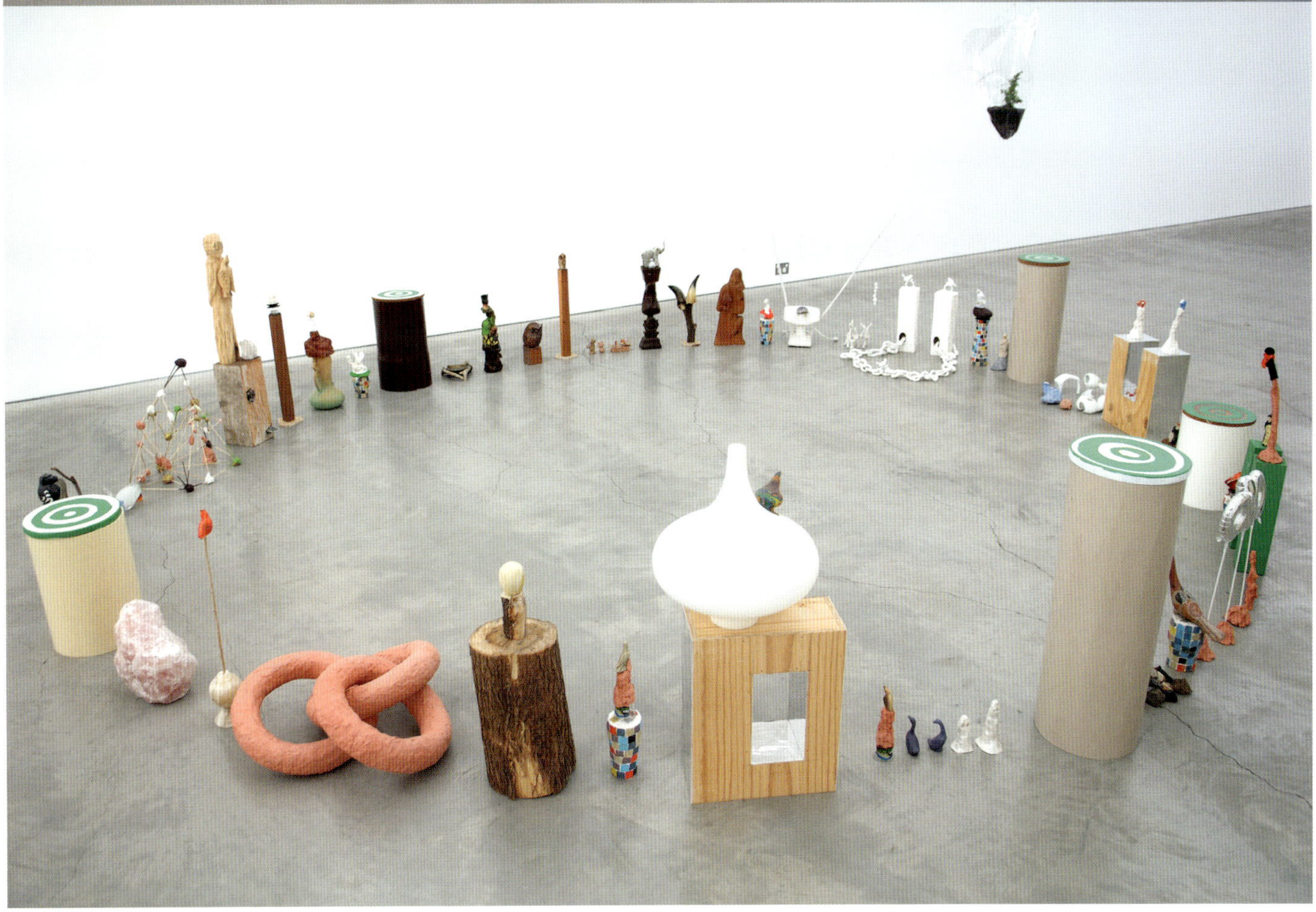

Mikala Dwyer:
Moon garden

20 December 2008 —
15 February 2009
Aratoi Wairarapa Museum of Art
and History, New Zealand

—

Moon garden 2008
plastic, plants, dirt, hessian, felt

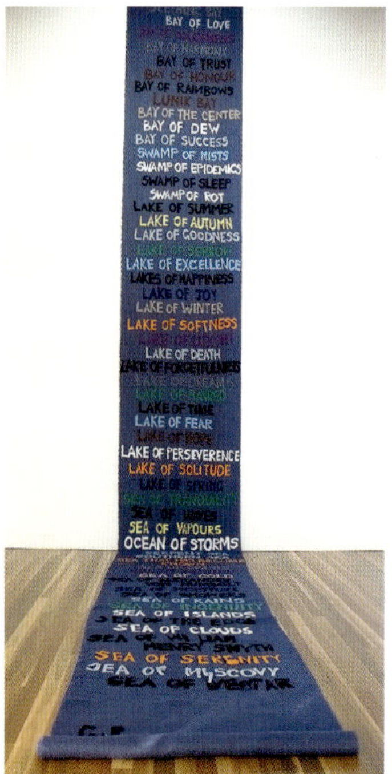

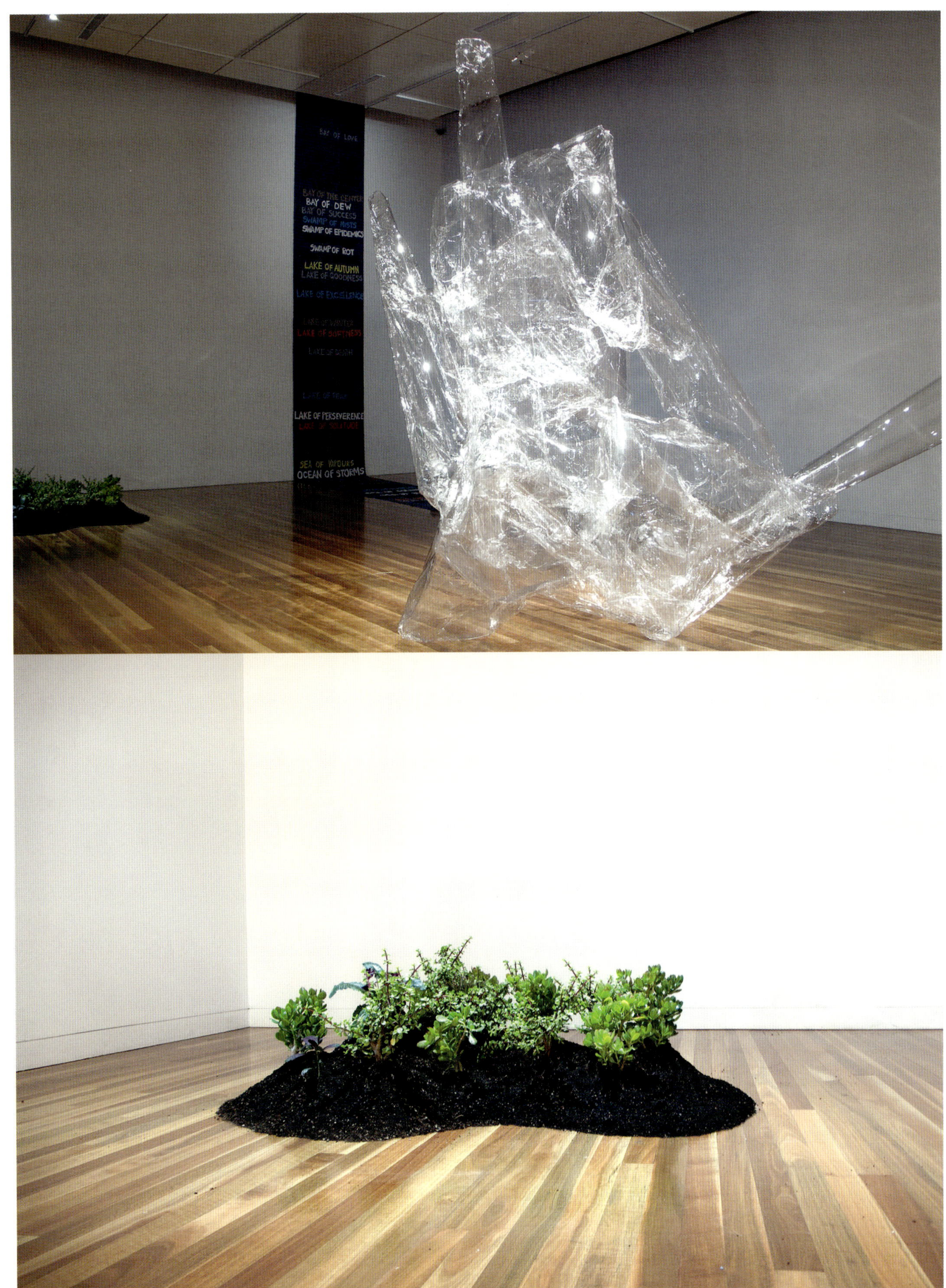
BAY OF LOVE
BAY OF THE CENTER
BAY OF DEW
BAY OF SUCCESS
SWAMP OF MISTS
SWAMP OF EPIDEMICS
SWAMP OF ROT
LAKE OF AUTUMN
LAKE OF GOODNESS
LAKE OF EXCELLENCE
LAKE OF WINTER
LAKE OF SOFTNESS
LAKE OF DEATH
LAKE OF FEAR
LAKE OF PERSEVERENCE
LAKE OF SOLITUDE
SEA OF VAPOURS
OCEAN OF STORMS

Mikala Dwyer:
Outfield

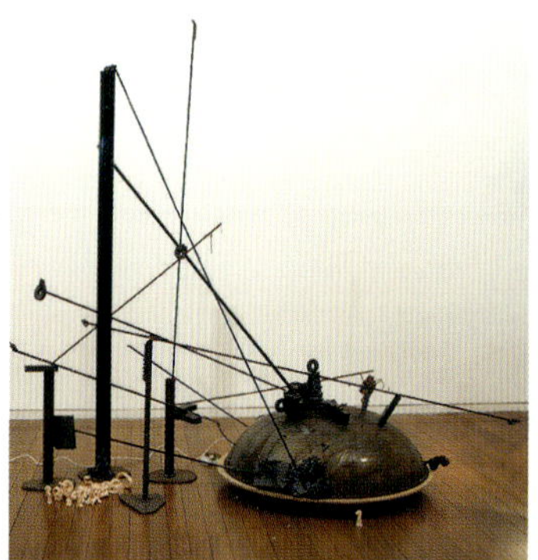

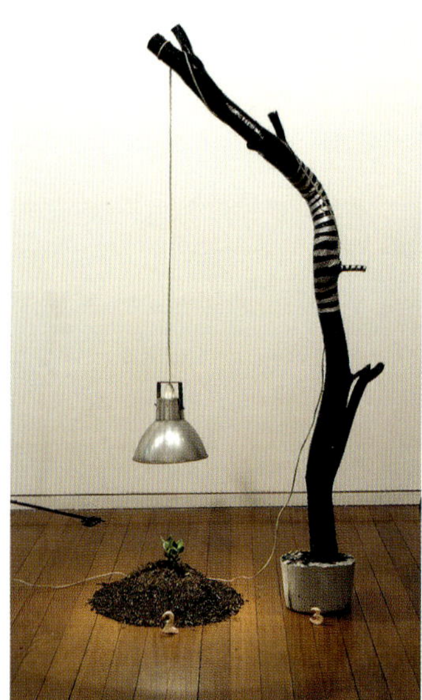

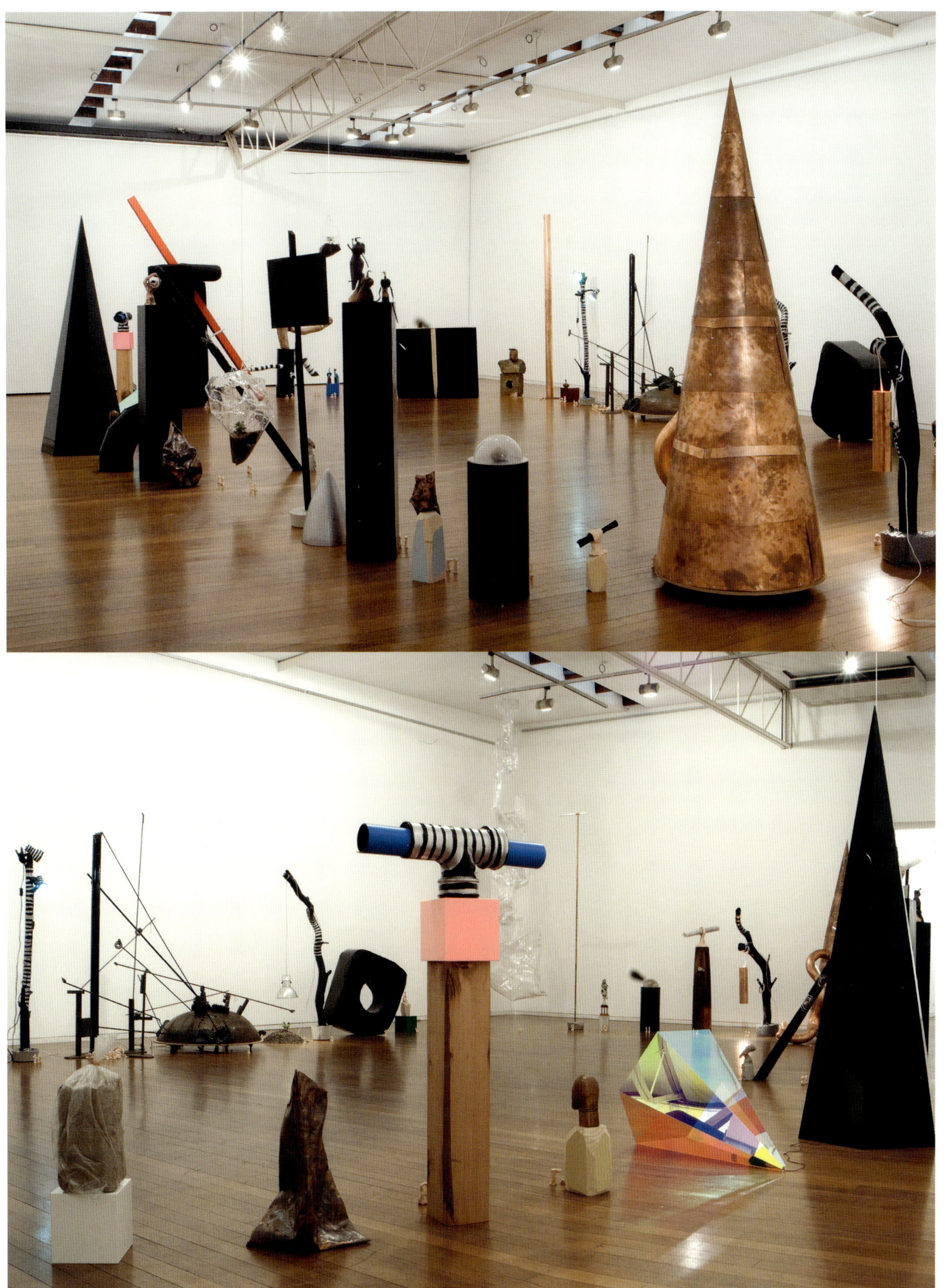

17th Biennale of Sydney
The beauty of distance:
songs of survival in a precarious age

12 May — 10 August 2010
Cockatoo Island, Sydney

—

opposite:

An apparition of a subtraction
2010
sandstone, audio, speakers, acrylic,
plastic, wood, mixed media

below from left:

Captain Thunderbolt's sisters
and **Red rockers** 2010
video performances
Justene Williams and Mikala Dwyer
Cockatoo Island, Sydney

**An apparition of a subtraction
(cave)** 2010
plastic, acrylic, lights, blankets

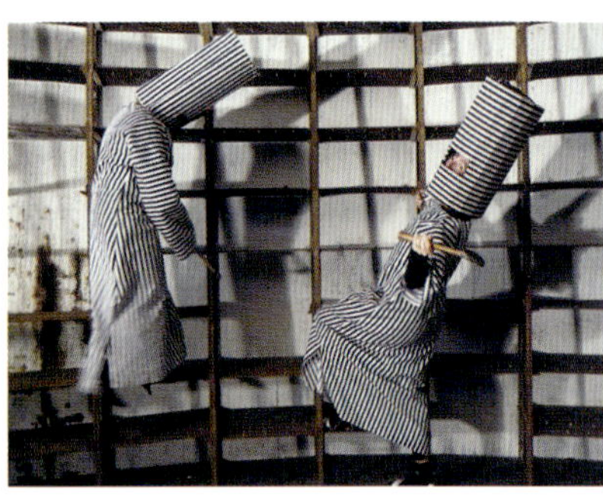

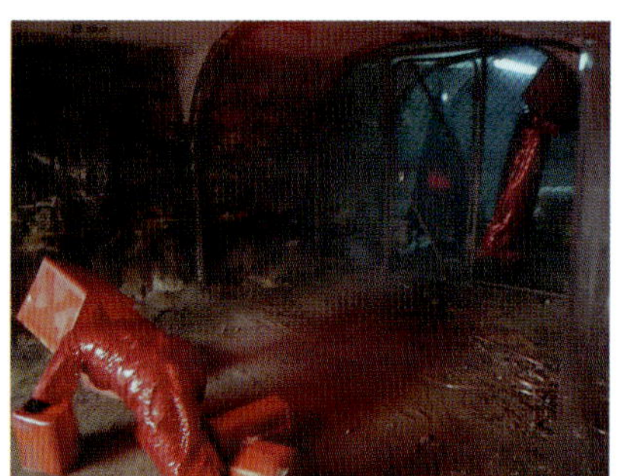

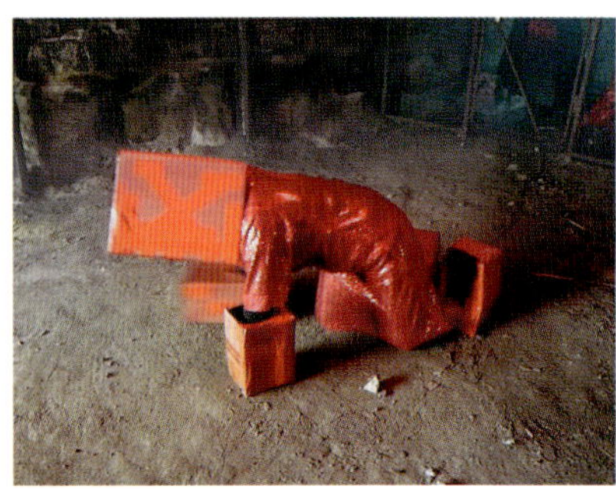

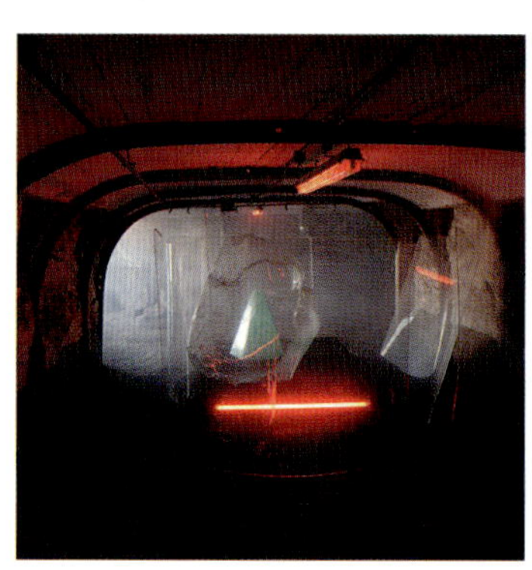

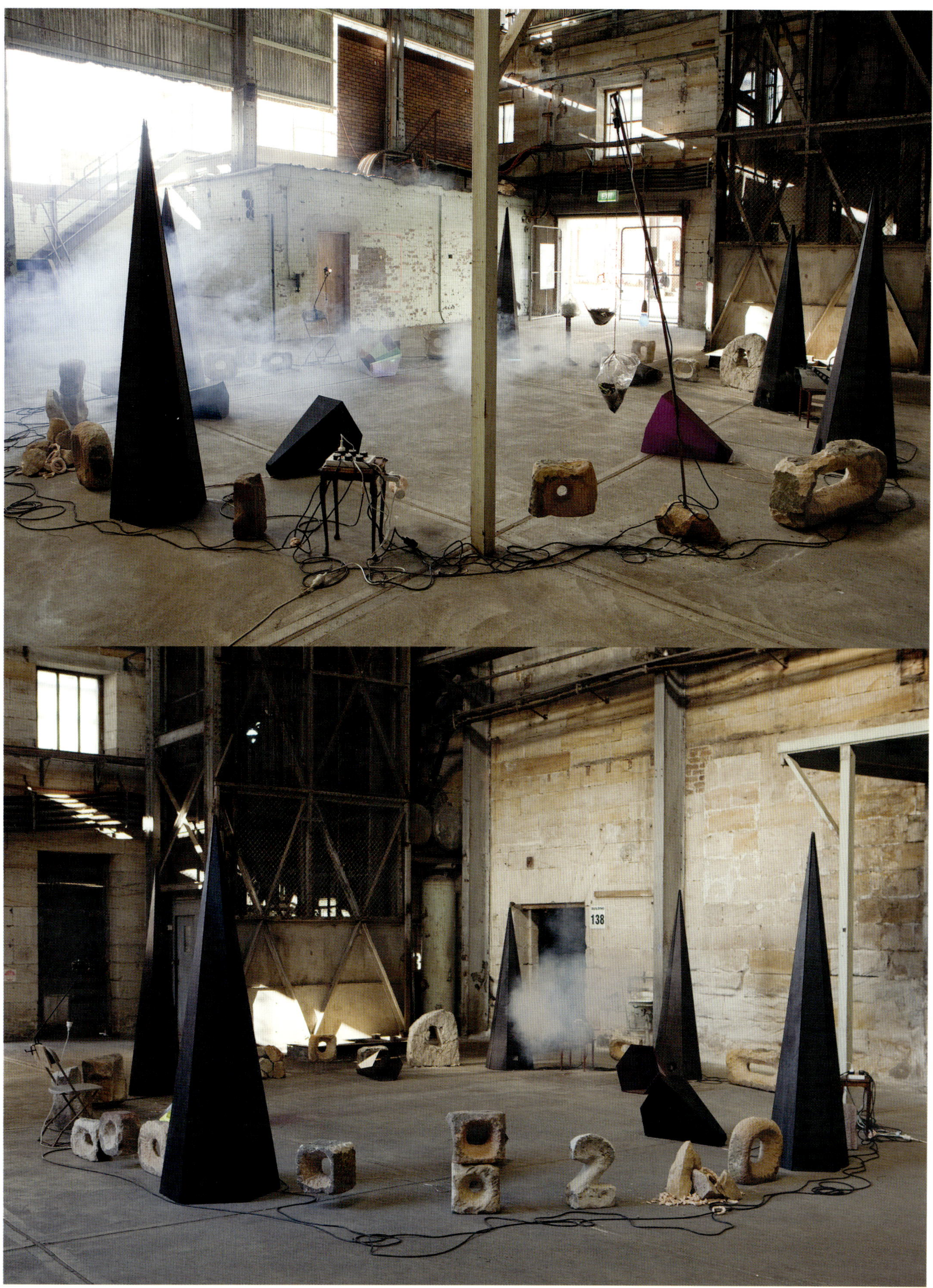

Mikala Dwyer:
Square cloud compound

10 September — 23 October 2010
Hamish Morrison Galerie, Berlin

—

opposite:

Square cloud compound 2010
fabric stockings, glass, beer,
champagne, plastic, ceramics,
found things, wood, rocks, lights,
paint, acrylic, cat and bird ornaments

below:

The silvering 2010
mylar, helium

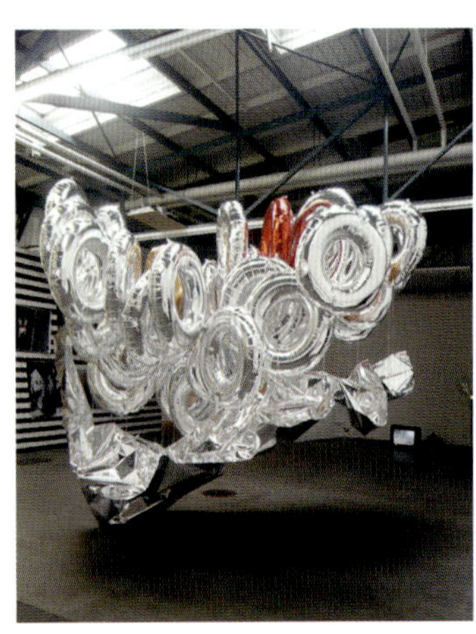

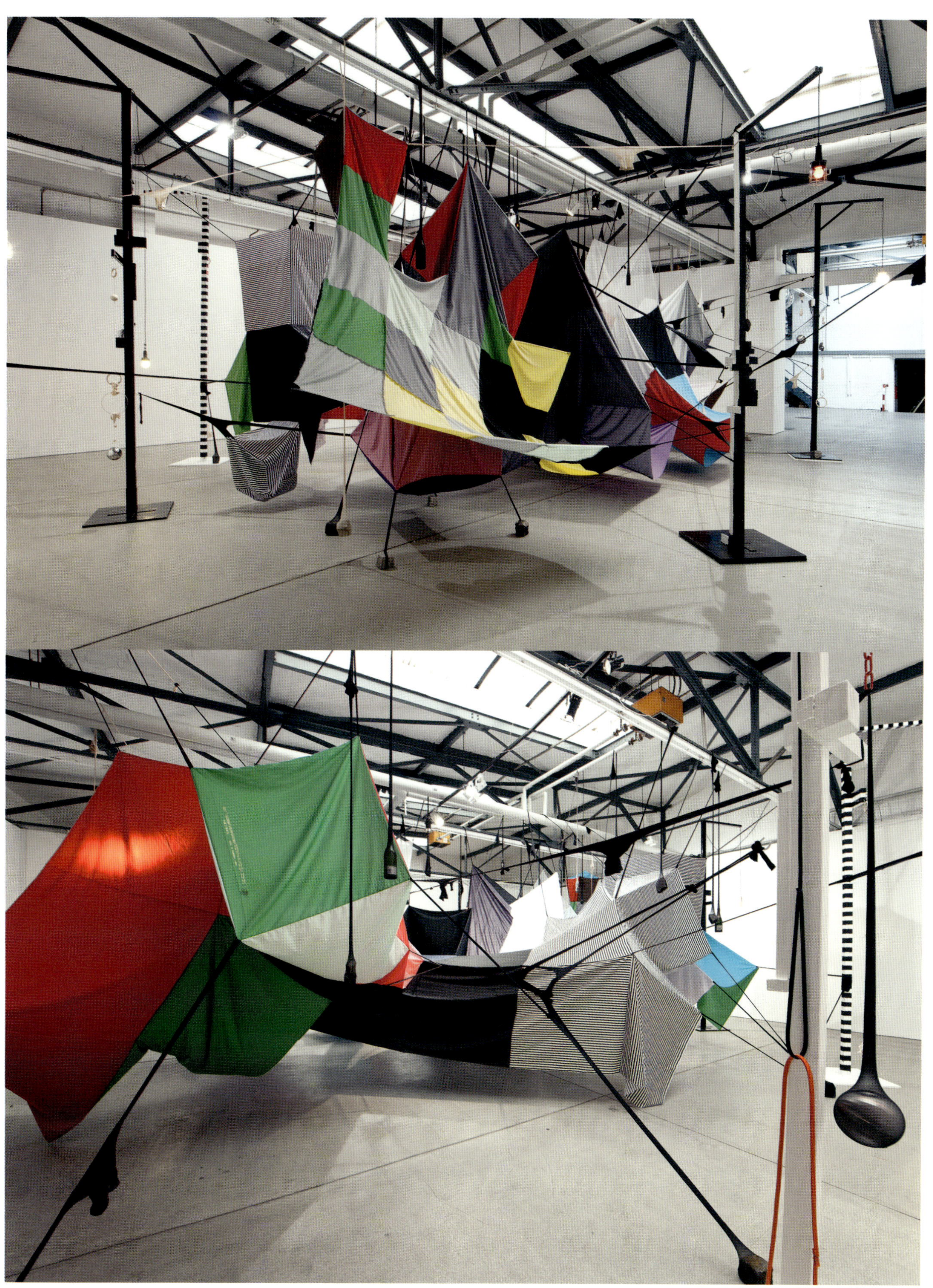

Mikala Dwyer:
Divinations for the real things

23 June — 21 July 2012
Roslyn Oxley9 Gallery, Sydney

—

opposite from top:

Diviner 2012
acrylic, steel, rope, bronze, glazed
ceramic, dirt, plastic, mandarin seeds

The things in things 2012
found objects, ceramic, glaze,
epoxy filler

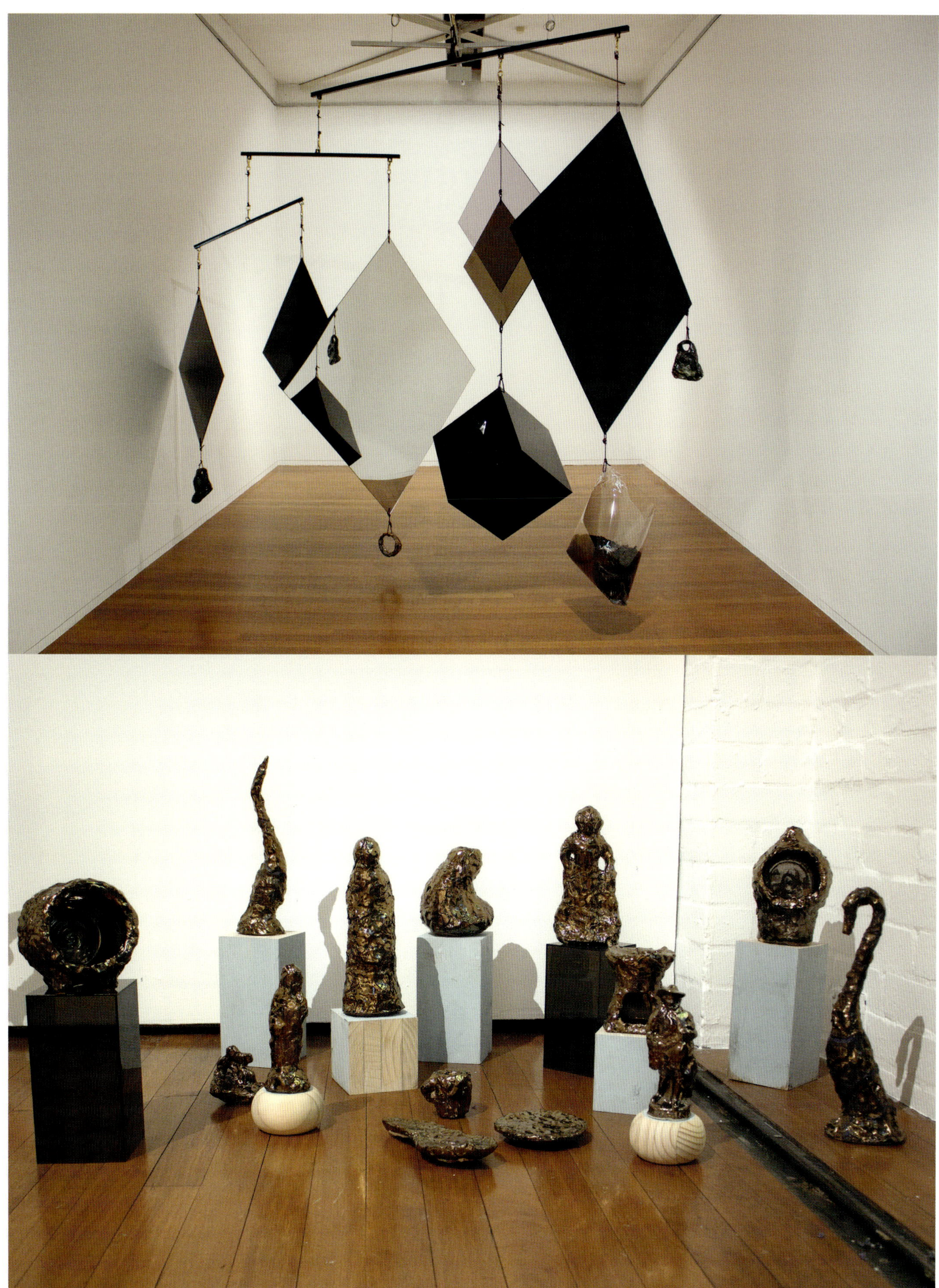

Mikala Dwyer:
Drawing down the moon

opposite from top:

The additions and the subtractions 2012
wood, fabric, acrylic, copper, coal, quartz, crystal, IKEA couch, wine, cigarettes, book, steel, magnets, found objects

Alterbeast (Carla Cescon, Mikala Dwyer and Tina Havelock Stevens) with Roland Souliere
Alphabet for ghosts 2011
acrylic, wheels, wood, synthetic polymer paint

below, clockwise from top right:

Costumes 2012
fabric, cardboard

Wall necklace 2012
acrylic, fabric, ceramic, steel, whiskey

Spell for a corner 2012
synthetic polymer paint on gallery wall

Lamps 2010–12 (detail)
wood, paint, stones, lights, fabric, found objects

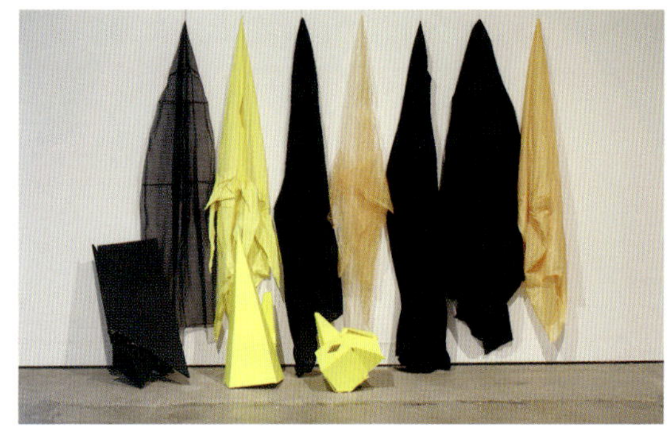

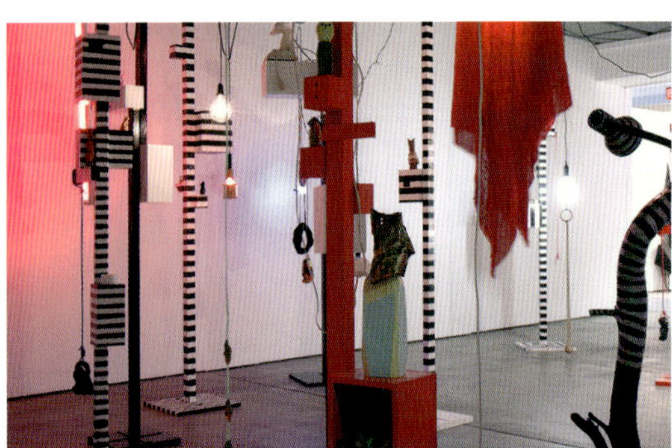

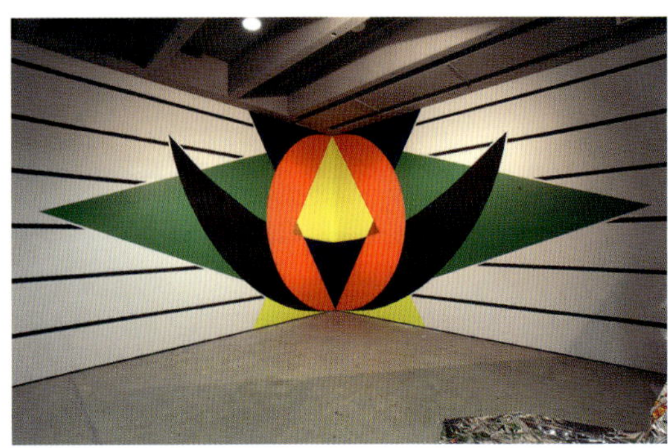

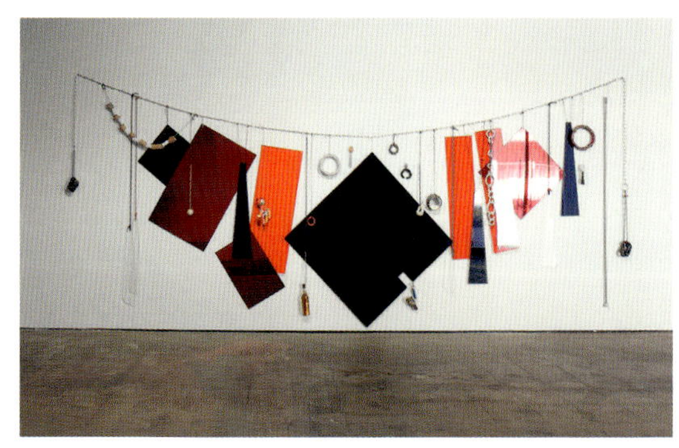

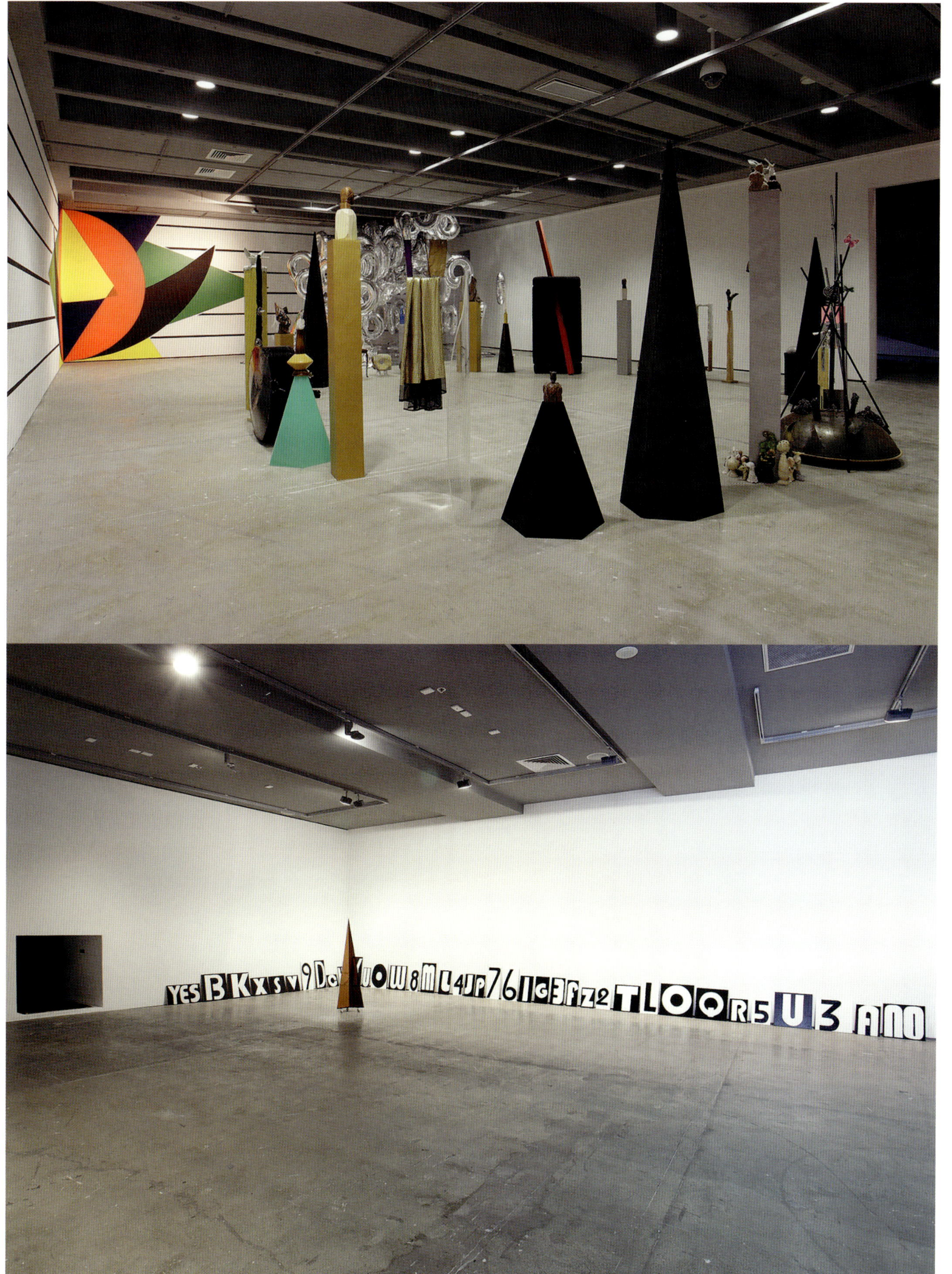

YES B K x s v 9 D c Y u O W 8 M L 4 J P 7 6 I G 3 F z 2 T L O Q R 5 U 3 A N 0

Mikala Dwyer:
Panto collapsar

27 January — 31 March 2012
Project Arts Centre, Dublin

—

opposite from top:

Panto collapsar 2012
mixed media

**The additions and the
subtractions** 2012
wood, metal, plastic, Marlboro
Gold cigarettes, whiskey, gold paint,
coins, spirit level, short-stem glasses,
clay, stones, video, semi-precious
stones, ceramic, papier-mache,
found objects

below:

**The additions and the
subtractions** 2012 (detail)

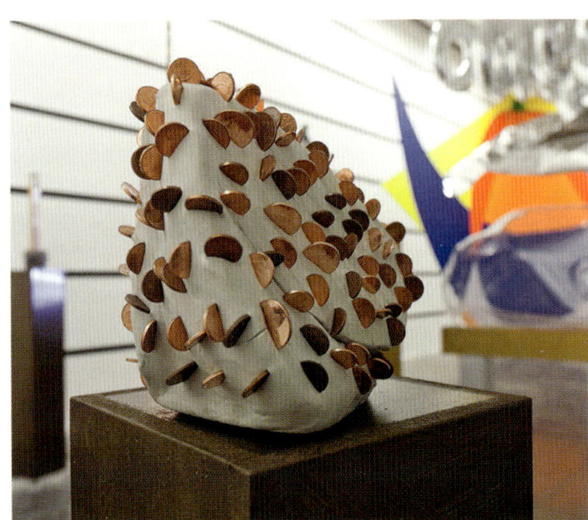

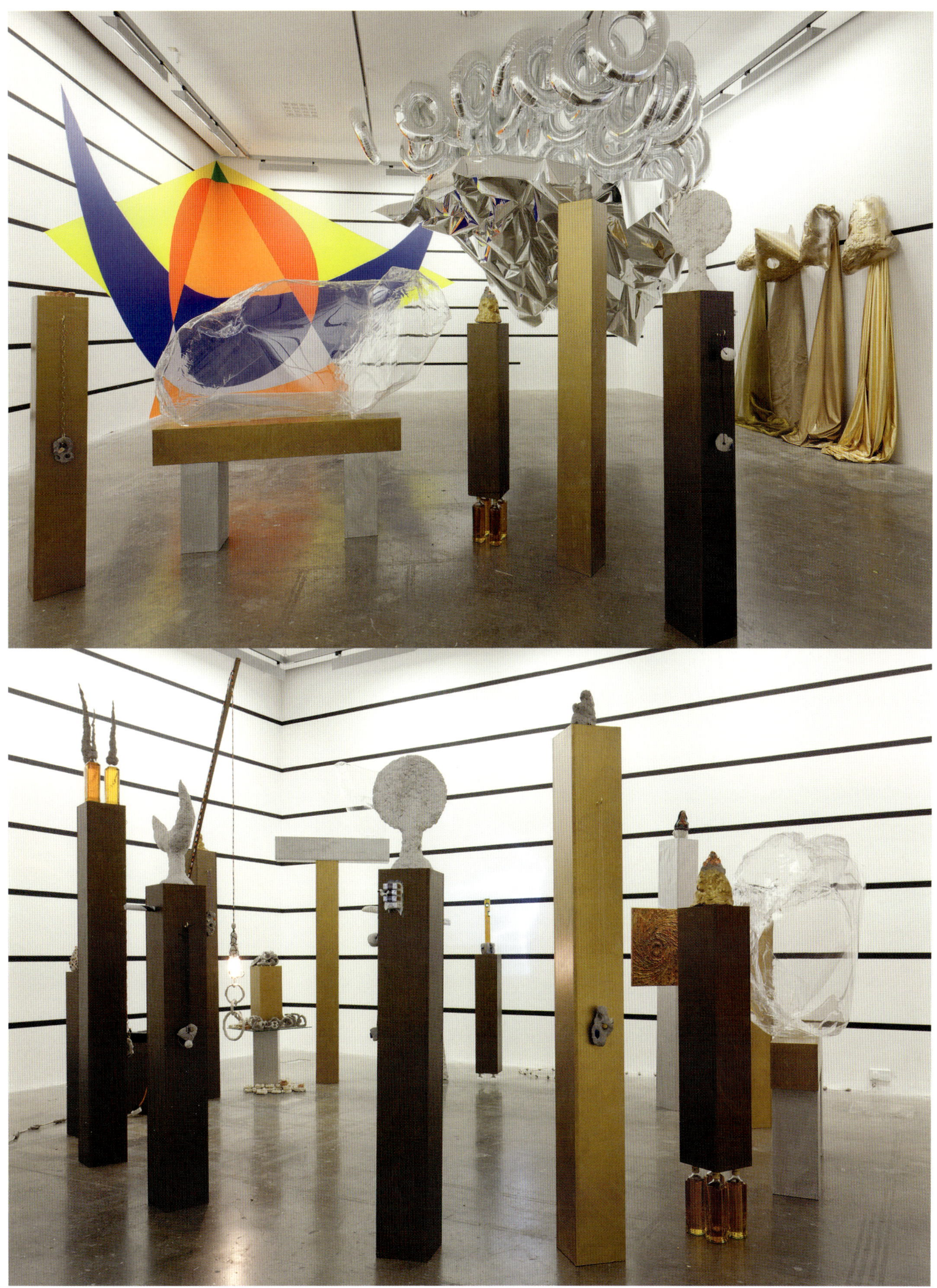

Mikala Dwyer:
Goldene bend'er

25 May — 28 July 2013
Australian Centre for Contemporary
Art, Melbourne

—

opposite from top:
Goldene bend'er 2013
costumes, objects, single-channel
documentation of performance with
sound, fabric, plastic, synthetic
polymer paint, acrylic, steel, shit
soundtrack: 'Circle piece' composed
by Laurie Scott Baker, performed by
Scratch Orchestra, 1970
Opening night performance

below from top:
Spell for a corner 2013
synthetic polymer paint on gallery
wall

Hollowwork (ringing) 2013
wood, Corten steel, polished
aluminium, paint, ceramics,
crackle goldene glaze
From original ring designs
by Dorothy Dwyer

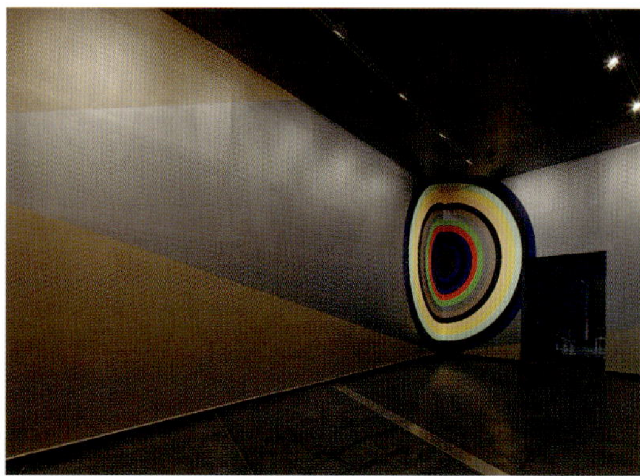

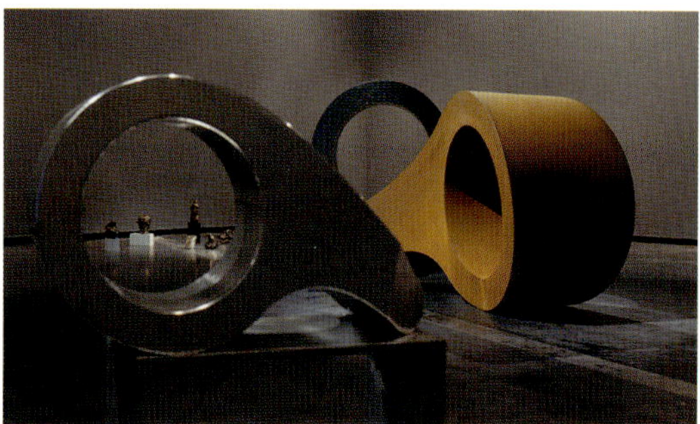

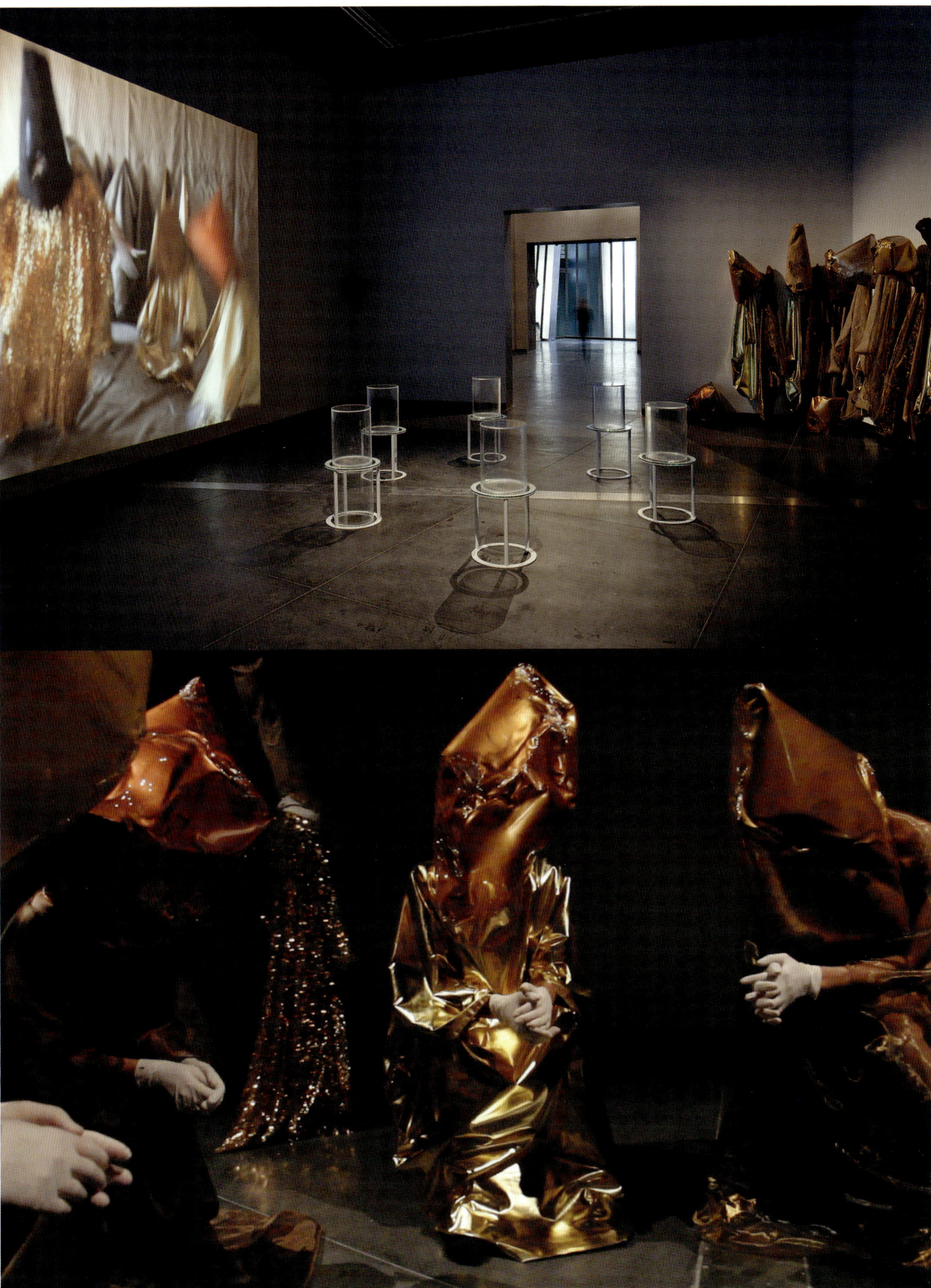

Mikala Dwyer:
Goldene bend'er

—

Agebbo skoven 2013
performance with costumes
at a Viking burial ground

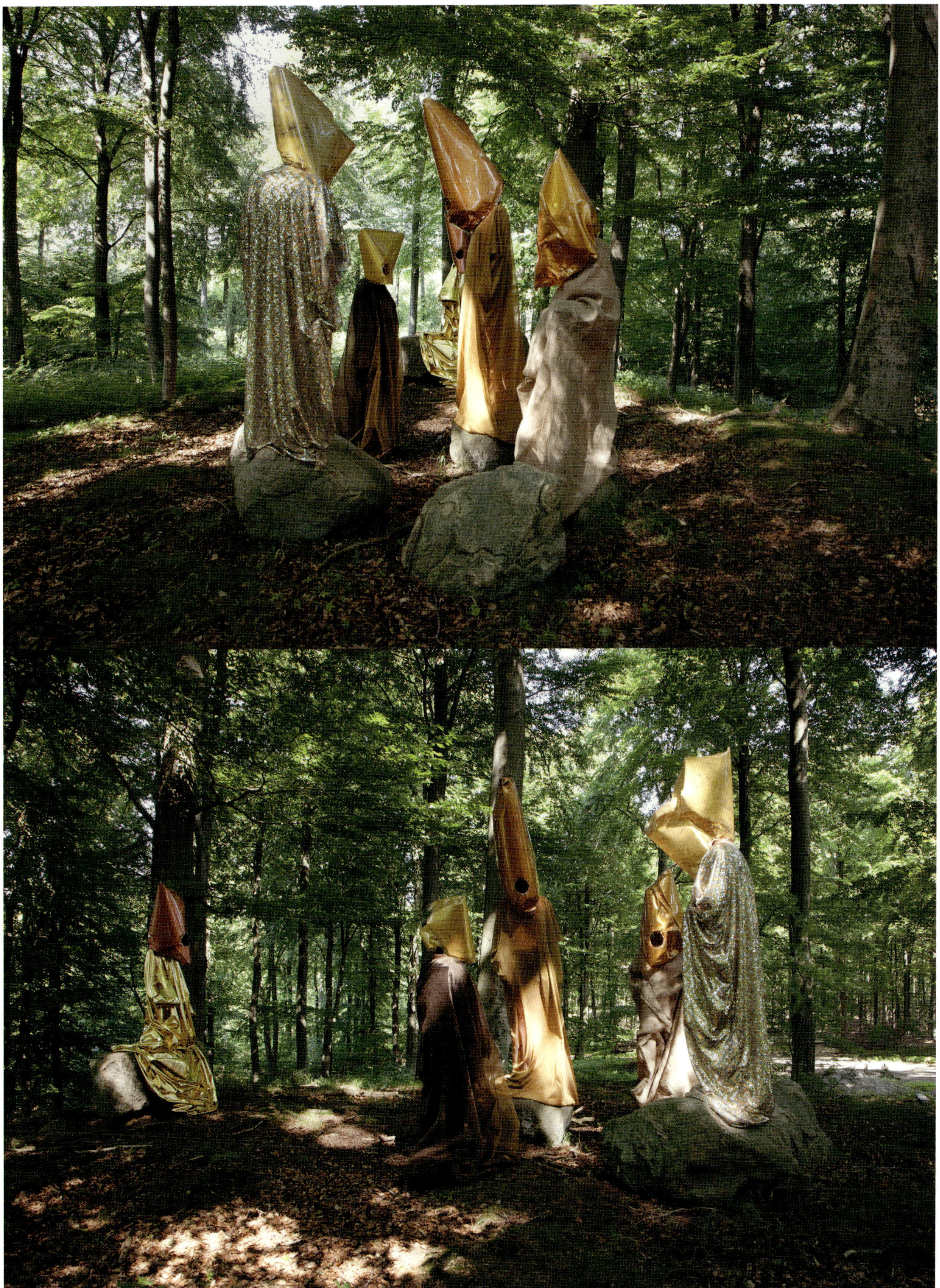

The end of the 20th century.
The best is yet to come.
A dialogue with the Marx Collection

14 September 2013 — 27 April 2014
Hamburger Bahnhof, Berlin

—

The silvering 2013
mylar, helium

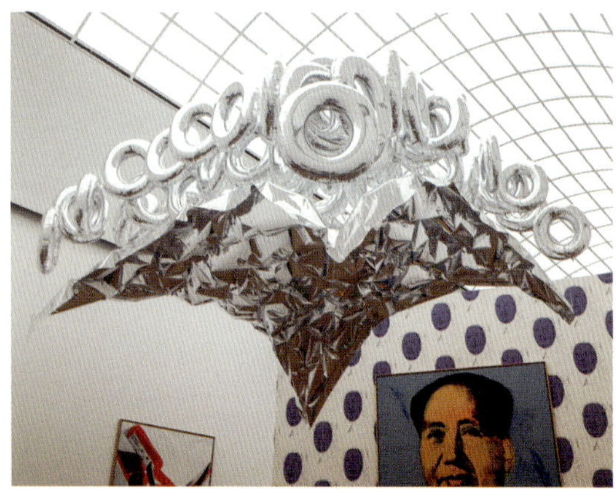

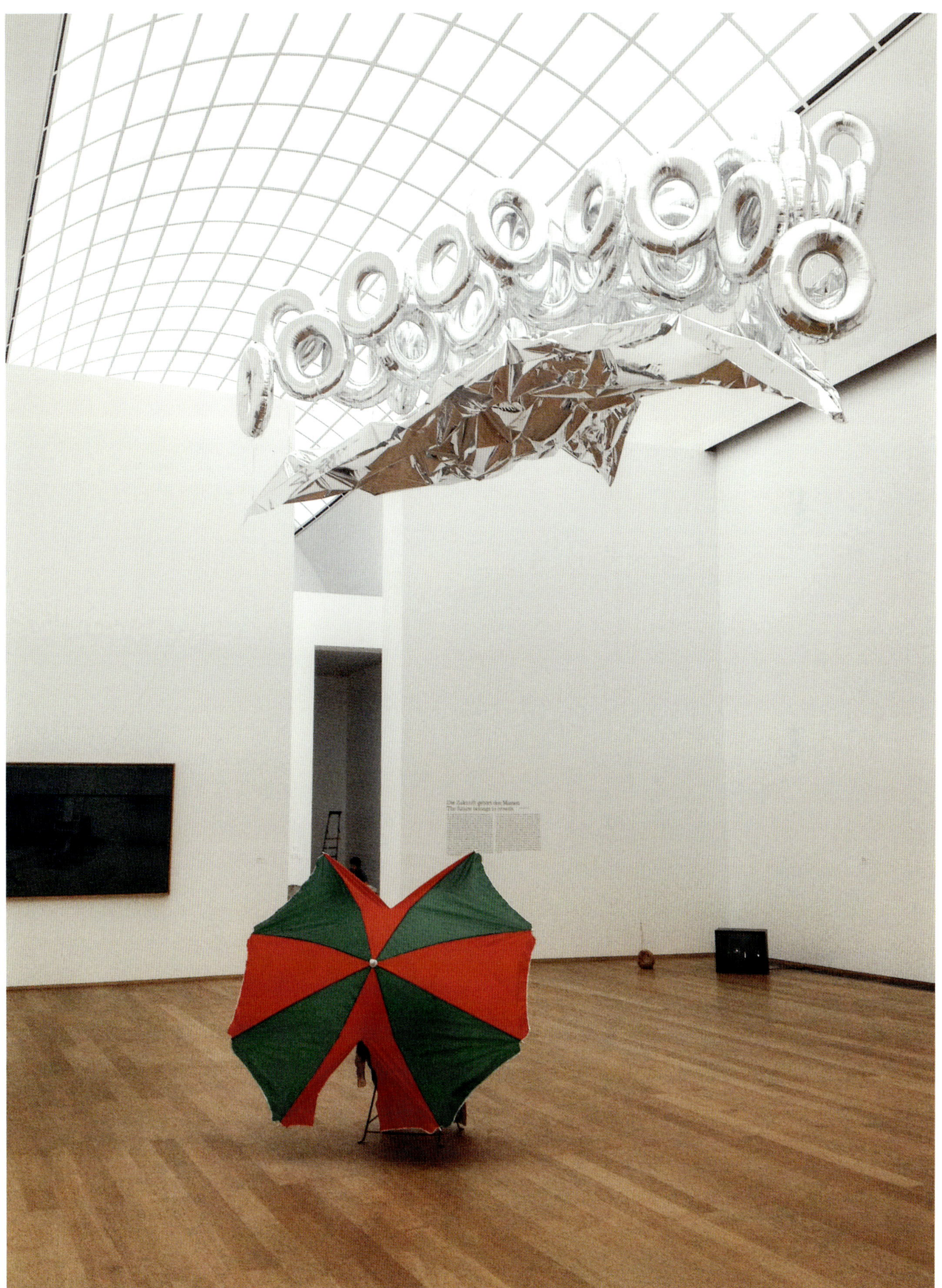
Die Zukunft gehört den Massen
The future belongs to crowds

19th Biennale of Sydney
You imagine what you desire

—

The hollows 2014
plastic, steel, rope

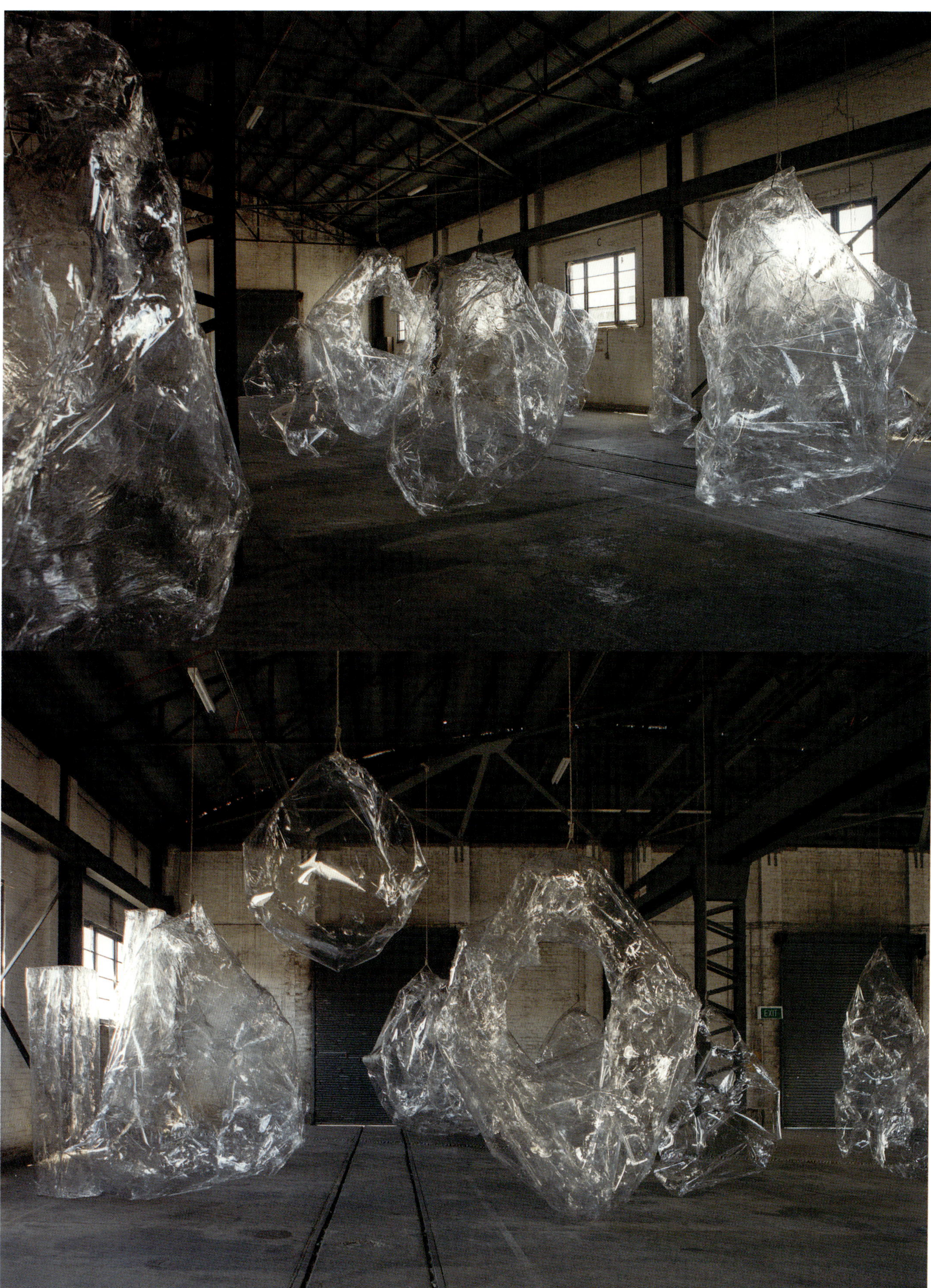

Mikala Dwyer:
The garden of half-life

5 September 2014 —
17 January 2015
University Art Gallery,
University of Sydney

—

The garden of half-life 2014
synthetic polymer paintings on wall;
coloured and ultraviolet fluorescent
lights; lampstands comprising
synthetic polymer paint on wood,
power cords, light fittings, found
objects, air-drying clay; four video
monitors playing *Dust*, *The cave*,
The dungeon, *The plane* and
Hypnosis, performed by Phillip
Adams, cinematography by Alejandra
Canales and Mikala Dwyer; clear,
mirror and black acrylic display
devices, some based on Piet Hein's
SOMA cube design; synthetic
polymer paint on PVC pipe; rocks
and minerals from Sydney University
Geo Science collection

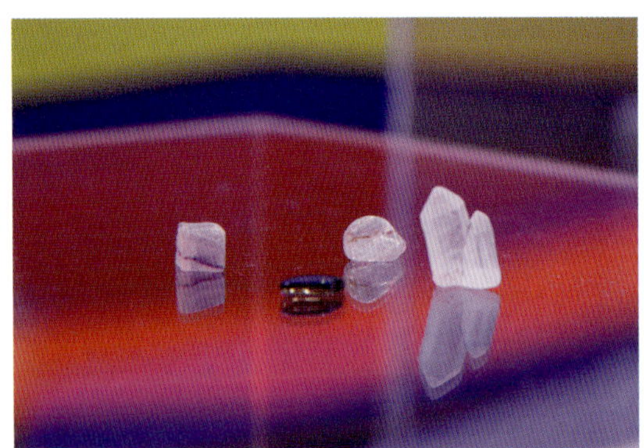

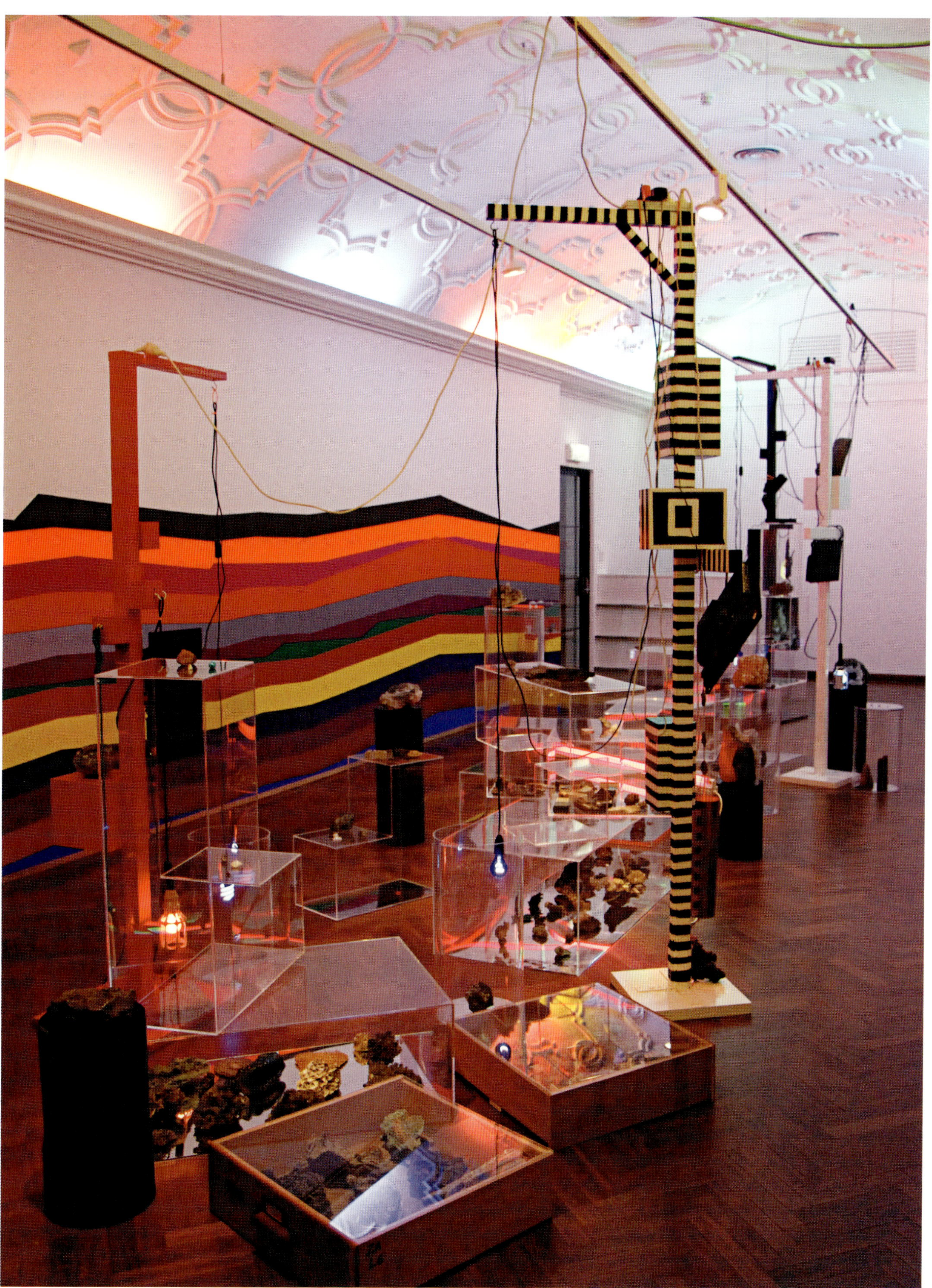

opposite:

St Jude's leftovers 2015
multi-site installation
mixed media

below, clockwise from top:

St Jude's leftovers performance
within Ulla von Brandenburg's
installation in Leoben, Austria as part
of Steirischer Herbst Festival, Graz.

**St Jude's leftovers (your thoughts
in lights)** with Negirvan Sarik and
Mohammad Haci, Radwerk III,
Vordernberg, Austria (external and
interbal views)

St Jude's leftovers, Graz Museum

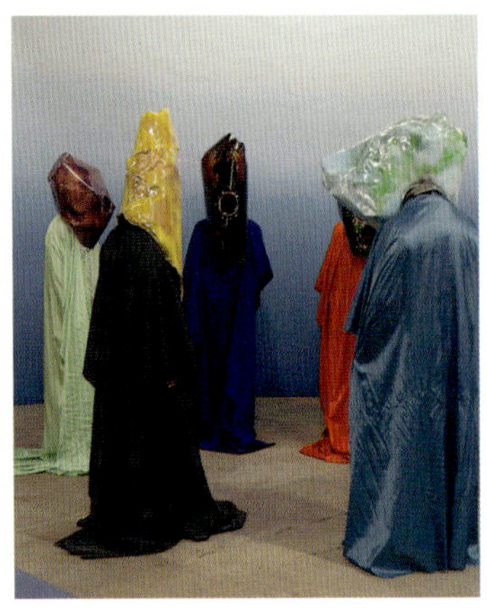

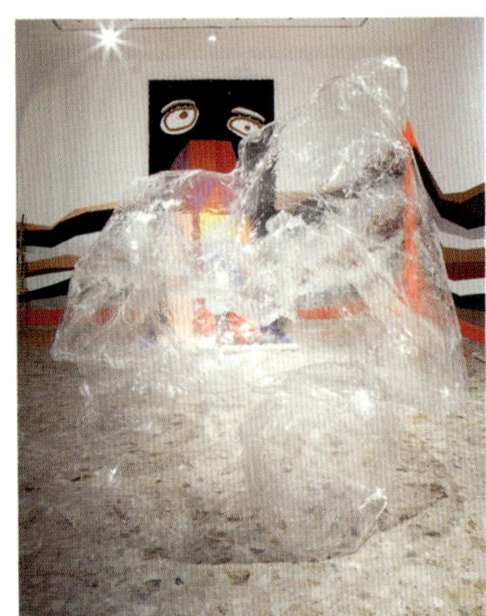

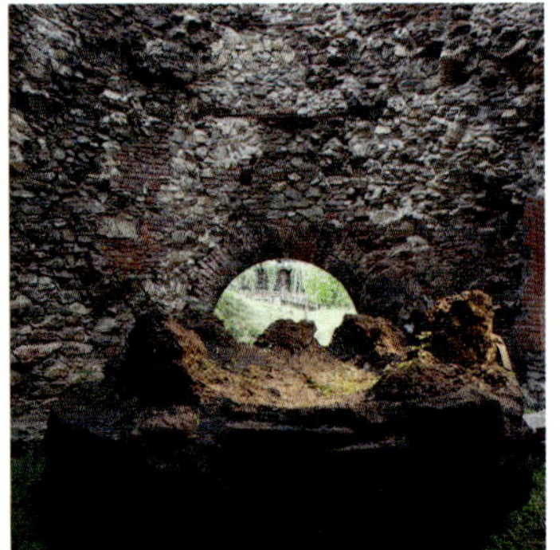

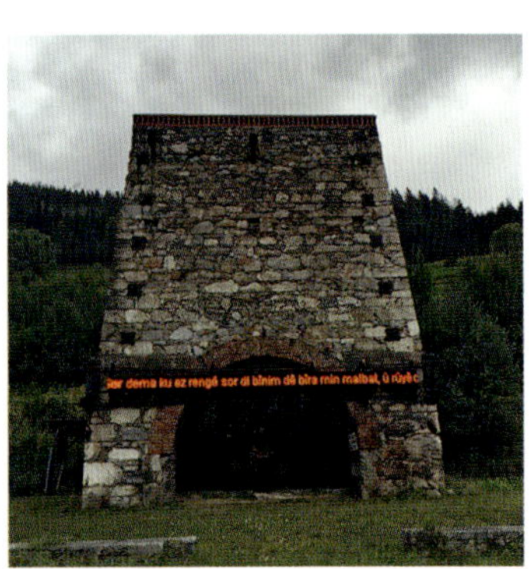

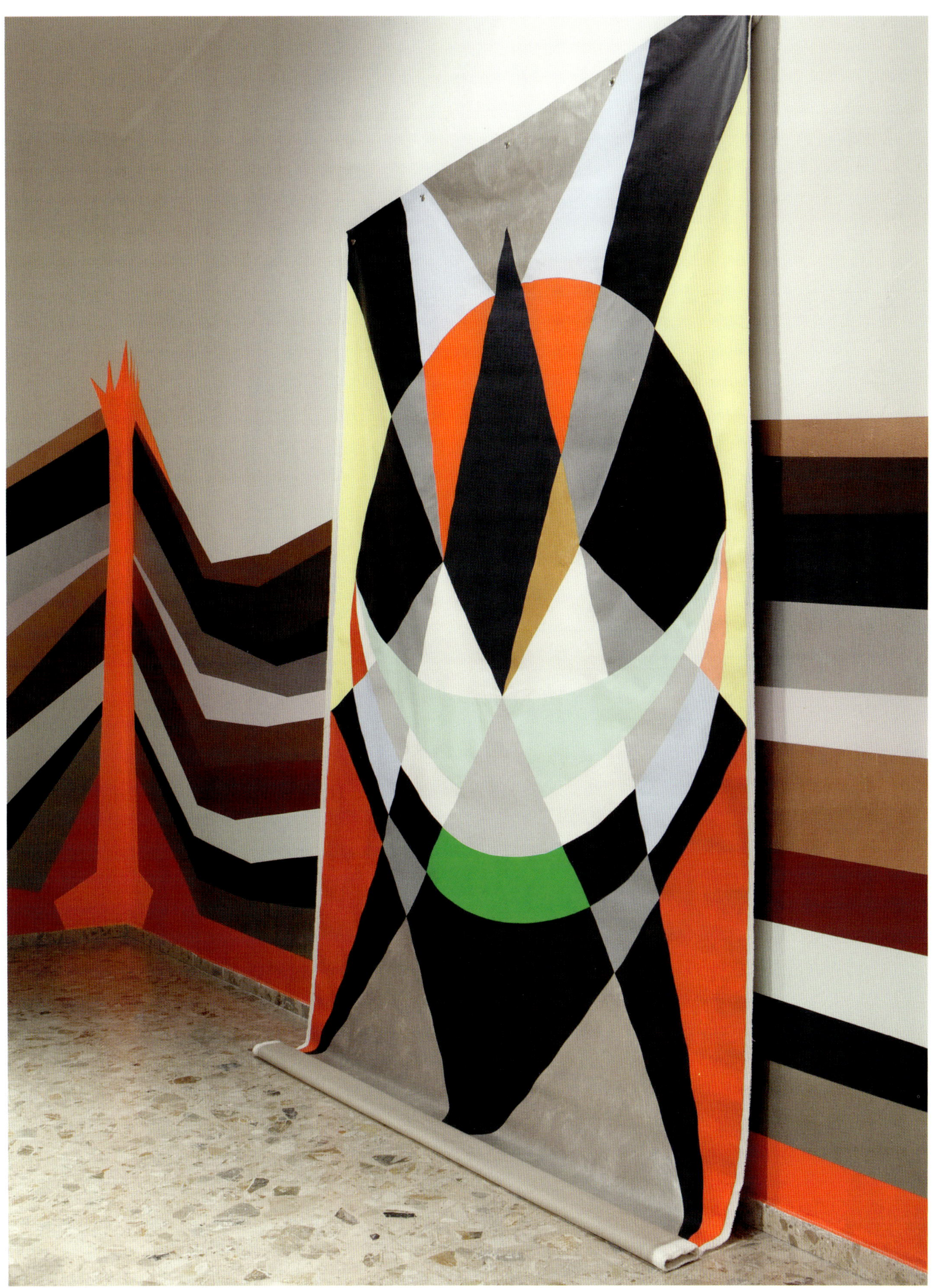

Mikala Dwyer:
The letterbox Marys

27 November — 18 December 2015
Roslyn Oxley9 Gallery, Sydney

—

opposite and below left:

The letterbox Marys 2015
acrylic, steel, fabric, Marys

below:

Green fairy necklace for wall 2015
acrylic, ceramic, brass, antler, ashtray,
string, uranium glass, absinthe, rock

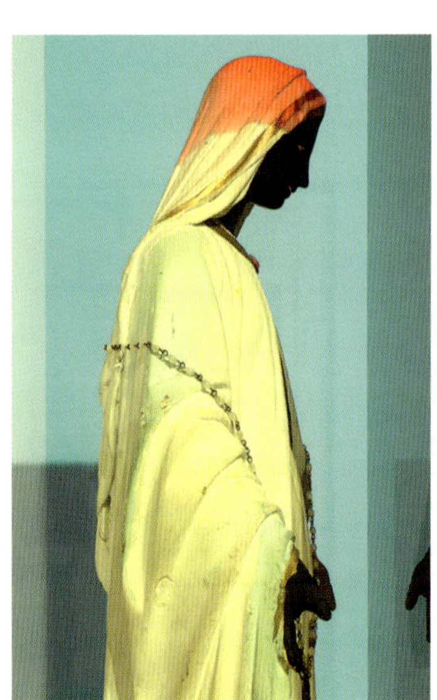

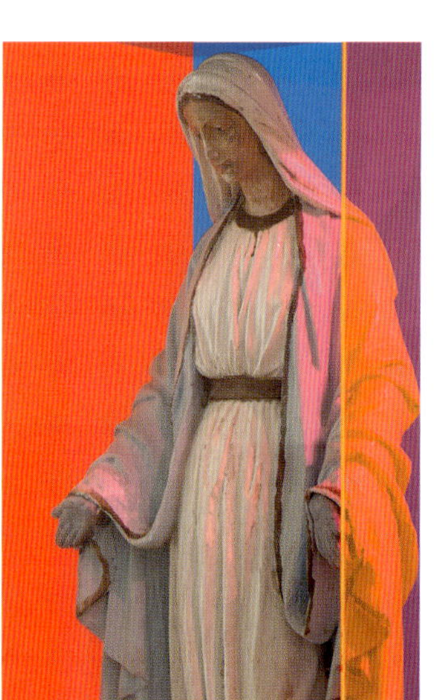

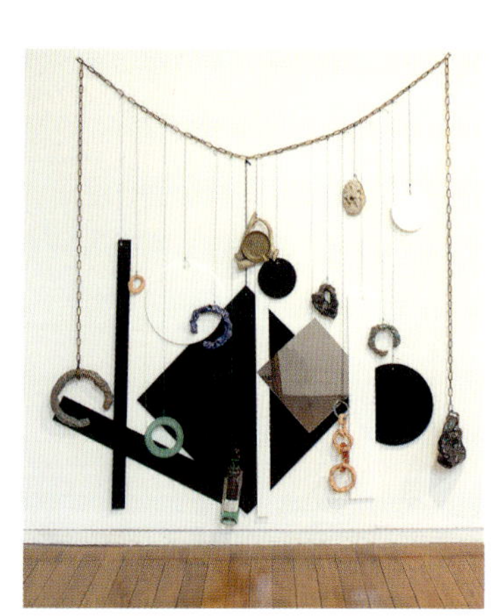

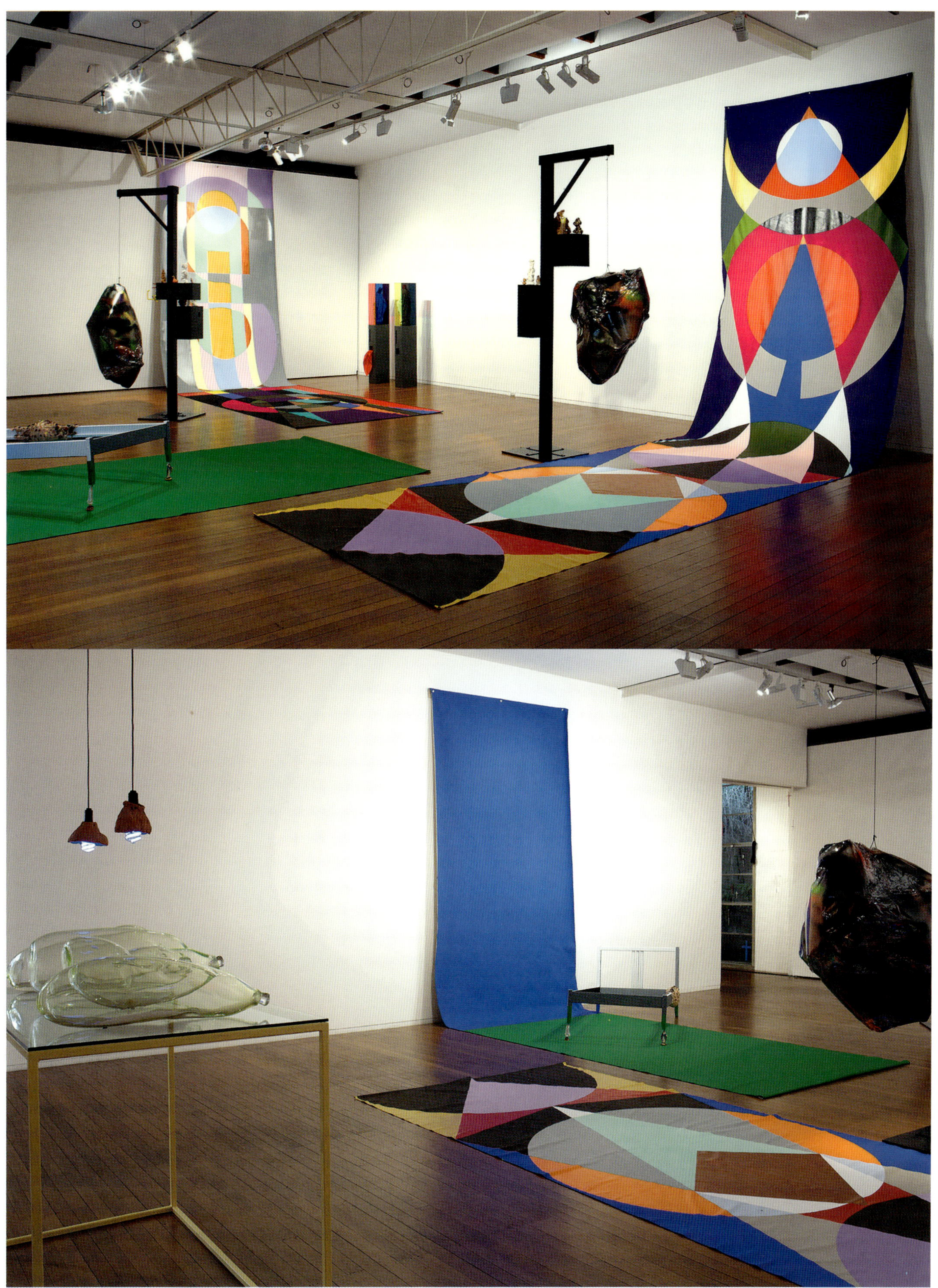

21 December 2015 —
21 February 2016
Museum of Contemporary Art
Australia, Sydney

—

opposite and below right:

Square cloud compound 2010
fabric stockings, glass, beer,
champagne, plastic, ceramics,
found things, wood, rocks, lights,
synthetic polymer paint, acrylic,
cat and bird ornaments

below left:

Spell for a corner 2015
synthetic polymer paint on wall

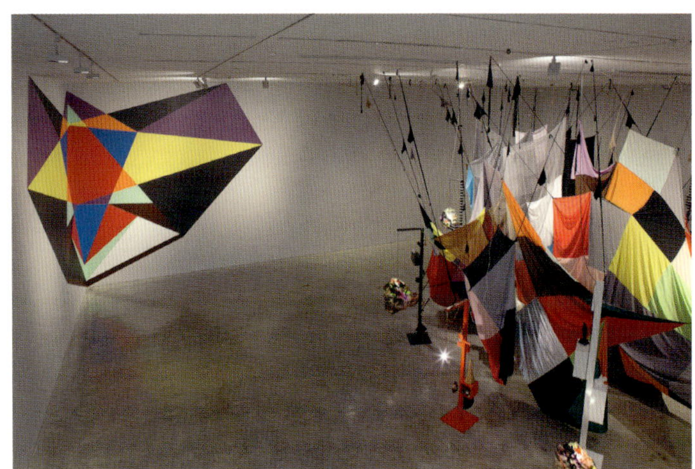

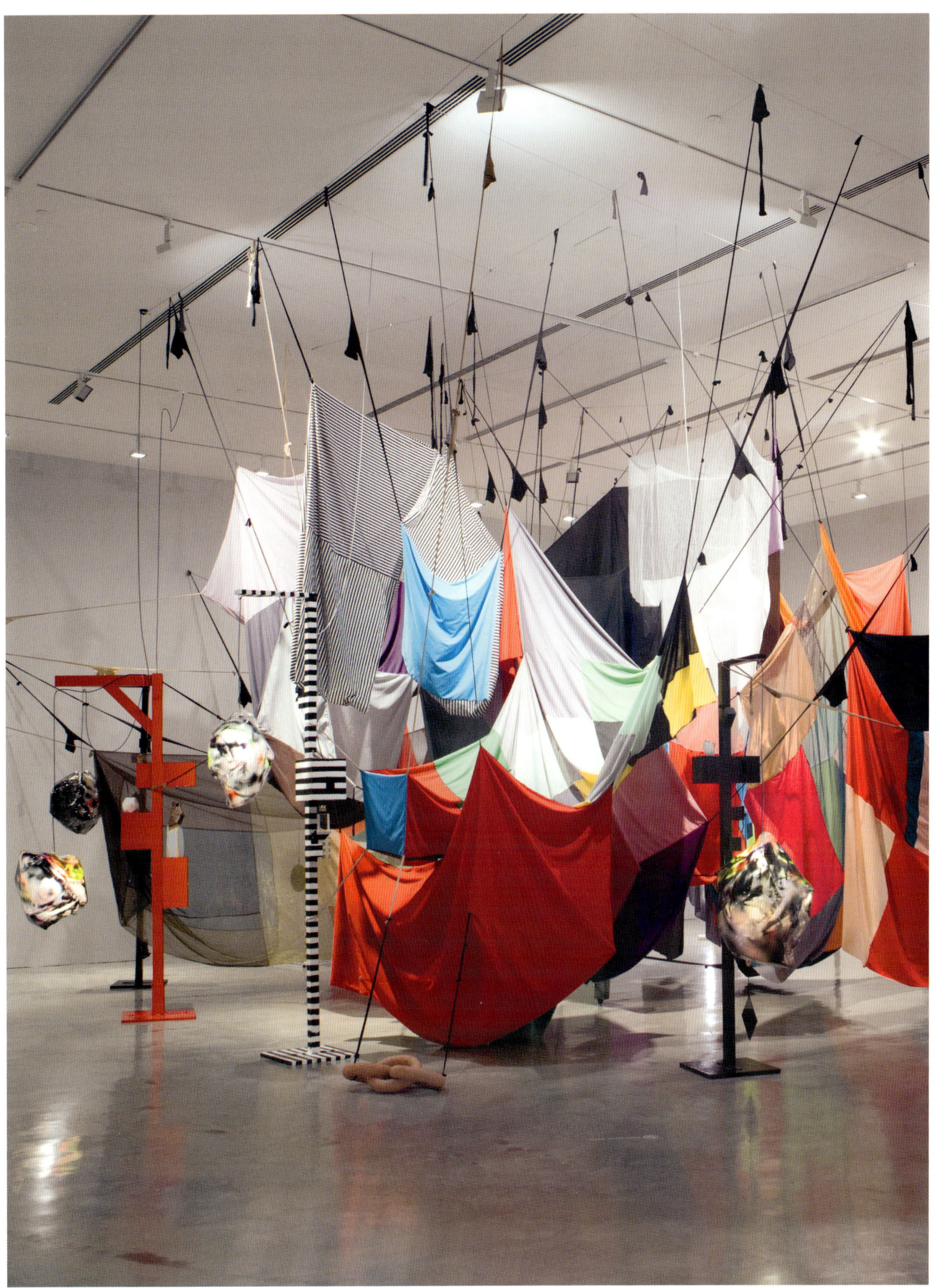

Riddle of the burial grounds

26 March — 27 July 2016
Extra City Kunsthal, Antwerp

—

bowls:
Ruth E Lyons **Afterings** 2015
salt
Supported by Irish Salt Mining Ltd,
Kilroot, Carrickfergus, Co Antrim,
Ireland and EU Salt Association

plinths:
Mikala Dwyer **Underlay** 2016
synthetic polymer paint on wood
Commissioned by Extra City Kunsthal

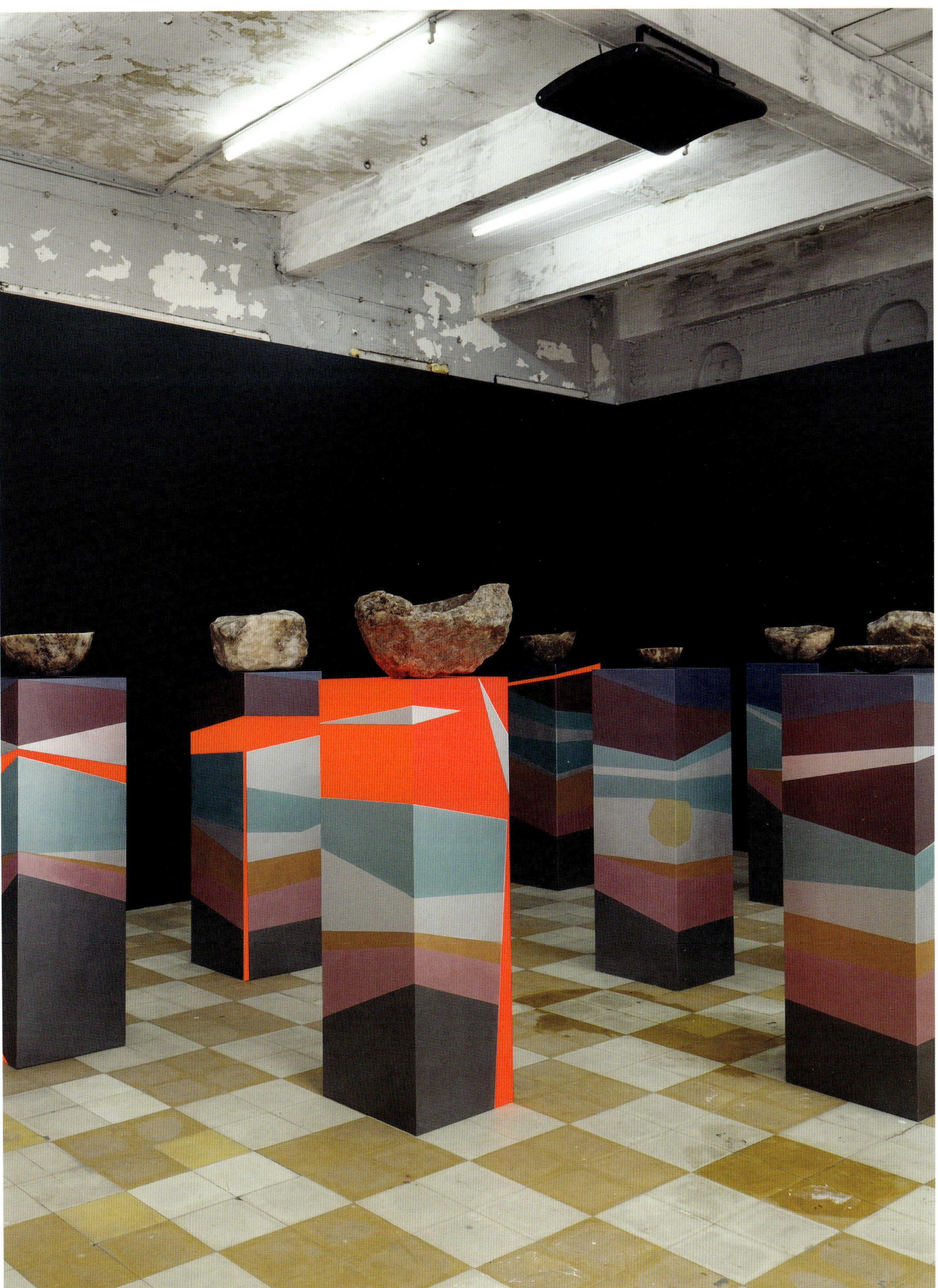

25—26 February 2017
Fondation Fiminco, Paris

—

The silvering 2017
mylar, helium

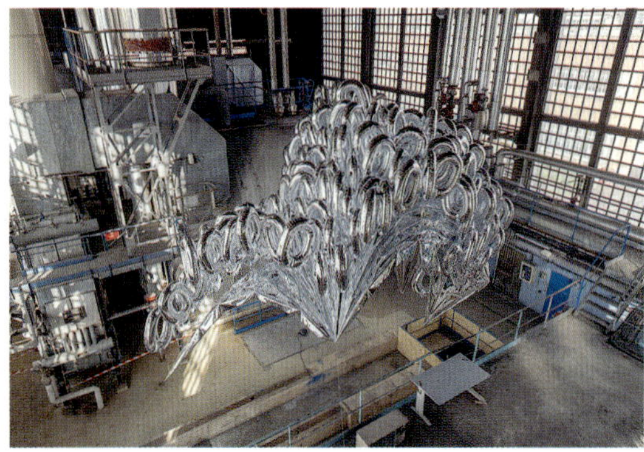

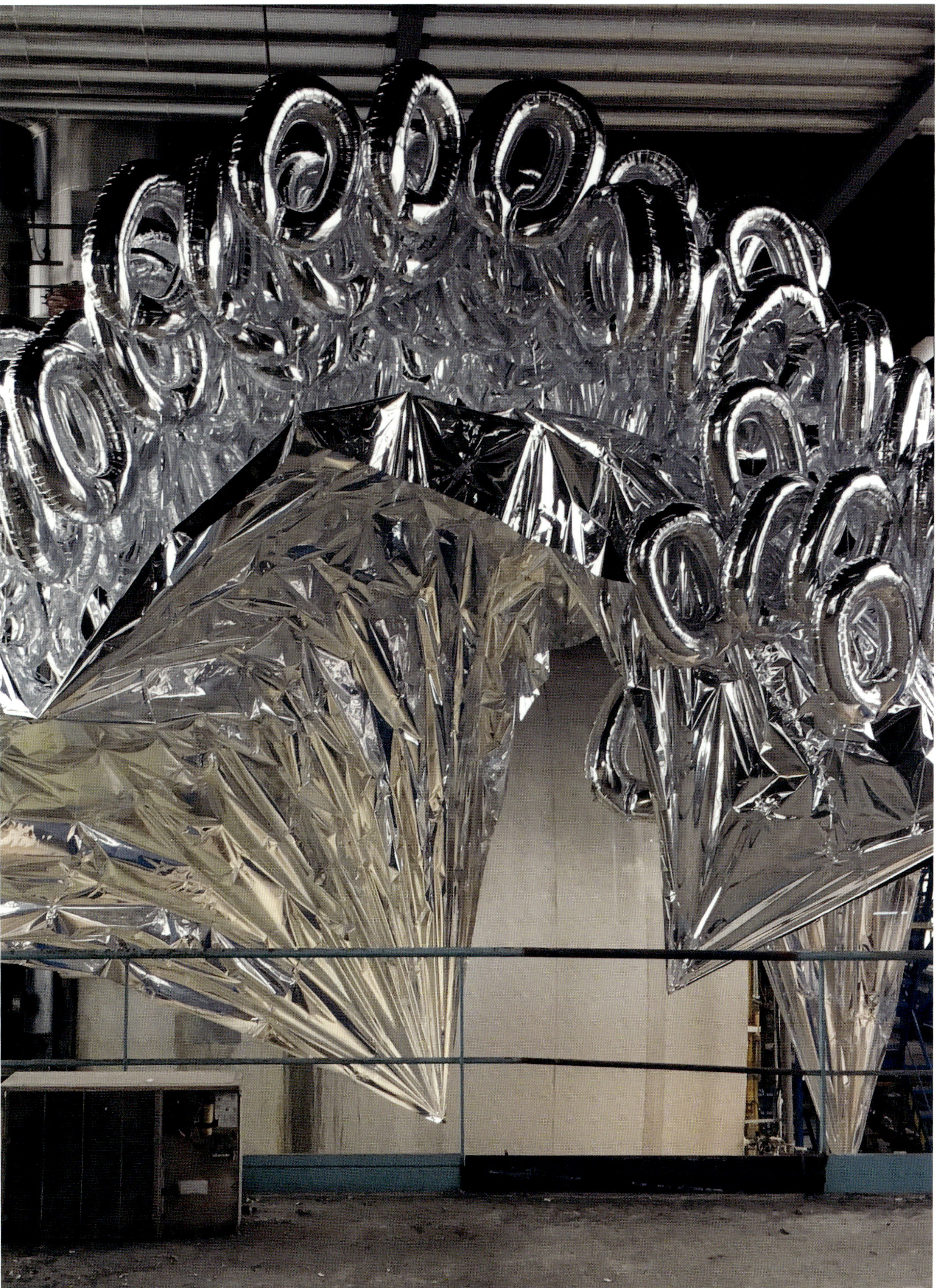

Monument for fishes:
a proposal for the future

Monument for fishes is a majestic totem to the sea and the idea of buoyancy as a symbol of optimism and resilience. It is also a poetic monument to the great Indigenous Eora fisherwomen of Sydney Harbour.

The abstract quality of **Monument for fishes** allows us to think in many directions. Its forms are accessible and philosophically open. They are vertical and curvaceous – both male and female but also beyond human. A powerful sense of gravity connects them to our bodily schema while their elevation captures the heights of our imagination. Monumental yet not static, they move with their site rather than against it, swaying languidly with the tides, winds and currents. Their sharply defined profiles are moderated by the active negative spaces between them, through which we perceive the ever-changing landscape of the harbour city.

Monument for fishes is a barometer of the harbour's energy cycles. At night its silhouetted forms, illuminated from within by coloured rings of light, become dancing, spectral presences inhabiting their location. In periods of calm from late evening to dawn, when reflections are more vivid, the rings of light and the softened shapes doubled in the water draw us into the depths and offer a more contemplative experience.

All qualities contain a suggestion of their mirror opposites, so with buoyancy there is also sinking and drowning, the idea that lightness could be subsumed by the sheer weight of the dark world beneath. This vast underworld of the sea is often thought of as a symbol for our collective unconscious. Hence these forms are totems to a great sense of unknowing. The work also nods to Kenneth Slessor's poem 'Five bells' (1939), a meditation on memory and time, and on the death of Slessor's friend Joe Lynch who drowned in Sydney Harbour, weighed down by beer bottles in his pockets.

While we may be familiar with the stuff boats are made of, the vertical configuration at an exaggerated scale here surprises, unsettling our inherent knowledge. This disassociation enables us to imagine new bodies and never-before-seen objects. Yet these majestic forms are based on the simplest of devices: the fishing float. The origins of fishing floats can be traced to the feathers attached to handmade fishing lines – like those that Indigenous Eora fisherwomen used to make. Fishing floats and buoys also inspired the sculpture's use of fluorescent orange and yellow, and black and white – colours that offer optical contrast and high visibility on the busy harbour. The addition of pure gold leaf introduces a wealth of symbolic meaning, and its soft, warm reflection of sun, moon and sky adds to the transcendent spirit of the work.

The seeming lightness of the five forms is paradoxically enabled by the weight of ballast in their rolling bases. Buffeted by the unpredictable watery ground, they become a mesmerising force in unison with the sea. Both monument and anti-monument, **Monument for fishes** rocks with a magical stability, much like the Eora fisherwomen as they balanced babies, fire and fishing in their tiny boats, but also marking the liquid beneath, the great ocean that fills our harbour and shapes the mythology, economy and geography of Sydney.

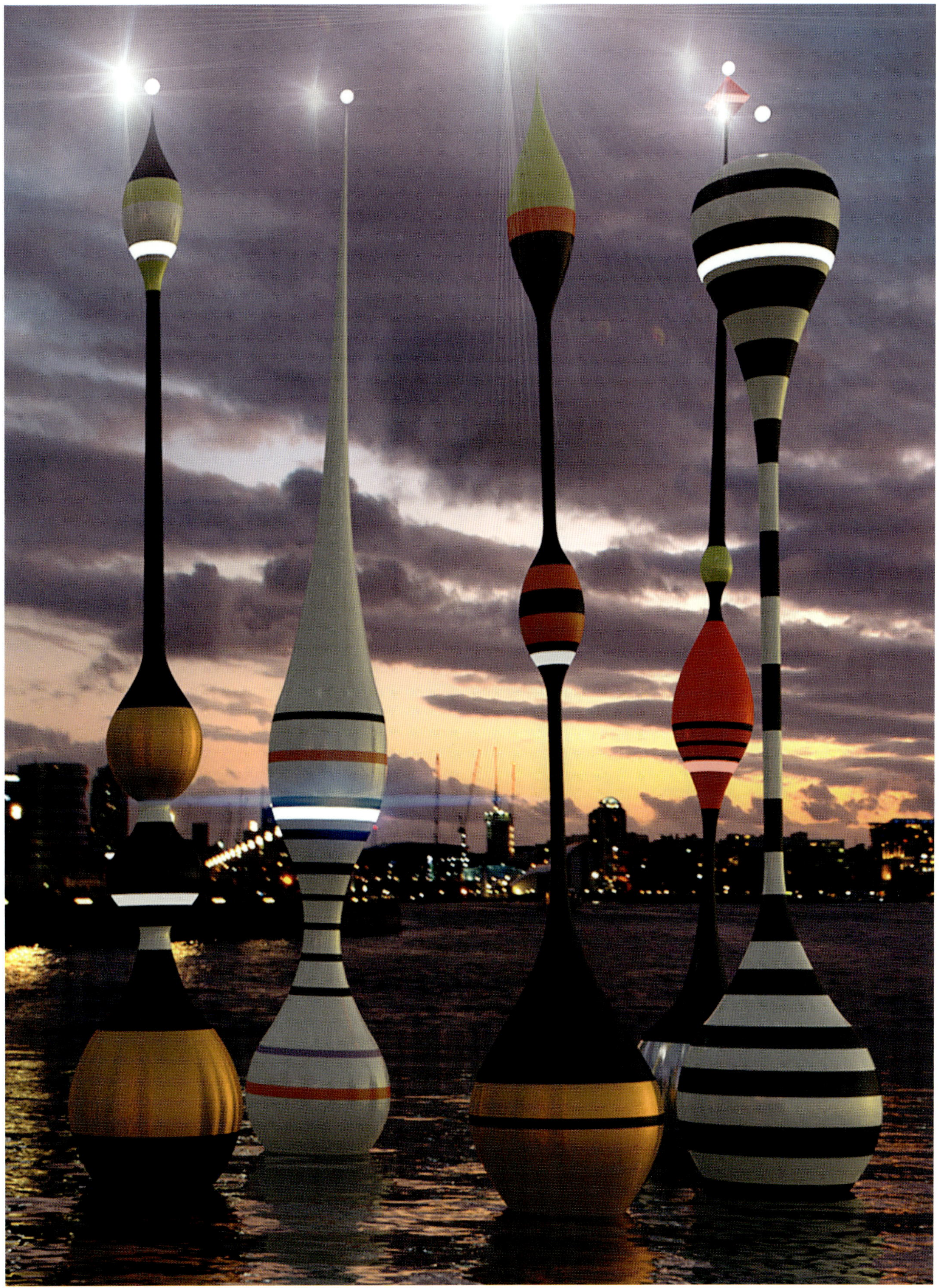

Ten questions with Mikala Dwyer

Interview by
Wayne
Tunnicliffe

MD — I didn't set about becoming an artist but found myself going to art school in 1983, when I was twenty-one. I was making up for lost time as I'd been expelled from school when I was quite young.

When I was sixteen I travelled to New Zealand and met some art students in Christchurch who were making hardcore conceptual sculptural works and I remember how bad I thought it was, how unfinished it seemed. But I think back now and realise that it was ahead of its time. I also visited many museums on my travels in Europe after I left Australia at the age of eighteen. It suddenly occurred to me how great art was – seeing work by artists like Alberto Giacometti and Niki de Saint Phalle opened up a whole new world for me.

When I came back I enrolled at Sydney College of the Arts (SCA) at a very exciting and dynamic time. SCA was an independent school with an innovative program and fantastic lecturers. It was wild. Instead of having modular electives we had people: artists who were travelling though Sydney came to the college and did workshops with students. The visiting artists were diverse and included Japanese actor and dancer Min Tanaka, performance artists Marina Abramovic and Ulay, Aboriginal elders, Anthony Howell from the performance group The Theatre of Mistakes, and Doc Neeson who was the lead singer of the rock band The Angels. We had real artists coming from all over the world doing intensive workshops and it was an amazing education.

After leaving art school I went straight to London and studied for more than a year at Middlesex Polytechnic, which also had a very good program. My previous teacher from the SCA, Adrian Hall, had taken up a post there. It was an exciting time to be in London in the mid 1980s. Sculpture was big, music was weird; it was the deep dark Thatcher years and strikes were long and horribly drawn out. Artist-run spaces were mushrooming as well, and it was the very beginnings of the group of artists who came to be known as the YBAs (Young British Artists), showing their work in artist-run galleries and warehouse exhibitions. I was involved in some alternate spaces with artist friends and was beginning to exhibit after art school in a lively context full of contradictions.

I returned to Sydney in 1988 and became involved in Firstdraft Gallery as one of its second group of artist directors. The gallery had been set up in 1985 by Narelle Jubelin, Tess Horwitz, Paul Saint and Roger Crawford, and after two years it was handed over to my group [from 1988–89], which included Adriane Boag, Astrid Kriening, Joanne McCambridge and myself. It was a great reintroduction to Sydney. Later, I ran a space called Black that was next door to a film production company of the same name, which gave me some pocket money to run it and free rein with the program. I began to be curated into exhibitions in other art galleries, one of the first of which was when Louise Pether included my work in an exhibition, **Delineations: exploring drawing**, at the Ivan Dougherty Gallery in 1989, where I crawled under the floorboards and made a work which consisted of projecting a super-8 film from under the floor and a wire spire that extended through a trapdoor to the ceiling. After that, things picked up.

Your mother was a jeweller and silversmith working in a modernist style and your father was an industrial chemist. Are there aspects of your upbringing that you draw on in your work?

For a long time I tried to defy my parents and rebel against them. My mother's Danish heritage of good design and her very formal aesthetic in her jewellery work – as well as her choice of furniture and everything around her – was there to reinforce her identity. She tended to create spaces that were very mid-century Danish and I hated that. I wanted the Queen Anne furniture and the frilly white curtains like everyone else had – I didn't want liverwurst sandwiches in my lunch box, I wanted Vegemite! Danes can be quite direct and there is an honesty there which at times can be a bit brutal. My mother was a very tough critic and said, 'You're not allowed to call yourself an artist, that's for other people to decide.' Now I think that was a fair-enough opinion.

My father was an industrial chemist – a very lovely and playful one, who was also very inventive, and some of his products became successful. He had quite a trippy mindset; he was more of a surrealist industrial chemist in some ways, and he was a profound influence on me. He always had a desk full of weird substances, from uranium yellowcake to unusual rocks and metals, and I loved going to his laboratory – a huge room full of glass beakers and things to cook stuff up in. It was perhaps more difficult for him to understand what I was doing and yet in some ways he connected to it more.

After my parents died I found notes and drawings by both of them that were uncannily like the things I was exploring, just in different scales and materials. I've realised that everything I've made has been genetically coded and passed down, as there are very similar forms and ideas that we were working on.

From early on you gravitated towards objects. What is the power of 'things' that you wanted to explore in your practice?

When I was at art school I spent the first year-and-a-half drawing quite obsessively – a lot of big expressionist drawings. Then, at the start of my second year, I suddenly stopped. I got to a point with drawing where I just didn't want to draw in two dimensions; I wanted to draw with objects and materials. I think my interest in objects is based on their ability to act like props, as three-dimensional mark-making in space, which hold ideas or become repositories of the memories we project onto them. They also have their own kind of voices and qualities and consciousness. I made the decision to stop drawing as such and to begin drawing again with objects, and I think to some extent that is still what I'm doing.

What led you to working with everyday materials?

I worked with what I could afford and what was available, as I still do. For my generation it was what you could find in the hardware store, or the two-dollar shop, or on the street. It was a way of refusing to be silenced by poverty: you could still make work, say something, and be an active agent with very limited means. Having nothing is a great point from which to start, and going out and having to find something means you must think on your feet. When you're thinking through ideas suddenly the world is very alive with stuff that can activate, or talk to or hold those ideas, and when you're working on something, walking down the street becomes a totally different experience.

I remember going and seeing punk bands and, rather than headbanging, I'd be shoe-gazing and looking at the floor and noticing the carpet and certain formations. It was a great inspiration, and something to do with the music and how it frees you up to look and think. When you're lost in the zone of making new work and you're excited about a train of thought or an emotional state, things become apparent, they appear like apparitions and present themselves to you in ways that they won't when you're not in that state of thinking and making.

The forms and materials come together to convey the emotions the work embodies. Cigarette butts, for example, are a great barometer of anxiety, while everyone can connect to the colour and the smell of a bandaid. The latter are super-weird in a gallery, but they talk about wounding and vulnerability, about containment and a pathetic gesture to patch something up that isn't going to hold. They talk about the skin, the border between outside and inside, between me and you; they're on that peripheral surface. I used bandaids early on at a time when I was interested in a surface that was porous, that could breathe. I also used neoprene or organza fabrics – which let light, air and water pass through them – to emphasise an idea about containment that wasn't fixed. I am still working with that idea in many ways: shapes that contain, or materials that convey borders, whether personal, psychological, architectural, sociological, political or economic. You can describe these borders or containments in ways that are very easy for people to access, then you can mix them up with other things as an alchemical brew of substances and ideas that complicate all these boundaries.

The psychic fortress that my circle works create, like **The divisions and subtractions** series 2017, also explores the irony that any fortress or closed system that emphasises containment also draws attention to its opposite – to openness, vulnerability and porosity. In many ways accentuating one thing activates its other, as when you make enough circles in an exhibition for people to start thinking about squares. Or when you excessively make squares and they end up being organic, as with **Square cloud compound** 2010, where I kept adding together very formal squares that should be a strong, organisational, stackable shape, but because they are made from soft fabric they ended up becoming a huge, messy organic structure.

The objects are not so important, they're props for people, props for conversations, props for movement, props to activate. The work is never totally situated in the object or the audience or the architecture – it's a continual interplay or movement between them all. I'm always trying to crack open an extra space that's like an extra dimension within these object-laden rituals.

The objects are often excessive so that they almost cancel each other out and you can't actually see them. For all their sculptural-ness and object-ness they tend to disappear when you put enough of them together so that you can create other states. You can create its opposite again, you can create a void, or a need for nothingness or emptiness. They're really elaborate sets in a way to create another space, another world, a momentary place that you can inhabit even if you're just going to walk through it, but it's not going to be like anywhere else you've been that day.

Your work is playful and engaging, but it can also be unsettling, as objects seem to have considerable autonomy and at times begin to take over. Is there a darker side to your practice?

Completely. One of my students the other day was talking about how violent some of the objects are. There is an impulse at times that is dark and violent, and there's a process of dark and violent urges coming into the world through art, which is therapeutic – they cease to be as violent as they could have been if you had literalised them. Rather than axe someone to death, I can put an axe behind a bandage on a wall and quieten it down, and somehow in that process I come out the other end happy – the impulses are really alleviated through the making!

Colour is also important and American artist Mike Kelley, whose work also has an underside, summed it up well when he said that colour is a great doorway or access point that people respond to and that allows them into the work. It's like that lovely family uncle who says 'Come sit on my knee', and everything seems normal and then suddenly it's not – it becomes sleazy and complex. You open a door and let people in, but then it's no longer sweetness and light and colour as you play with a contrasting darkness and twist it in another direction. Putting the nice and the nasty together is an animating force that can create a liveliness and it brings the work back to where it's closer to a performance, as if someone has just left the room. My work is closer to performance at times as I'm not interested in well-made objects, I'm more interested in when the viewer can sense the making of it. And yes, anyone can do it – you can do it and your four-year-old should do it – which comes back to a punk ethos in some ways.

You've directly drawn on occult or spiritualist practices at times, such as conducting séances or asking tarot card readers to help resolve sculptural conundrums. Is this part of your interest in questioning logic and rationalism and their hidden ideologies?

Ever since I can remember I've been interested in alternative knowledges, such as the occult, but for a long time I didn't open that up into my work. At one stage I hit a block so I went to a clairvoyant to find out if she could help me see what the work would be. It was an interesting experiment as

I'm a parallel sceptic and believer, which is a complicated position to occupy. The clairvoyant described a work in great detail in a very open way, and not in the language of painting or sculpture that you might expect. She described something quite nebulous and beautiful and I wondered: 'How am I going to make that?' I tried making exactly what she described and it was a disaster and ended up in the skip, and yet I found after two years I had made what she said but not in a literal sense. **Square cloud compound** and **The additions and the subtractions** works all connect to this experience.

The additions and the subtractions series is also connected to the death in 2007 of Stephen Birch, a good friend and a great artist. I visited his studio after his death and saw all these wonderful unfinished experiments, and in some ways my subsequent circle sculptures respond to his unfinished work and a desire to explore his ideas further on his behalf. Thinking about the occult and the afterlife, whether you believe or not, is another way to free yourself up, another lateral thinking tool.

Which leads me to Catholicism. You were brought up a Catholic and, in recent years, Christian religious references have appeared in your work. What are you exploring by incorporating Catholic iconography?

Catholicism is an impossible one to shake; I think everyone agrees that once a Catholic always a Catholic, no matter how much you decry it or even despise it a little. In these works I was looking at my own personal mythologies, and what has shaped my thinking, and asking myself why I come up with particular forms. Is the Catholicism still there and does it influence what I make? I'm trying to get underneath my thinking to explore formative influences and to find out what they mean. It's the illogic of belief that Catholics are particularly good at, such as the magic act that happens in Communion with the transubstantiation of bread and wine into the body and blood of Christ, which I find fascinating. There are also alternate theologies in the Catholic Church, such as the Virgin Mary as a co-redeemer, alongside Jesus, providing direct access to God, which then opens up the possibility of many redeemers and Christianity no longer being a monotheistic religion. Whether we like religions or not, they have a hold on us and don't tend to go away too quickly.

You often work with other artists on projects and with people from different fields – in a sense you draw together creative people in your practice, in your teaching, and your participation in artist-run projects. Is this community of makers important to your practice?

I think it goes back to the bandaid, to open forms and open systems that can be infected and contaminated by each other. Like many artists, I often want to work alone in my studio and not talk to anyone, but I find when I force myself to open up and invite others in – like when I was making the **The divisions and subtractions** work in 2017 – that it's a very positive experience. It's not generosity though, in offering other artists exposure by participating in my exhibitions, it's because I'm devouring and cannibalising them into my work! But it's an exchange and part of my process of derailing my habits and patterns of thinking – I am quite a fixed thinker, but by inviting people in or being with students or by exposing myself to work by other artists I open up my thinking to more lateral possibilities.

I fail again and again, I'm stubborn and I'm fixed and I want things my own way. I've found though that with people like Nick Dorey, Stevie Fieldsend, Hany Armanious, Andre Bremer, Adriane Boag and Matthys Gerber, if I shut up and listen when they come into my studio and let things unfold they show me things that I would never have thought of myself. It's not a collaboration necessarily, but they've given nuance to and enriched the work. They've put their energy in there too, so that the work is not just mine but a community of objects and a community of people, as you never really make your work on your own.

August 2017

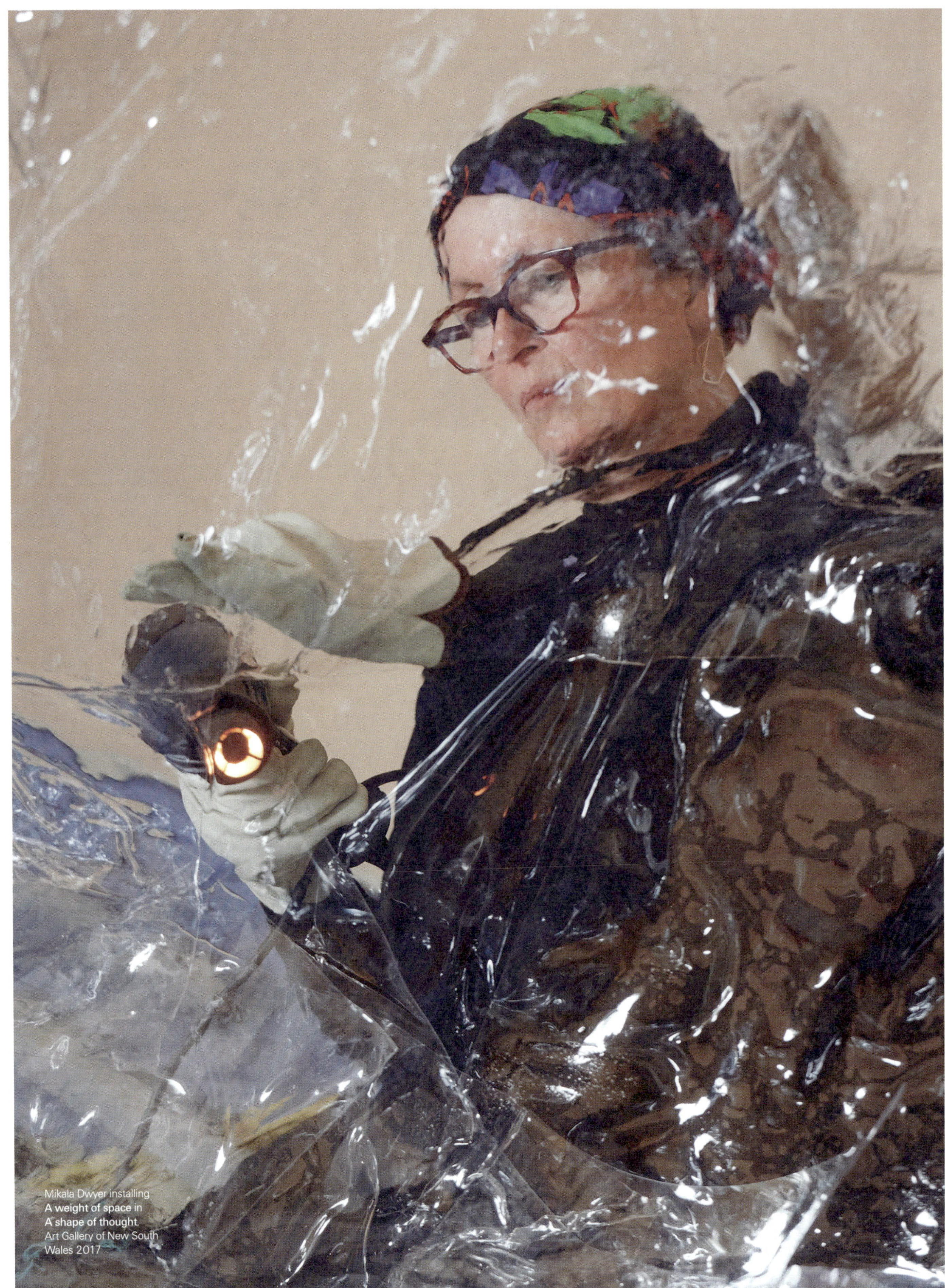

Mikala Dwyer installing
A weight of space in
A shape of thought,
Art Gallery of New South
Wales 2017

Mikala Dyer: A shape of thought 2017—18

Mikala Dyer:
A shape of thought

26 August 2017 — 4 February 2018
Art Gallery of New South Wales,
Sydney

—

Comprising:

The silvering 2017

Square cloud compound 2010
Costumes 2017

A weight of space 2017
Hollowwork (ringing) 2013

The divisions and subtractions
2017

The letterbox Marys 2015–17
   Backdrop for Saint Jude 2015
   Backdrop for rounders 2016
   Backdrop for base matter 2016
   Earthlings 2015
   Possession 2015
   Puzzle (after Piet Hein /
     Kumbel Kumbell) 2015
   Shadow lamp I 2015
   Shadow lamp II 2015
   Sigil for heaven and earth 2015
   The angel 2015
   The letterbox Marys 2015
   Wall charm 2017

opposite and pages 108–11:

The silvering 2017
mylar, helium

Georg Baselitz **Oven soot** 2015
(in background)

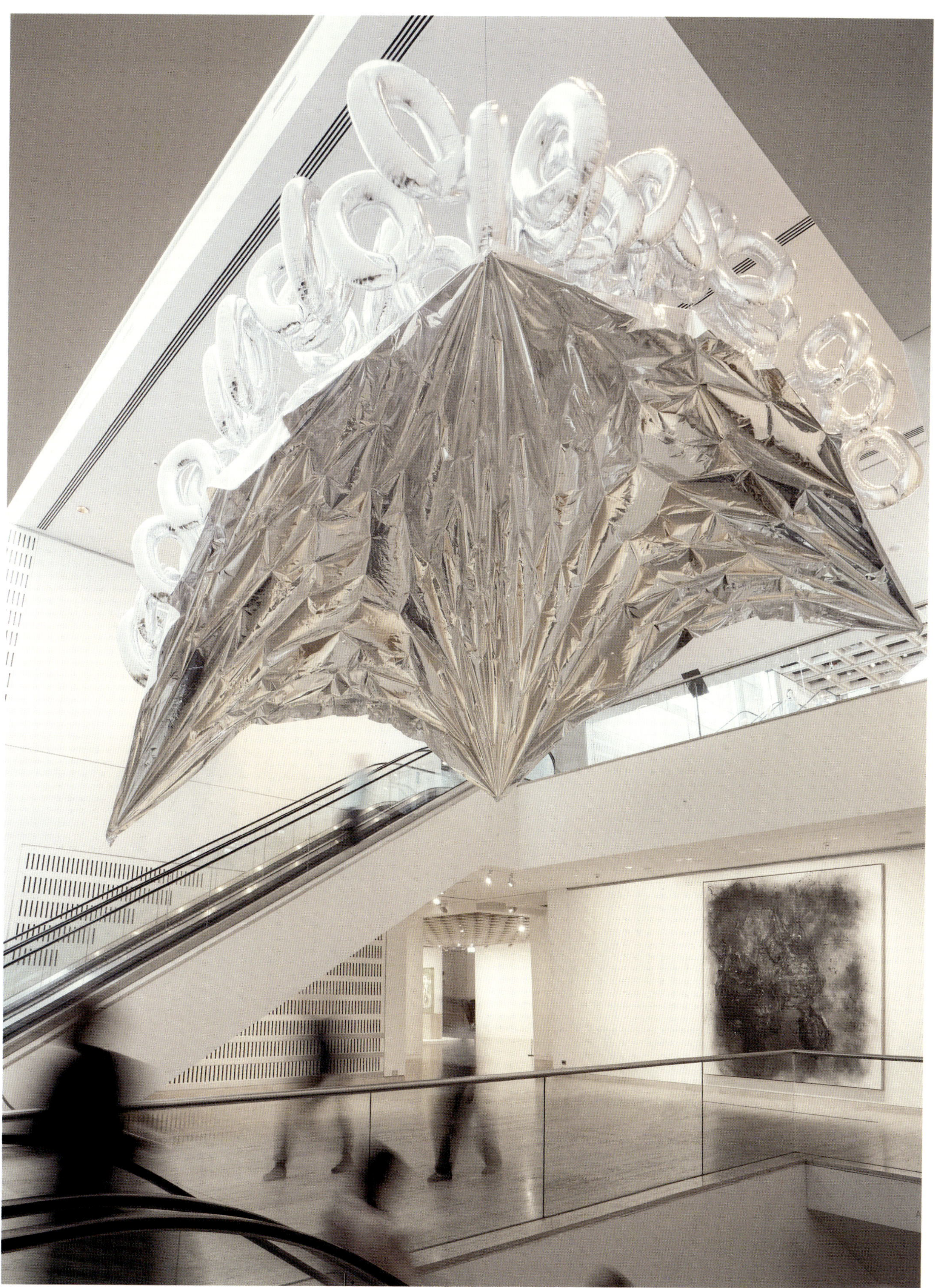

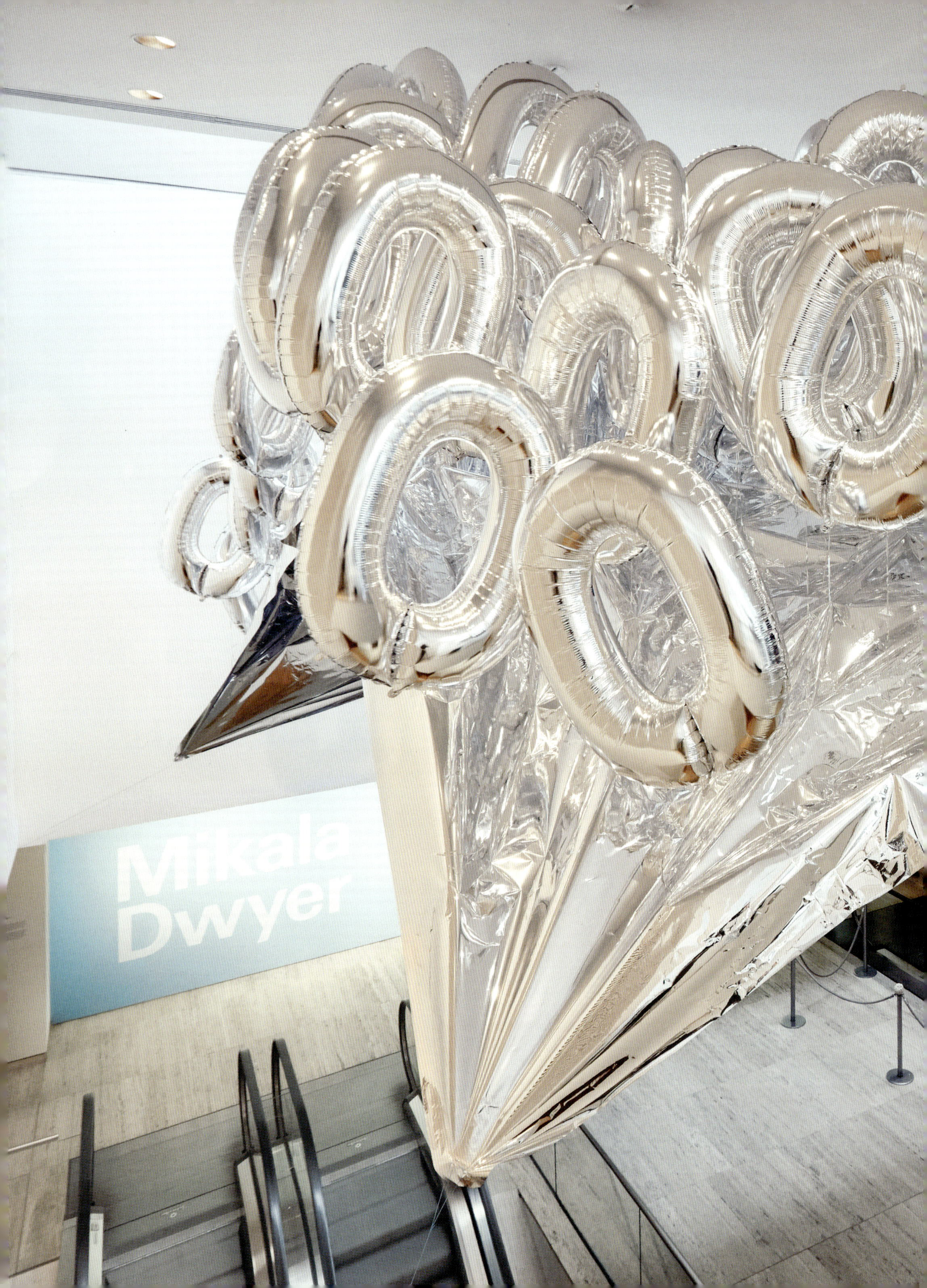

Mikala
Dwyer

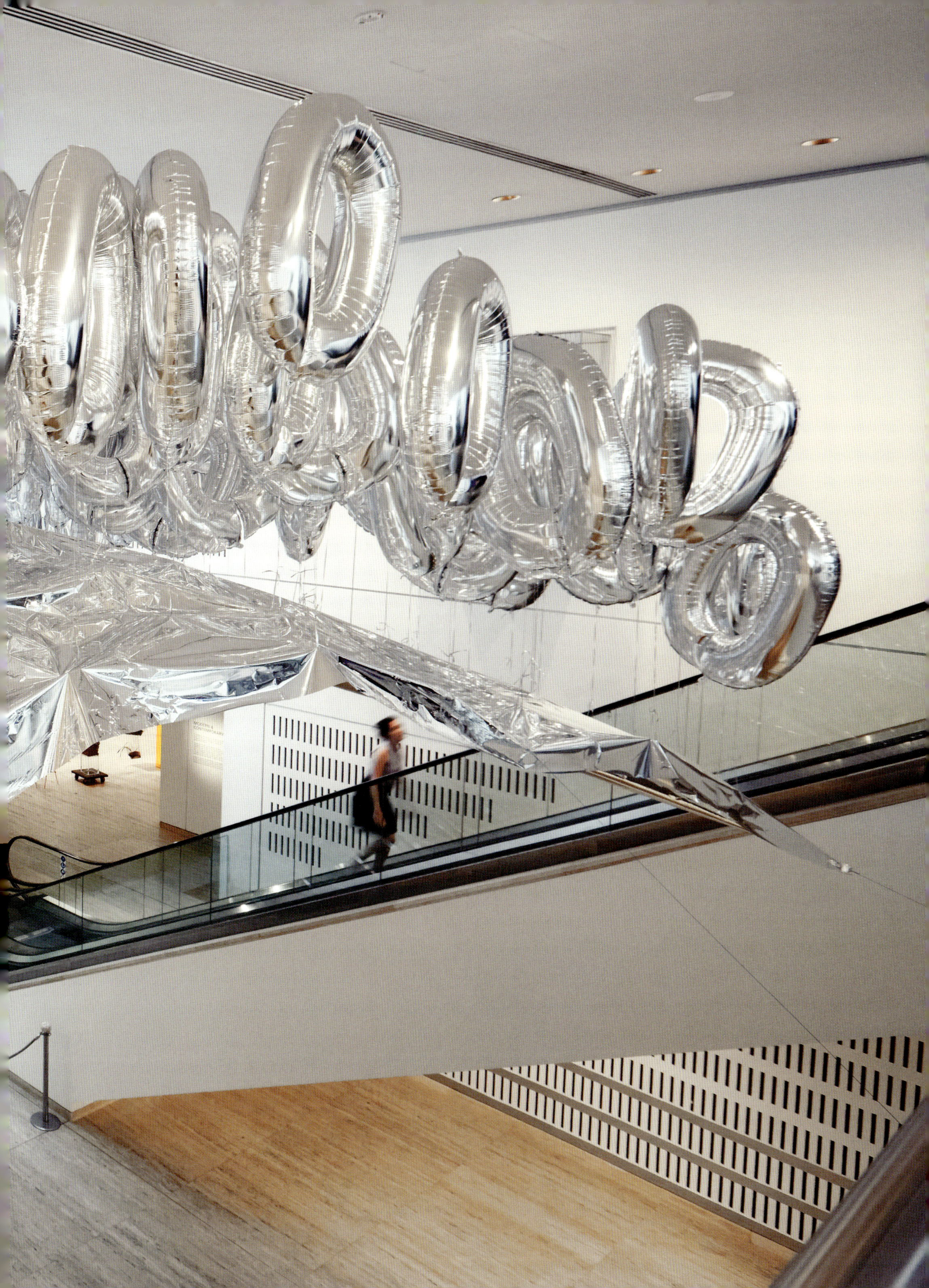

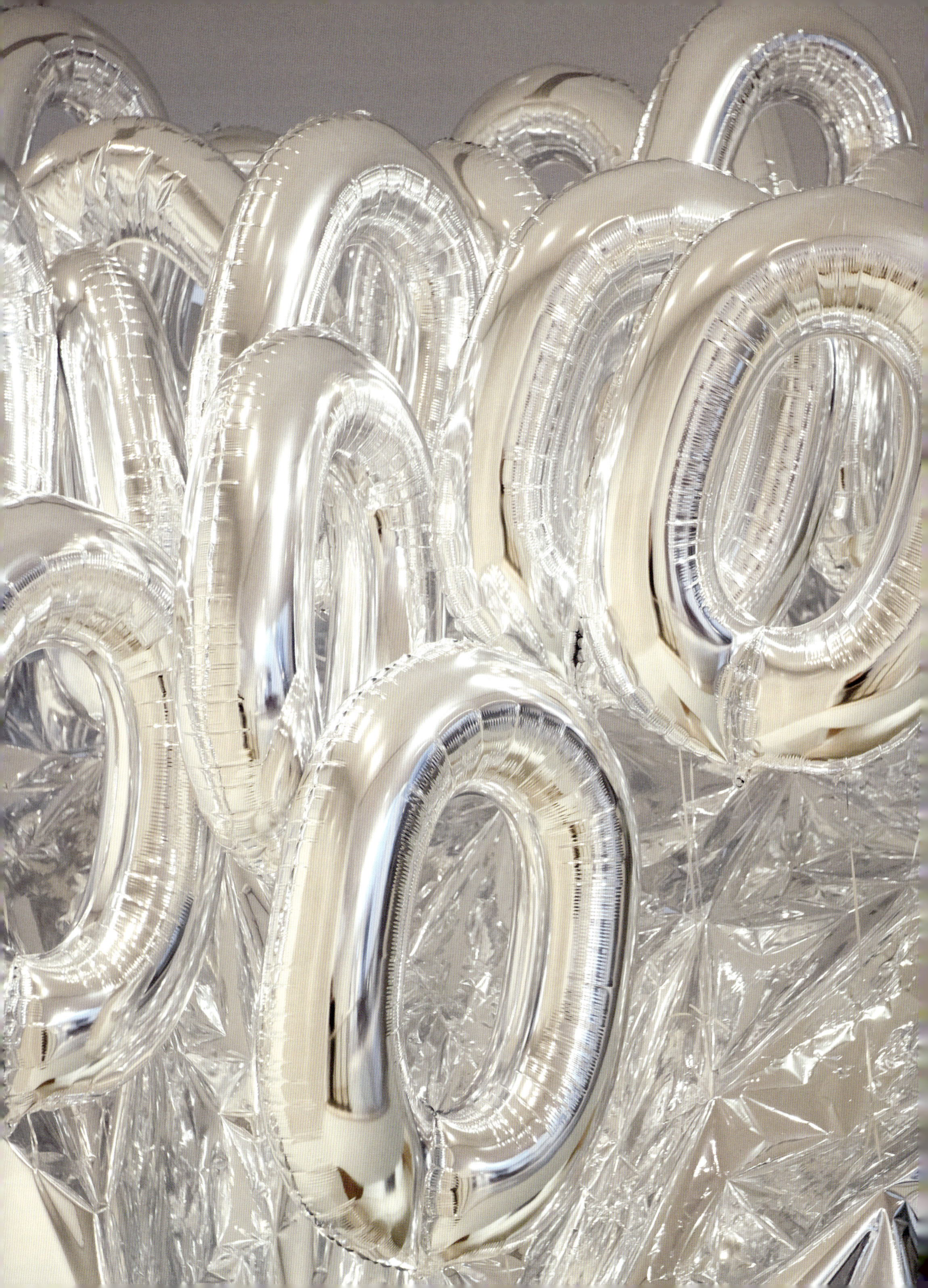

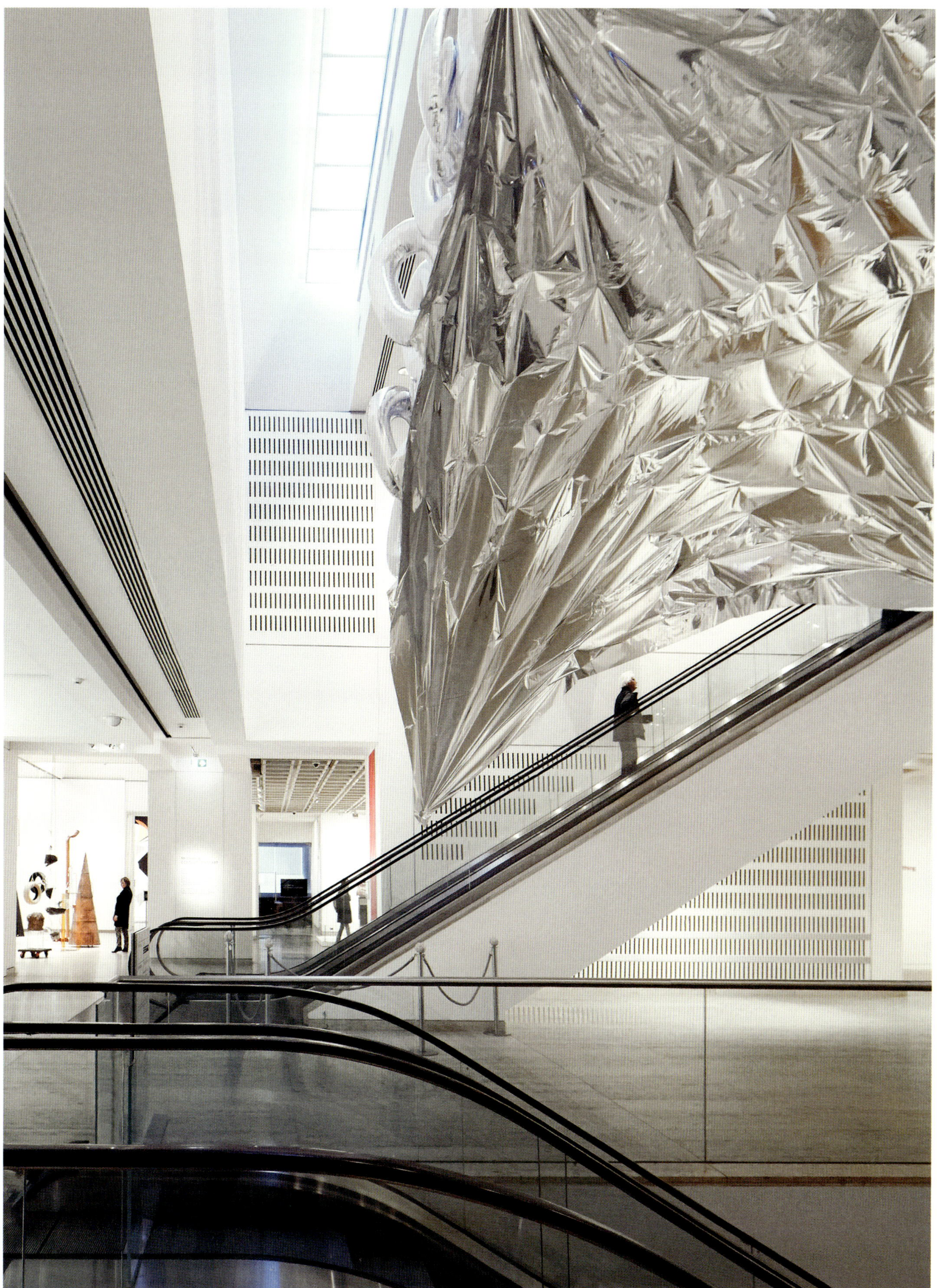

Mikala Dwyer:
A shape of thought
26 August 2017 — 4 February 2018
Art Gallery of New South Wales,
Sydney

—

opposite and pages 114–16:

Square cloud compound 2010
fabric stockings, glass, beer,
champagne, plastic, ceramics,
found things, wood, rocks, lights,
synthetic polymer paint, acrylic, cat
and bird ornaments
Museum of Contemporary Art,
Australia, Sydney, purchased
with funds provided by the
MCA Foundation, 2015

page 117:

Costumes 2017
4 parts: fabric, plastic, spay enamel

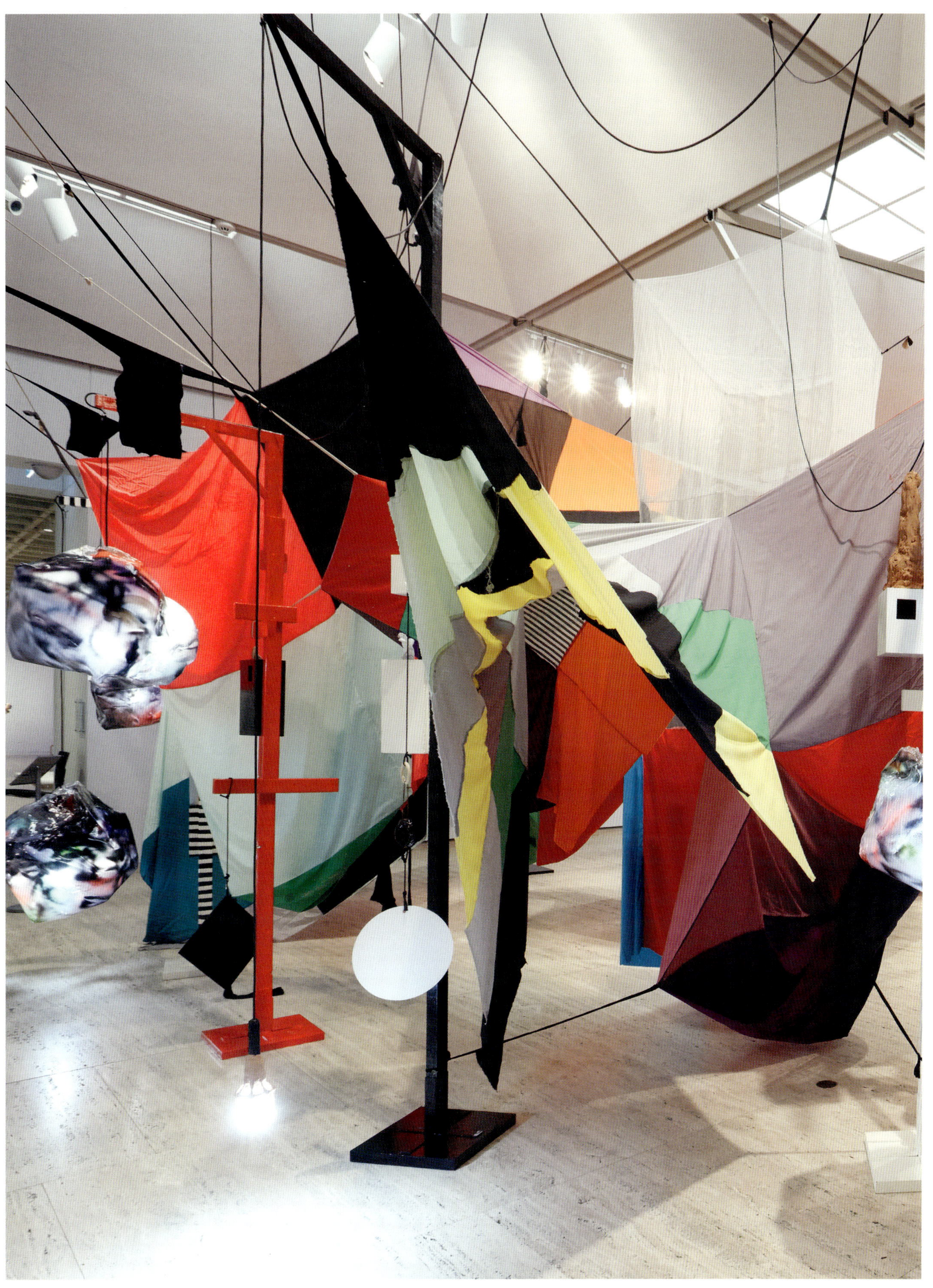

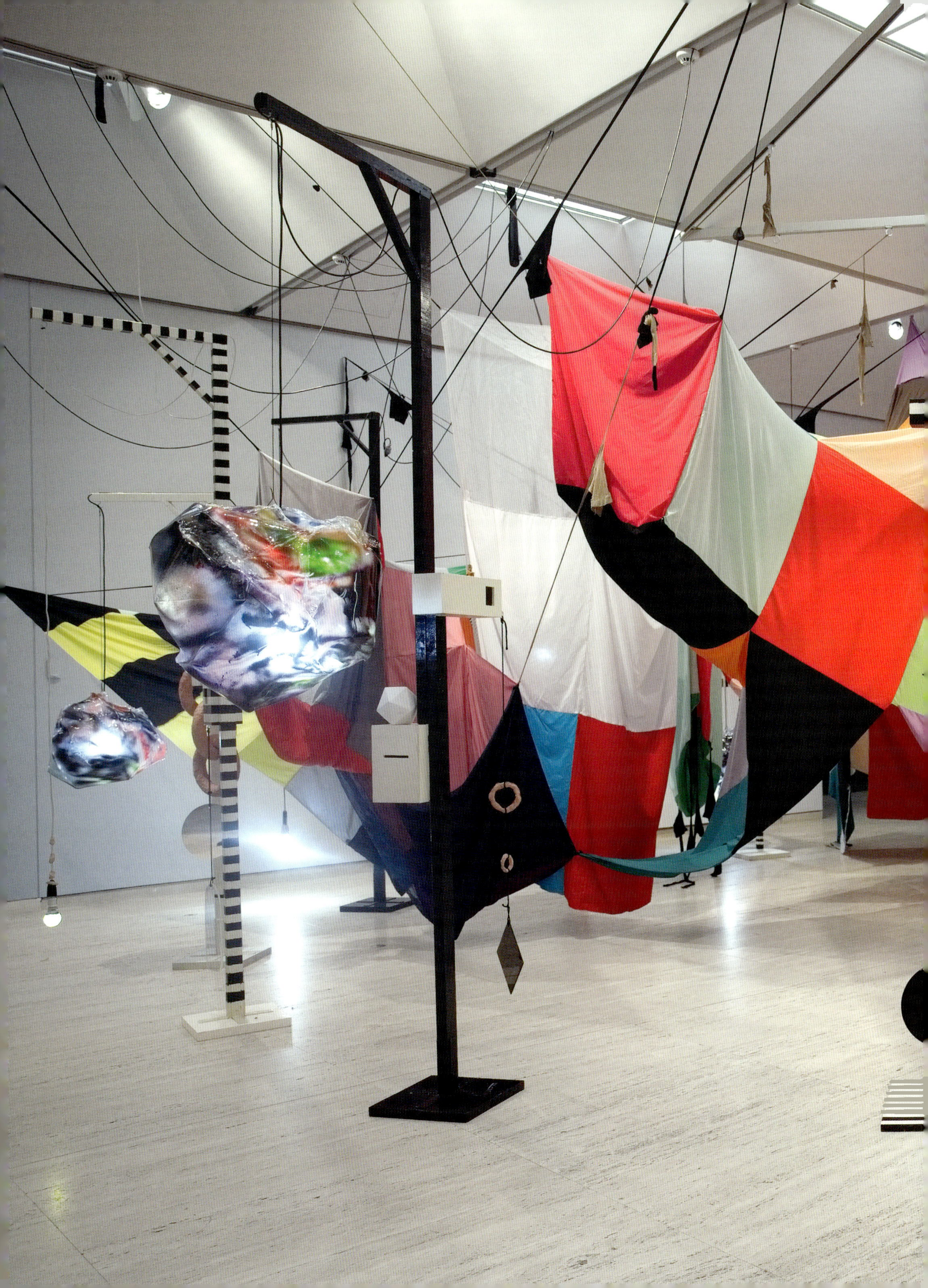

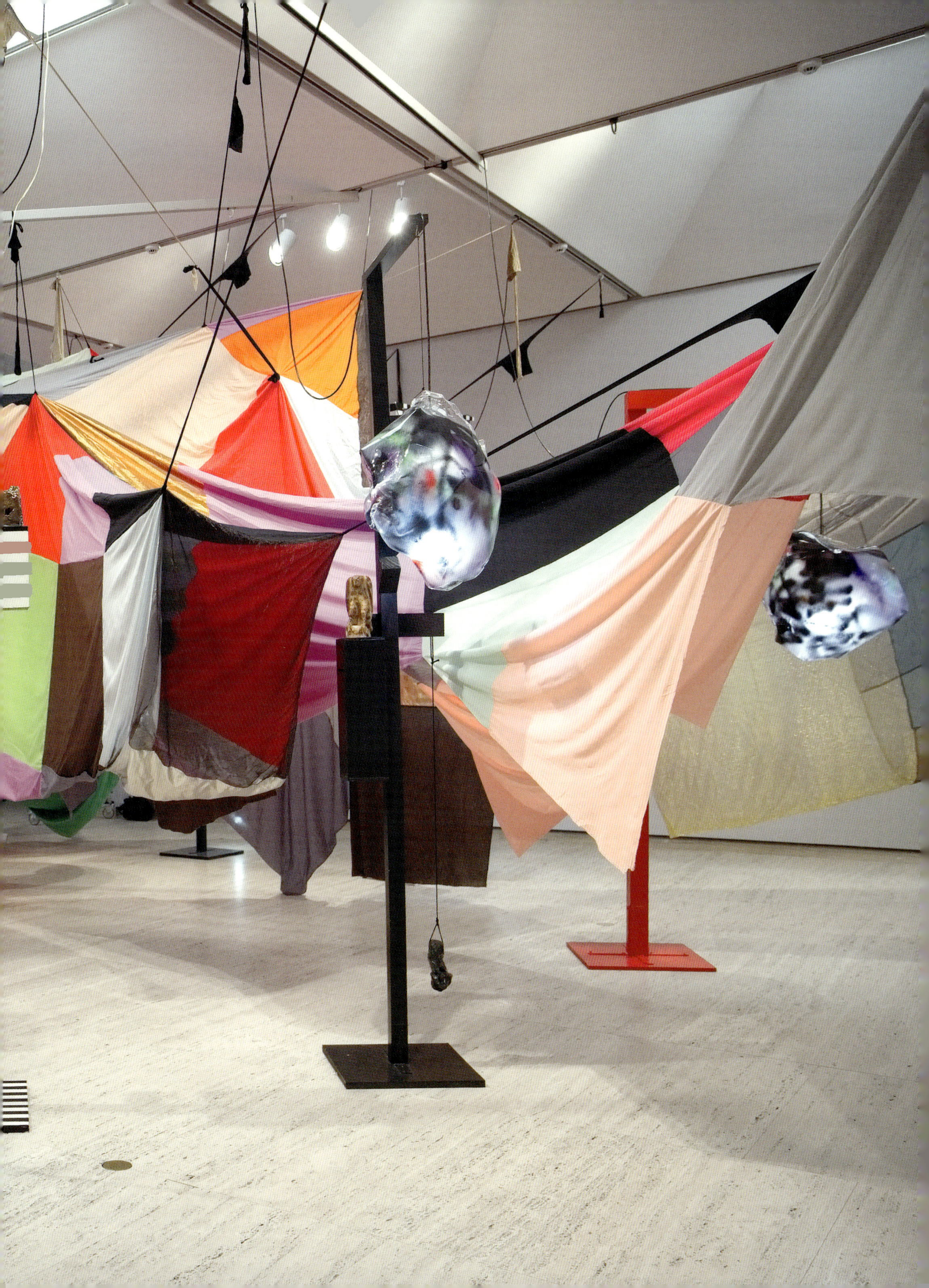

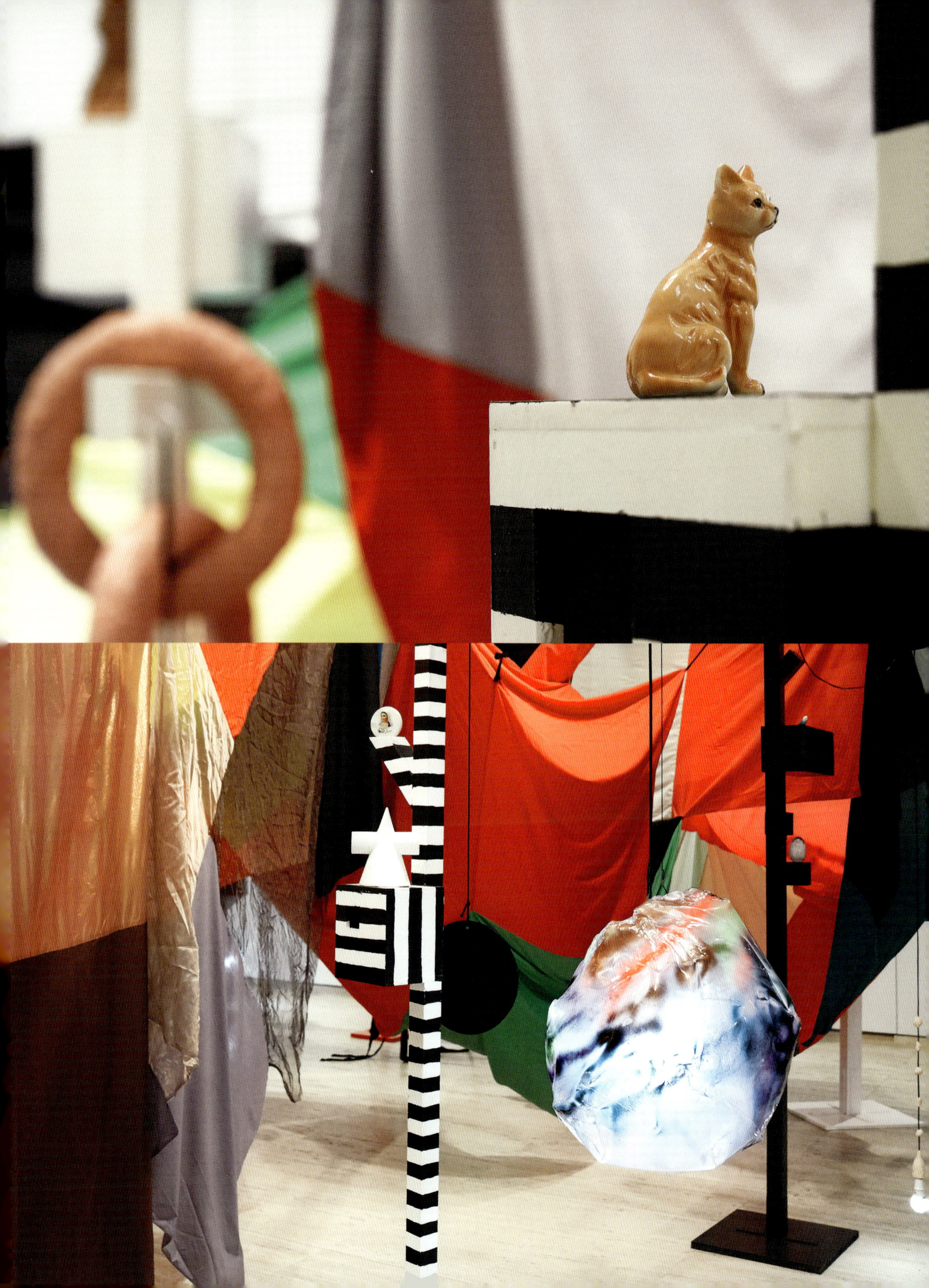

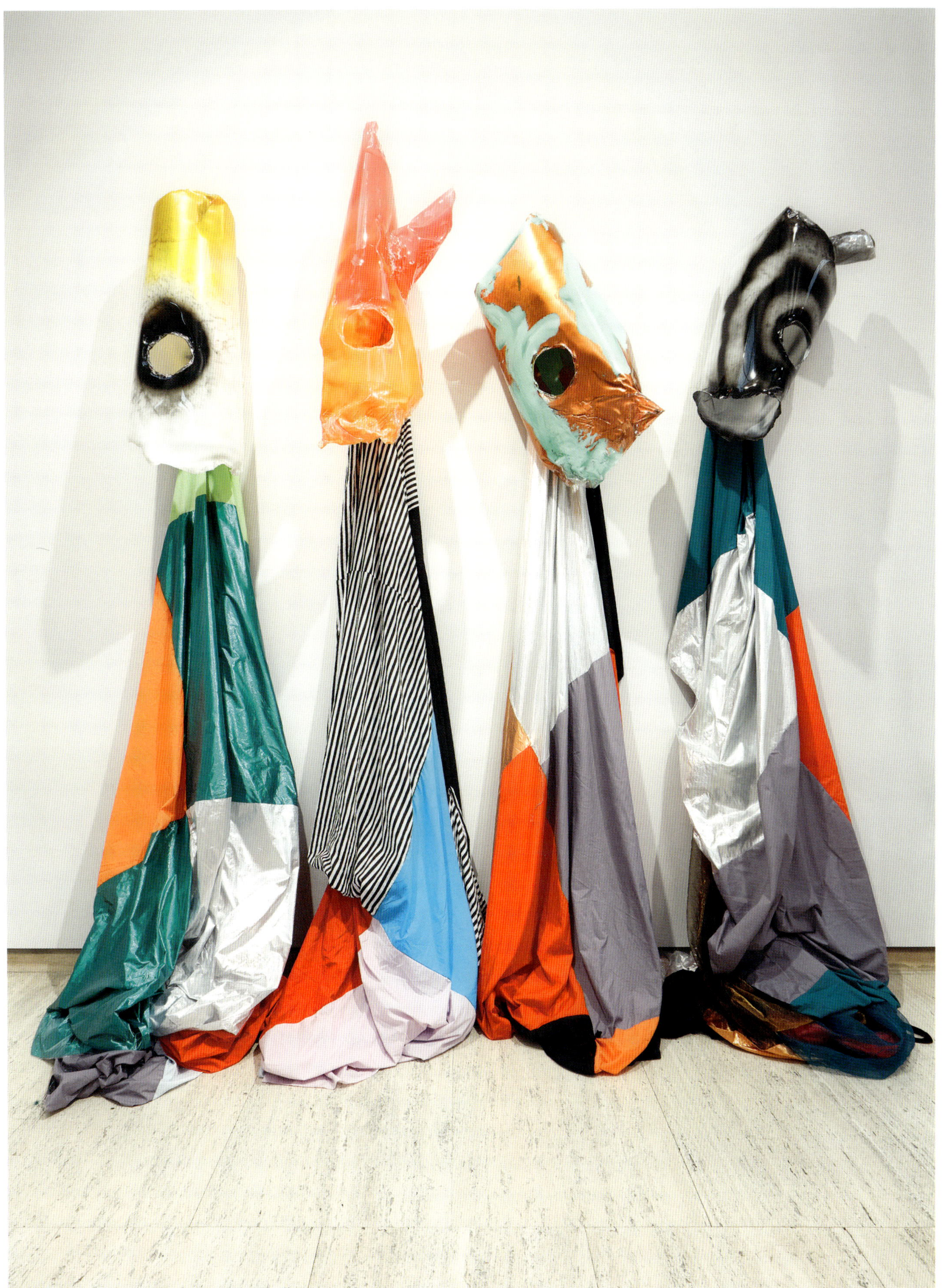

Mikala Dwyer:
A shape of thought
26 August 2017 — 4 February 2018
Art Gallery of New South Wales,
Sydney

—

opposite and pages 120–23:

Hollowwork (ringing) 2013 (detail)
aluminium

A weight of space 2017
(background)
plastic, steel, rope

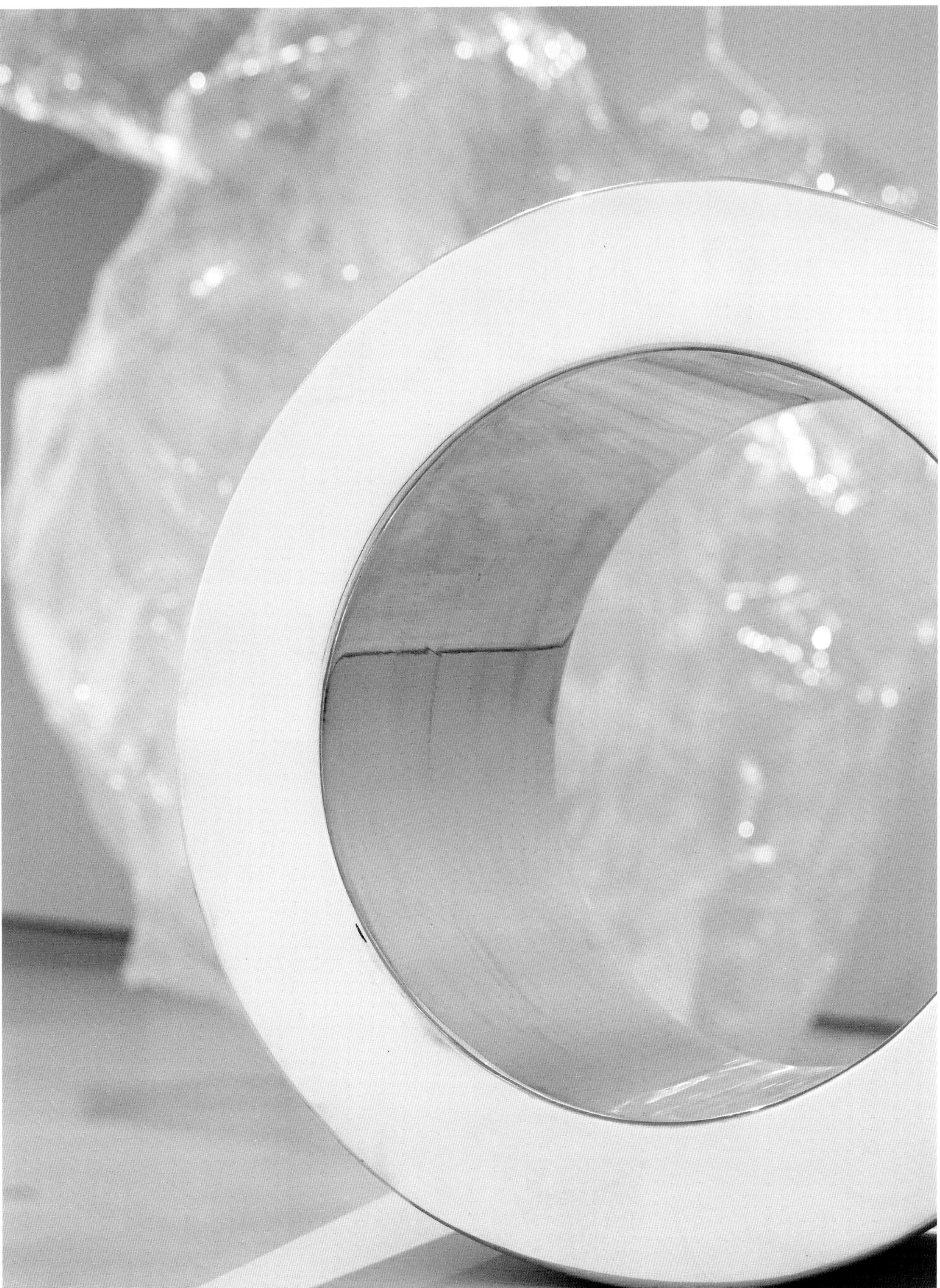

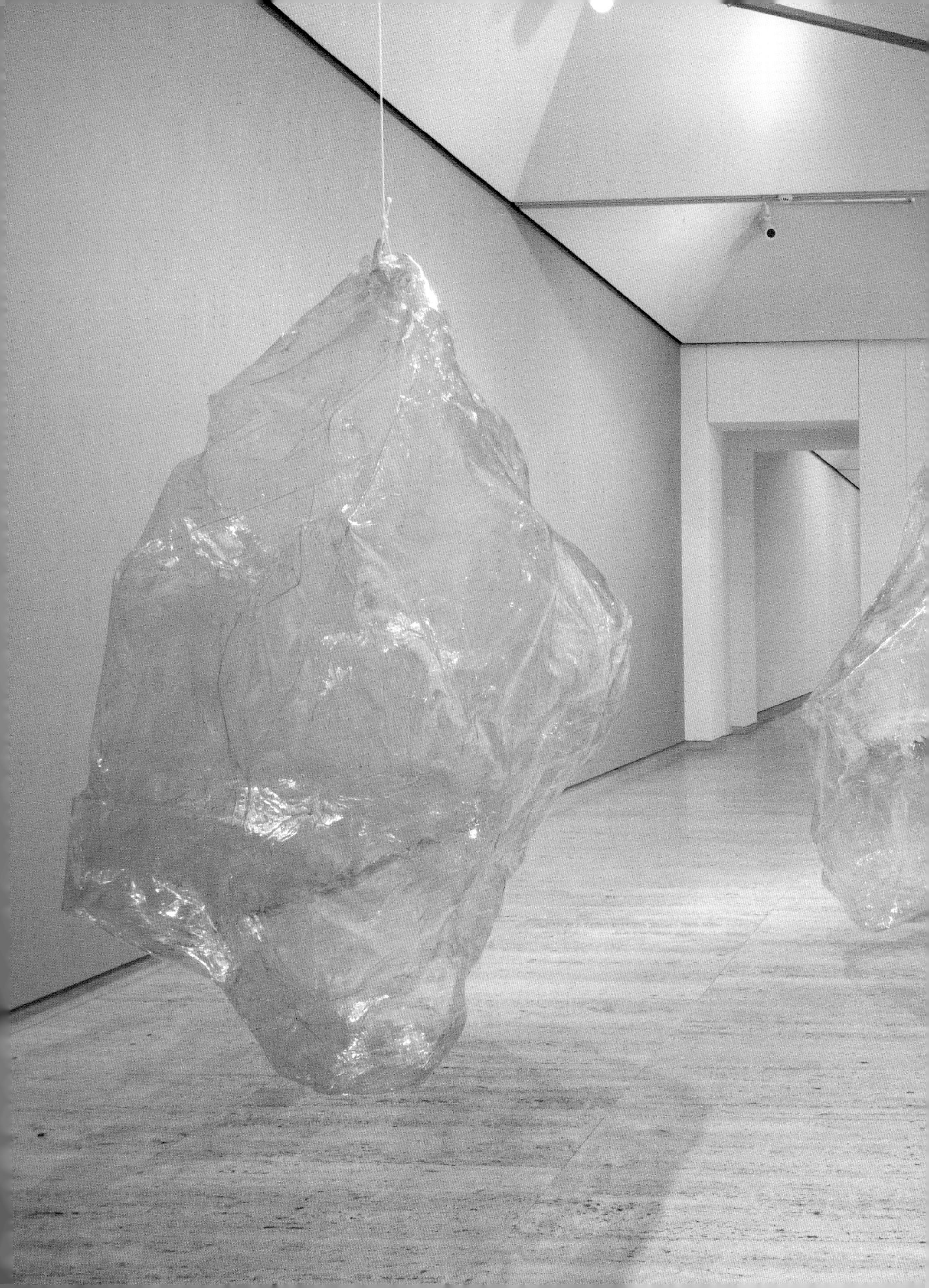

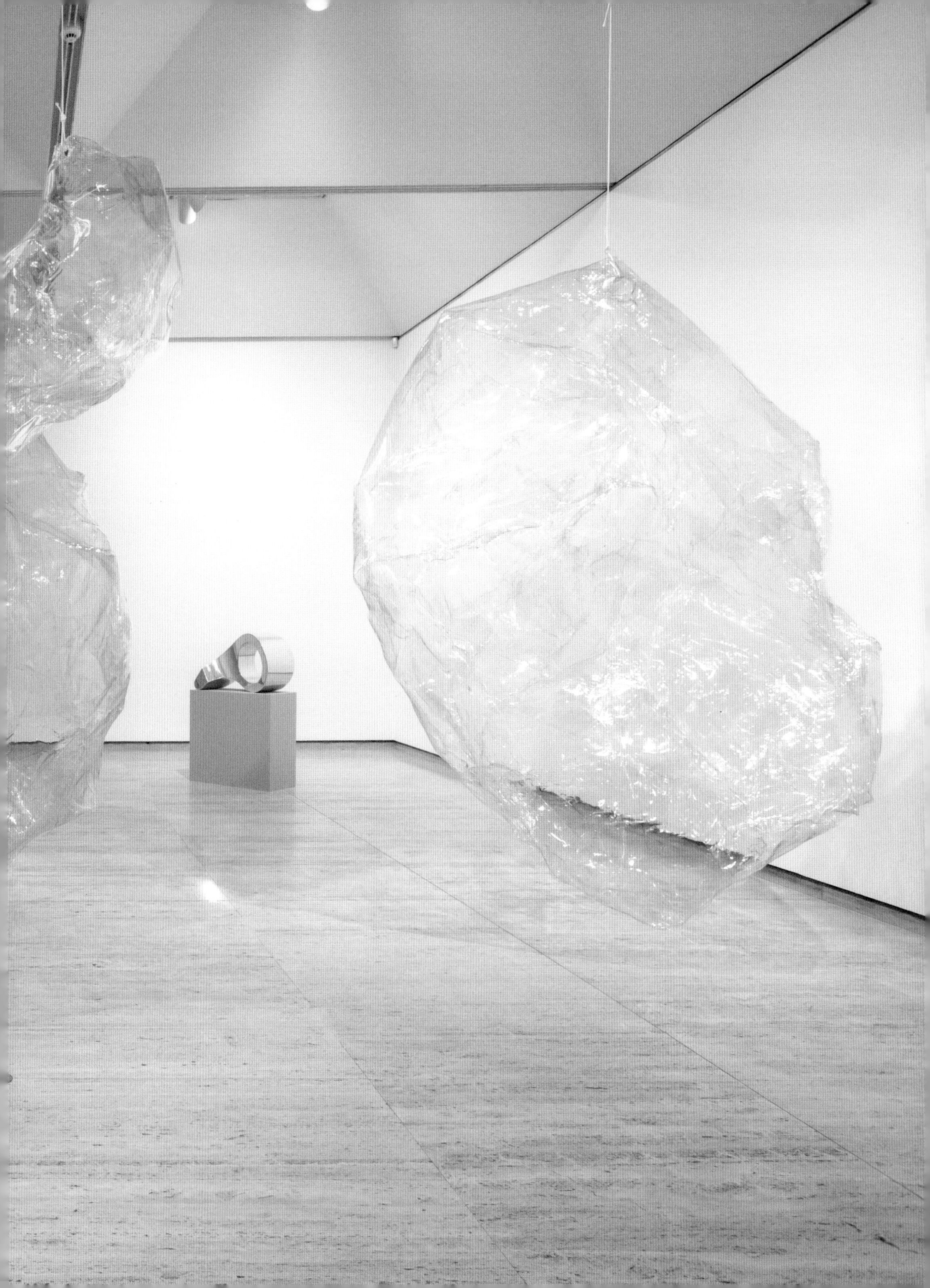

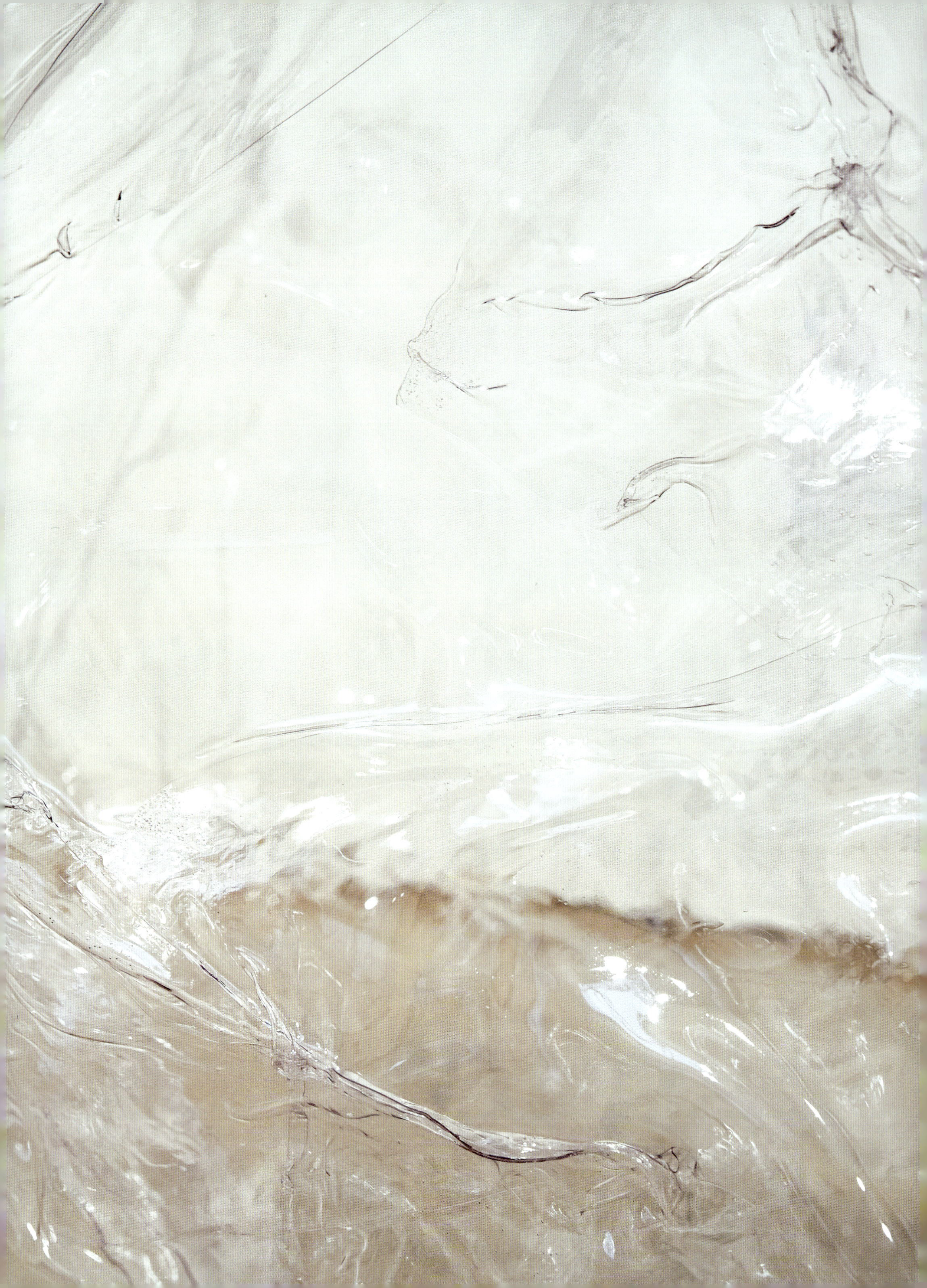

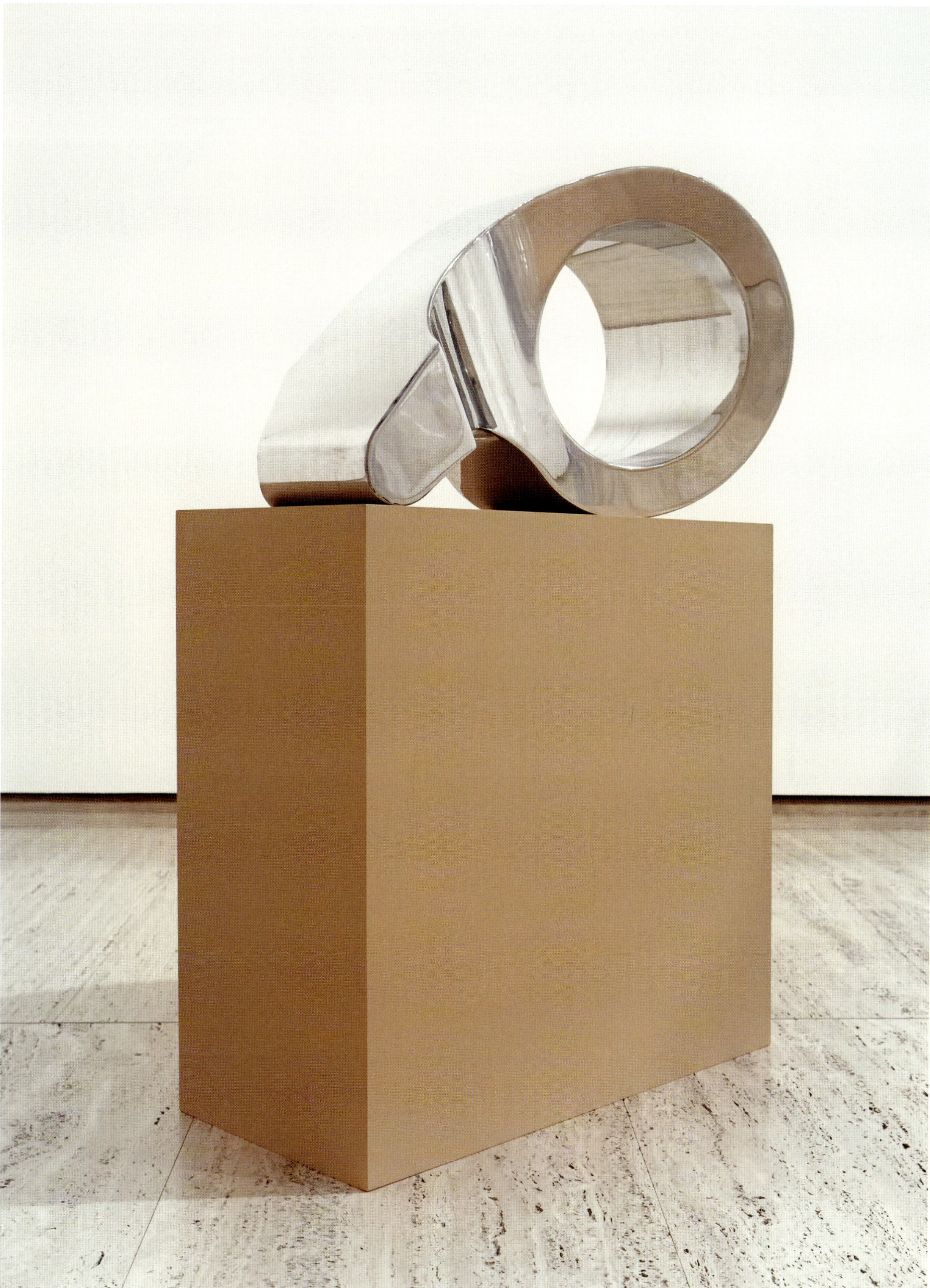

Mikala Dwyer:
A shape of thought
26 August 2017 — 4 February 2018
Art Gallery of New South Wales,
Sydney

—

opposite and pages 126–29:

Mikala Dwyer with Hany Armanious,
Adriane Boag, Andre Bremer, Nick
Dorey, Stevie Fieldsend, Matthys
Gerber

The divisions and subtractions
2017
mixed media

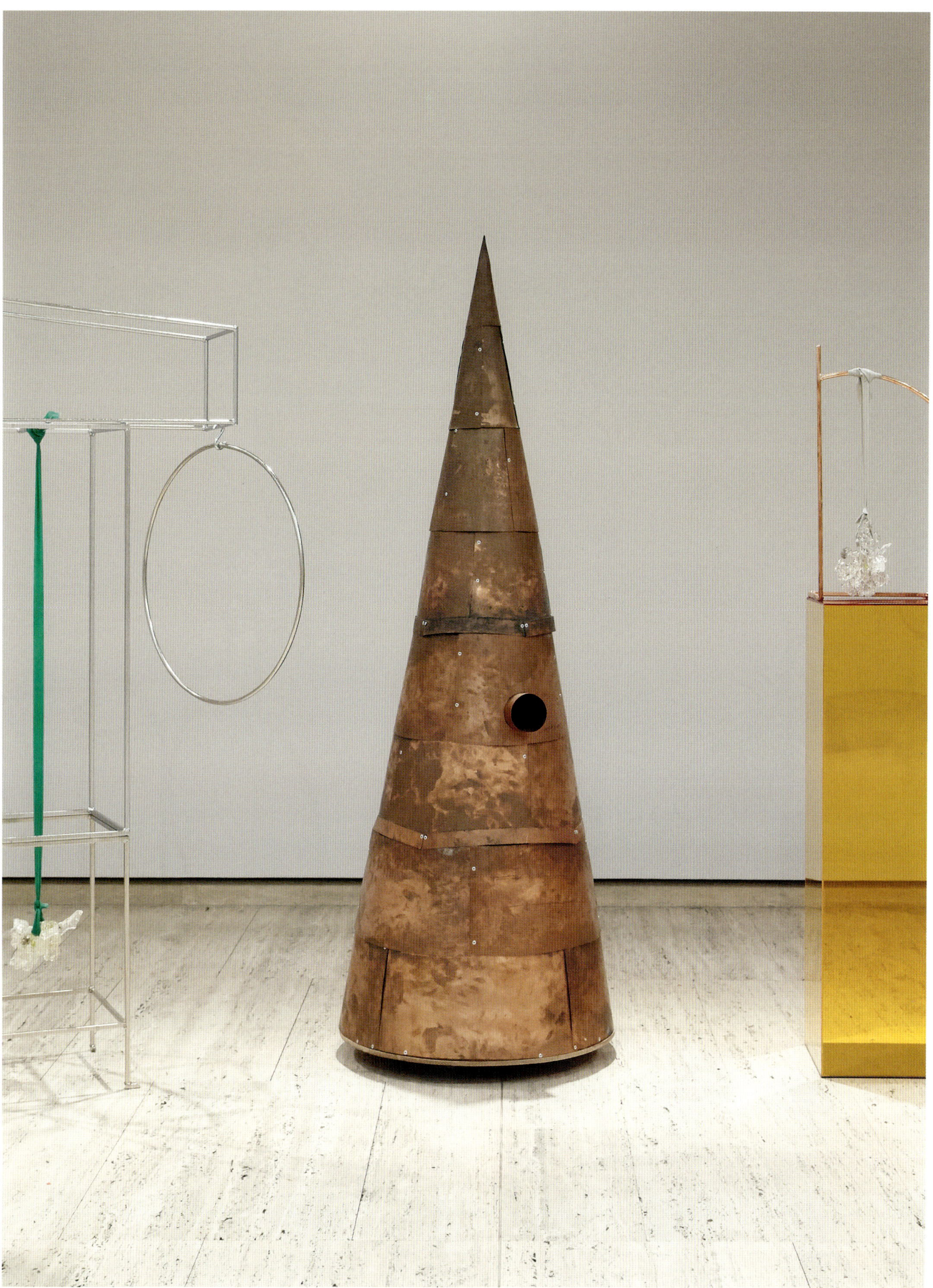

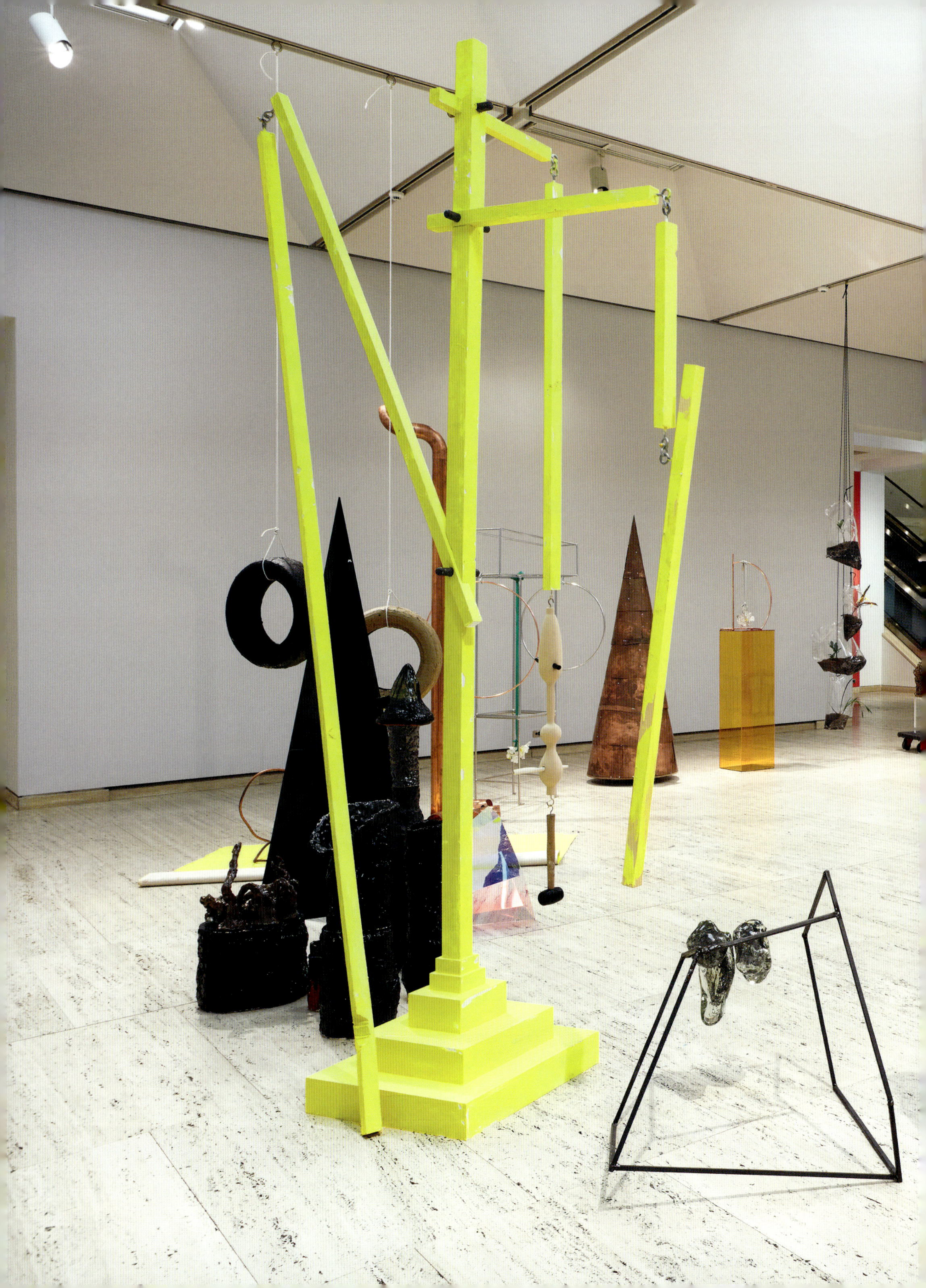

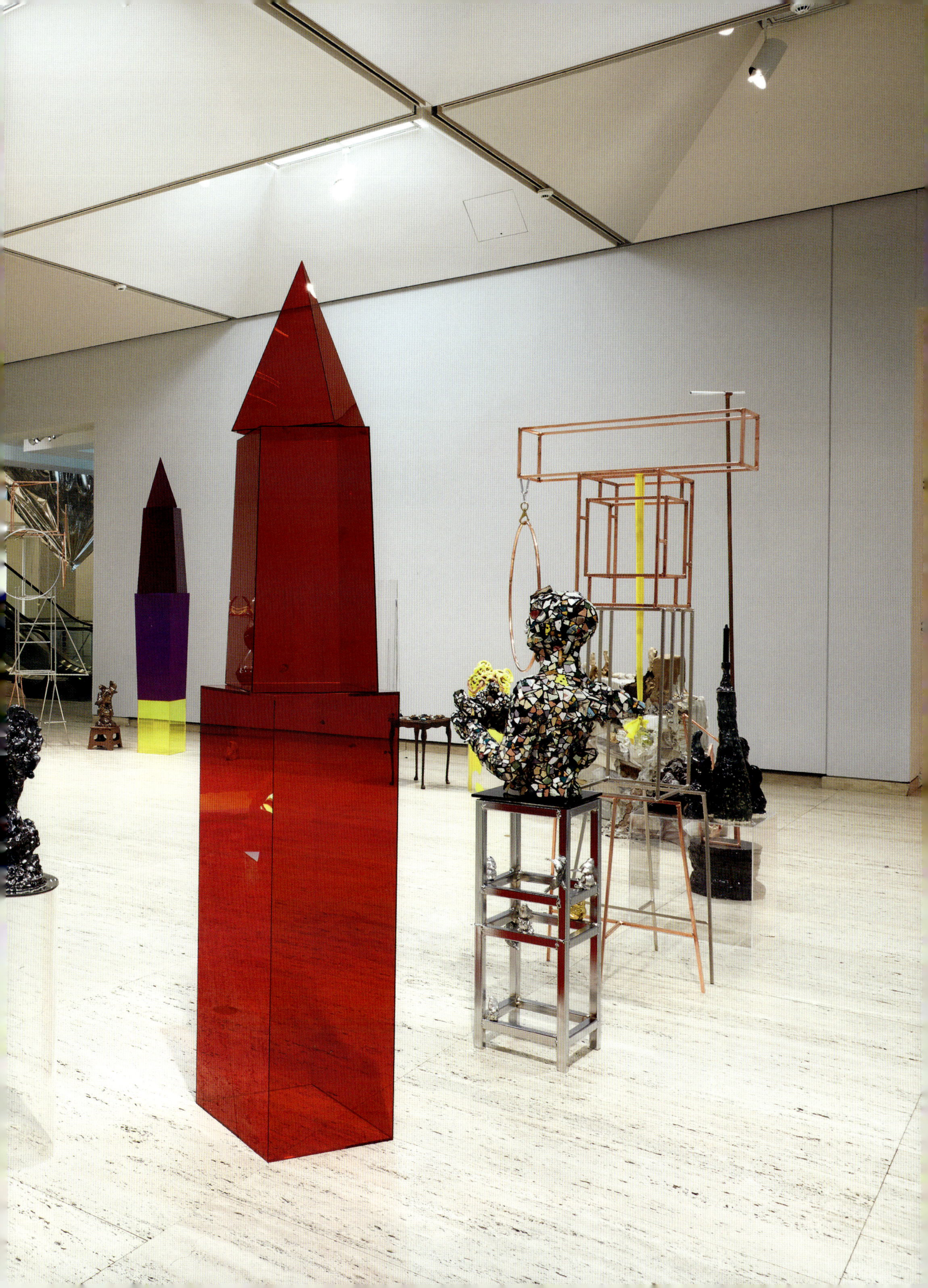

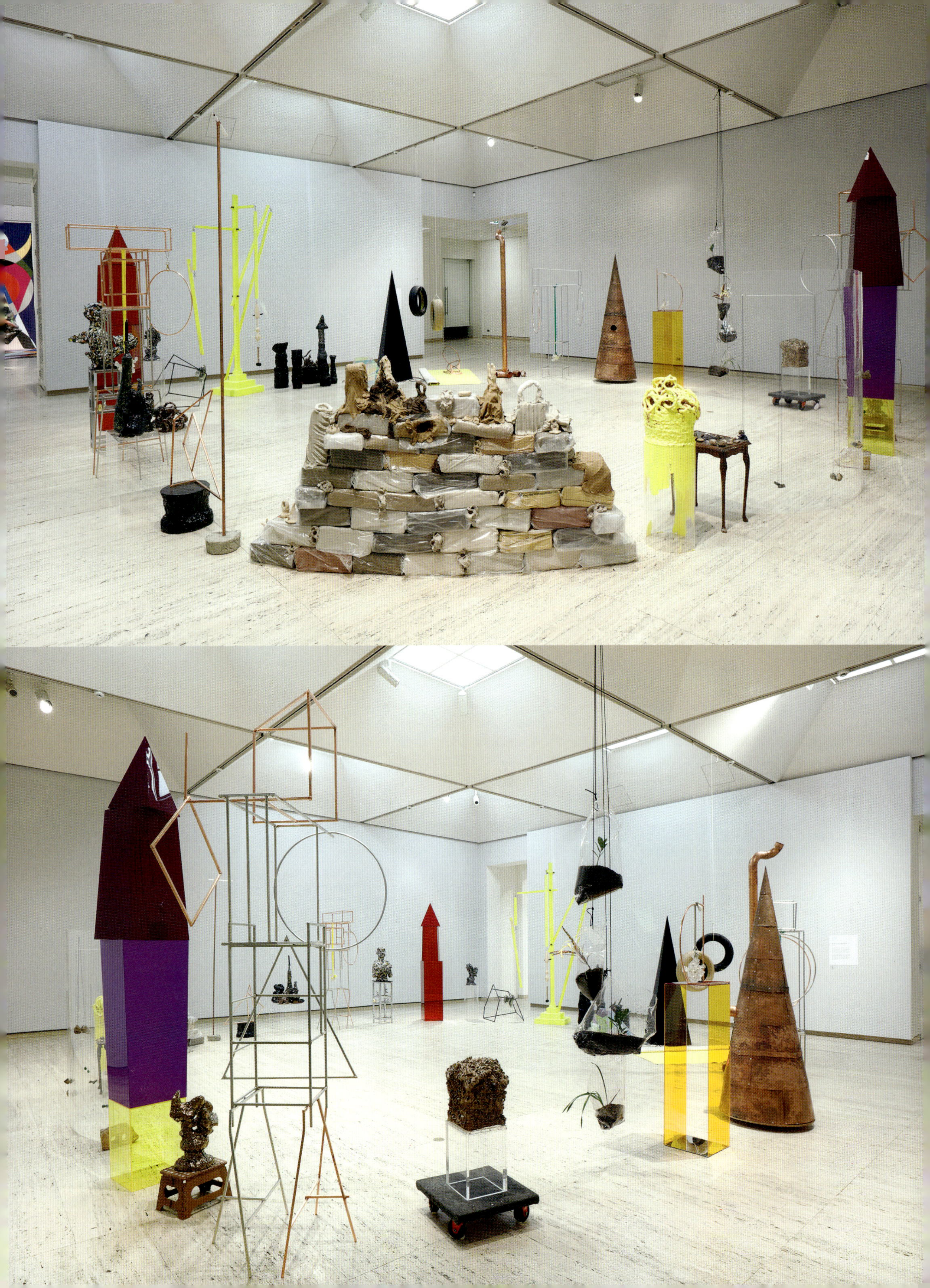

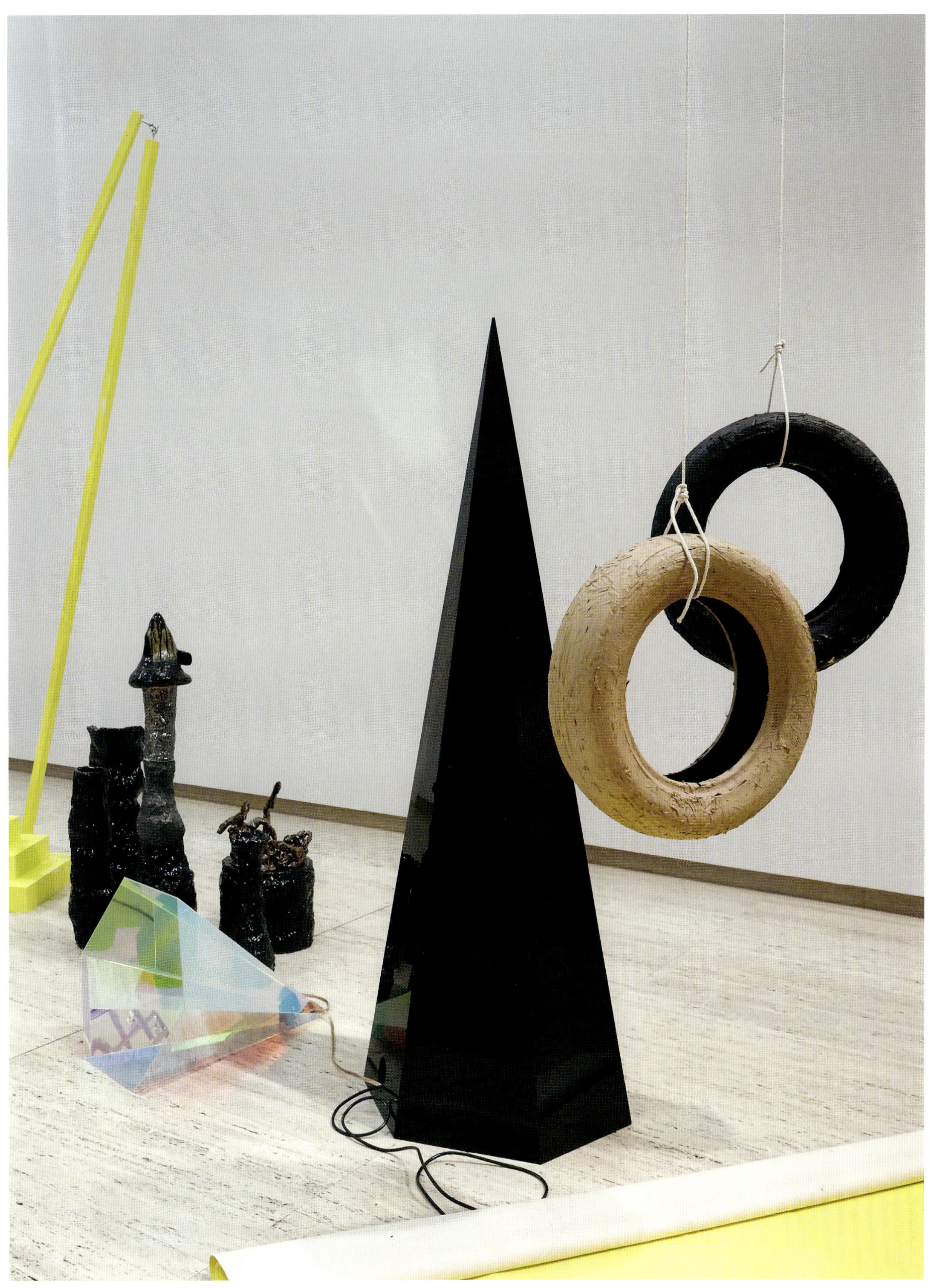

Mikala Dwyer:
A shape of thought
26 August 2017 — 4 February 2018
Art Gallery of New South Wales,
Sydney

—

opposite:

The letterbox Marys 2015 (detail)
acrylic, steel, fabric, Marys

below and pages 132–35

The letterbox Marys 2015–17
installation of various artworks

clockwise from below:

Backdrop for Saint Jude 2015
synthetic polymer paint on canvas,
ceramic, scientific glass

Earthlings 2015 (foreground)
uranium glass, glass, blacklight, holy
water, mercury sol (homeopathic),
brimstone (sulfur), salt (pink lake), clay

Wall charm 2017 (wall)
mixed media

banners from left:

The angel 2015
synthetic polymer paint on canvas

Possession 2015
synthetic polymer paint on canvas,
IKEA bed, polyurethane, coins, stones,
gems, Marys

Sigil for heaven and earth 2015
synthetic polymer paint on canvas

Backdrop for rounders 2016
synthetic polymer paint on canvas

**Puzzle (after Piet Hein / Kumbel
Kumbell)** 2015 (foreground)
acrylic

Backdrop for base matter 2016
synthetic polymer paint on canvas

Shadow lamp I 2015
wood, plastic, acrylic paint, hooks

Shadow lamp II 2015
wood, plastic, acrylic paint, ceramic

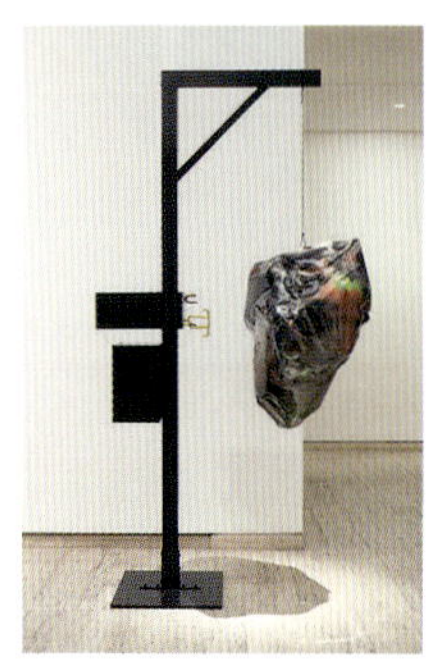
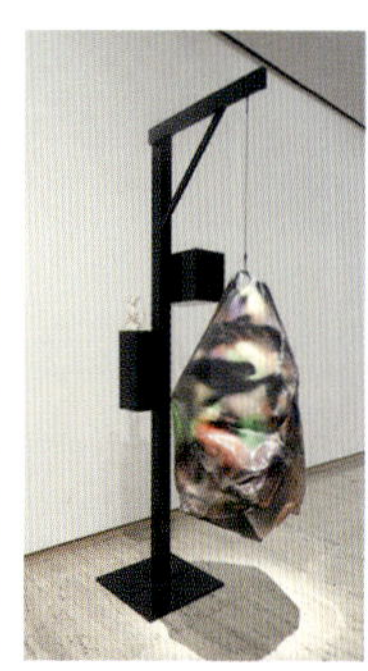
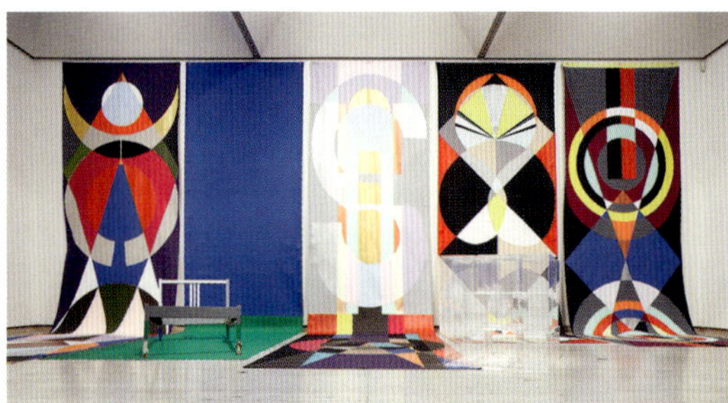
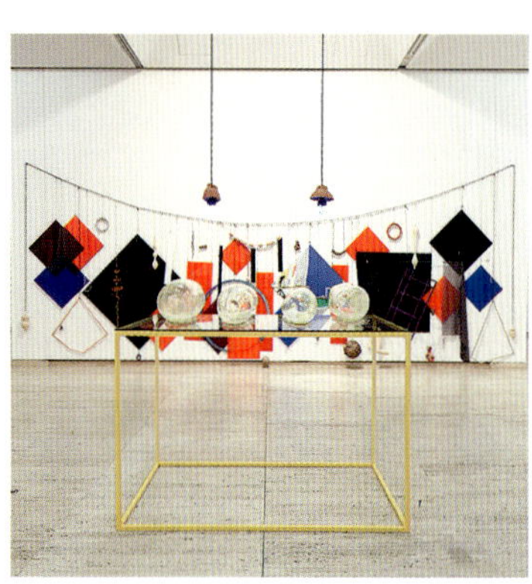
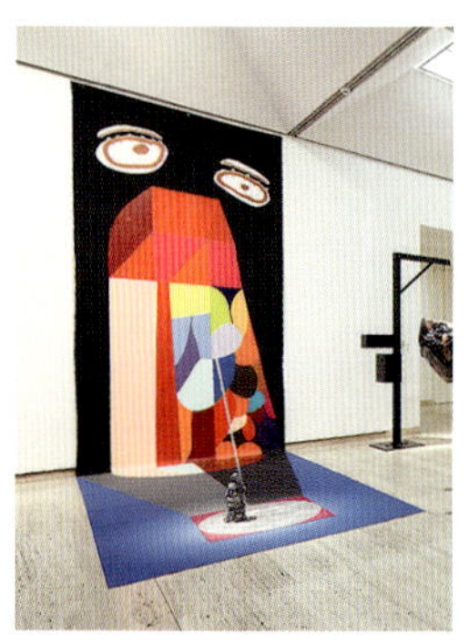

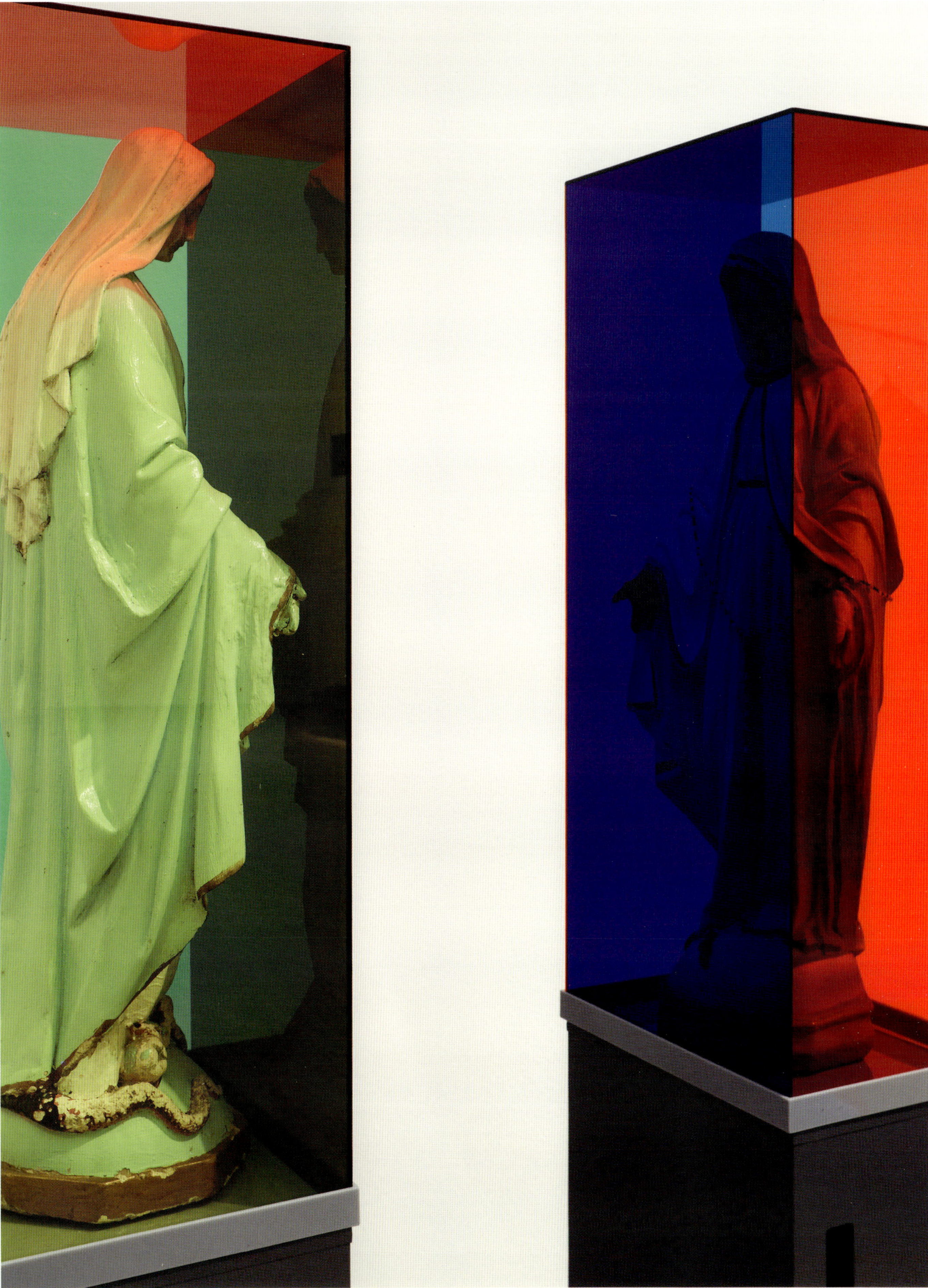

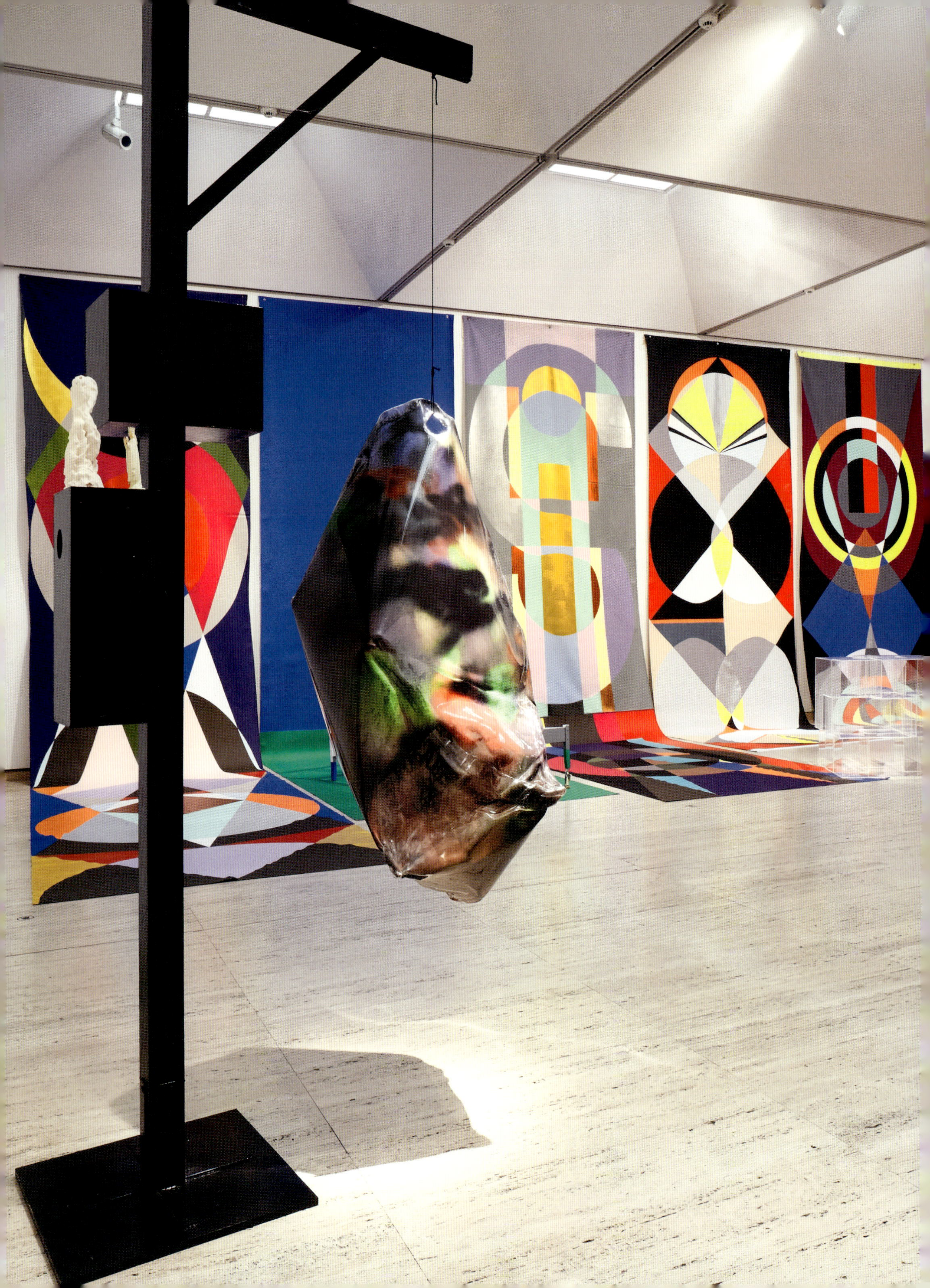

Mikala Dwyer

Mikala Dwyer (b 1959) studied at Sydney College of the Arts, University of Sydney; University of New South Wales, Sydney; Middlessex Polytechnic, London; and Berlin University of the Arts, Berlin.

Dwyer has established a significant and prominent practice with many solo and group exhibitions in Australia and internationally. She has received numerous scholarships, grants and awards, and her work is held in public collections throughout Australia and New Zealand.

Dwyer is also a highly regarded art teacher in Sydney and has held positions as lecturer at the University of Western Sydney (1995–99) and Sydney College of the Arts, University of Sydney (since 1999).

Contributors

Susan Best is professor of art theory and deputy director (research and postgraduate) at the Queensland College of Art, Griffith University. Her research focuses on modern and contemporary art with an emphasis on women's art and Latin American art. She is the author of *Visualizing feeling: affect and the feminine avant-garde* (2011) and *Reparative aesthetics: witnessing in contemporary art photography* (2016). In 2012 *Visualizing feeling* was awarded the prize for best book by the Art Association of Australia and New Zealand. Currently, she is writing a new book titled 'Impersonality: self and other in post 60s body art'.

Helen Hughes is research curator at Monash University Museum of Art and lecturer in art history and curatorial practice at Monash Art Design & Architecture (MADA) in Melbourne. She is a co-founder and co-editor of the contemporary art journal *Discipline*; an editor of the peer-reviewed online art history journal *EMAJ*; on the editorial advisory board of *Broadsheet*; and a member of the *Art + Australia* advisory group, A+A Associates. In 2016 she co-curated, with Victoria Lynn, *TarraWarra Biennial 2016: endless circulation* and co-edited, with Janine Burke, *Kiffy Rubbo: curating the 1970s*. Other recent books include *Impresario: Paul Taylor* (2013, co-edited with Nicholas Croggon) and *Making worlds: art and science fiction* (2013, co-edited with Amelia Barikin).

Wayne Tunnicliffe is curator of *Mikala Dwyer: A shape of thought* and head curator of Australian art at the Art Gallery of New South Wales where he works across the Australian collection and exhibition programs, as well as overseeing the Brett Whiteley Studio in Surry Hills. His many exhibitions and publications at the Art Gallery of New South Wales include *The National* 2017 (with Anneke Jaspers), *Pop to popism* (2014–15), *The John Kaldor Family Collection* (book, 2012), *Wilderness: Balnaves contemporary: painting* (2010), *Tim Johnson: painting ideas* (2009), *Adam Cullen: let's get lost* (2008), *Contemporary: Art Gallery of New South Wales contemporary collection* (book, 2006), *Robert Owen: different lights cast different shadows* (2004) and *Simryn Gill* (2002). Most recently he was curatorial advisor for the exhibition *Australia's impressionists* at the National Gallery in London (2016–17).

Acknowledgments

The production of this book and the *A shape of thought* exhibition has involved dedicated work by members of staff from across the Art Gallery of New South Wales. In particular, I acknowledge (for the book) publishing manager Julie Donaldson and publication designer Analiese Cairis; (for the exhibition) assistant curator Nick Yelverton, exhibition manager Katy Preston, exhibition registrar Sophie Moran, conservators Frances Cumming and Melanie Barrett, head of installation Nik Reith, lighting technician Kane Hancock, digital producer Francesca Ford, public programs producer Alexandra Gregg, education manager Leeanne Carr and photographer Mim Stirling.

Wayne Tunnicliffe

My thanks go to Wayne Tunnicliffe, David and Olive, Stephanie and Mr Mak, Sofia Freeman, Stevie Fieldsend, Matthys Gerber, Andre Bremer, Nick Dory, Hany Armanious, Adriane Boag, Katie Louise Williams, Lionel Doolen, Anny Mokotow, Margo Ray, Helen Hughes, Susan Best, Jonathan Blake, Canbora Bayraktar, Vashti Tregonning, Louise Hasselton, Margaret Harris, Joan Grounds, Marcus Dillion and Simon Ray. Thank you also to Artspace, Sydney; the students of Sydney College of the Arts, University of Sydney; and the Art Gallery of New South Wales installation team: Nik Reith, Brett Cuthbertson, Julia Bavyka, Tim Dale, Jake van Dugteren and Stevan McBride. I acknowledge and am grateful for the support of my gallerists: Roslyn Oxley (Roslyn Oxley9 Gallery, Sydney), Anna Schwartz (Anna Schwartz Gallery, Melbourne) and Hamish McKay (Hamish McKay Gallery, Wellington), as well as Sarah Cottier and Ashley Barber, Hamish Morrison and Our Neon Foe.

Mikala Dwyer

Haylock, Brad. 'Goldene bend'er: Mikala Dwyer', *Vault Magazine*, issue 4, August 2013, pp 10–15

Hein, Piet. 'Astro-gymnastics', *Mikala Dwyer: the garden of half-life*, University Art Gallery, University of Sydney, Sydney, 2014, pp 10–12

High tide: new currents in art from Australia and New Zealand, Zachęta National Gallery of Art, Warsaw and Contemporary Art Centre, Vilnius, 2006

Kent, Rachel. 'Minimalism past and present', *The infinite space: women, minimalism and the sculptural object*, Ian Potter Museum of Art, University of Melbourne, Melbourne, 1998, pp 3–10

King, Natalie. 'Mikala Dwyer', *Art + Text*, no 49, September 1994, pp 74–75

Leonard, Robert. 'Mikala Dwyer interviewed by Robert Leonard', *Mikala Dwyer: drawing down the moon*, Institute of Modern Art, Brisbane, 2012, pp 57–62

Long, Declan. 'Circles of possibility: approaching the art of Mikala Dwyer', *Mikala Dwyer: goldene bend'er*, Australian Centre for Contemporary Art, Southbank, VIC, 2013, pp 33–37

Lynn, Victoria. *Australian perspecta 1993*, Art Gallery of New South Wales, Sydney, 1993

Michael, Linda. *Primavera 1992*, Museum of Contemporary Art, Sydney, 1992

Michael, Linda. *No, not ever: the nail polish series*, BARBERism, Newtown, NSW, 1994

Michael, Linda. 'The little temples of love for the dead things', *Mikala Dwyer*, Museum of Contemporary Art, Sydney, 2000, pp 7–11

Michael, Linda. 'Mikala Dwyer: *Hanging eyes 2*', *Fieldwork: Australian art 1968–2002*, National Gallery of Victoria, Melbourne, 2002, pp 112–13

Michael, Linda. 'Mikala Dwyer', *Mystic truths*, Auckland Art Gallery Toi o Tāmaki, Auckland, 2007, pp 31–35

Michael, Linda. 'Mikala Dwyer', *Before and after science: 2010 Adelaide Biennial of Australian art*, Art Gallery of South Australia, Adelaide, 2010, p 48

Michael, Linda. 'The real thing', *Mikala Dwyer: goldene bend'er*, Australian Centre for Contemporary Art, Southbank, VIC, 2013, pp 4–7

Michael, Linda, Andrew McNamara and Ann Stephen. *Future primitive*, Heide Museum of Modern Art, Bulleen, VIC, 2013

O'Dwyer, Rebecca. 'This must be the place: Mikala Dwyer's *Panto collapsar*', *Rebecca O'Dwyer* (blog), 15 February 2012, ebeccaodwyer.wordpress.com /2012/02/15/this-must-be-the-place -mikala-dwyers-panto-collapsar/. (accessed 31 August 2017)

O'Neil, Emma. 'Mikala Dwyer: MCA collection', *Art AsiaPacific*, no 98, May/June 2016, p 118

Parker, Luke. 'Interview with Mikala Dwyer', *Mikala Dwyer: the garden of half-life*, University Art Gallery, University of Sydney, Sydney, 2014, pp 61–65

Paton, Justin. 'Mikala Dwyer', *Good work: the Jim Barr and Mary Barr collection*, Dunedin Public Art Gallery, Dunedin, 2001, p 9

Poppelwell, Martin. 'Das up 2001', *Mikala Dwyer: an Australian artist's project*, City Gallery Wellington, Wellington, 2002, pp 24–28

Porch, Debra. *9 lives: Michael Butler, Mikala Dwyer, My Le Thi, Nguyen Minh Thanh, Nguyen Quang Huy, Nguyen Van Cuong, Albertina Viegas, Regina Walter, Paul White*, Casula Powerhouse Arts Centre, Casula, NSW, 1999

Rankin-Reid, Jane. 'Shirthead', *Art + Text*, no 46, September 1993, p 78

Ratliff, Melissa, Dougal Phillips and Lisa Girault with David Elliott. 'Mikala Dwyer', *17th Biennale of Sydney: the beauty of distance: songs of survival in a precarious age*, Biennale of Sydney, Woolloomooloo, NSW, 2010, p 274

Ross, Toni. 'Mikala Dwyer', *Contempora5*, National Gallery of Victoria, Melbourne, 1999, p 13

Ross, Toni. 'Embodied reason, functionalist magic, animate objects', *Mikala Dwyer: drawing down the moon*, Institute of Modern Art, Brisbane, 2012, pp 75–86

Ross, Toni. 'Encountering Mikala Dwyer's art with Eva Hesse and minimalism', *Mikala Dwyer: goldene bend'er*, Australian Centre for Contemporary Art, Southbank, VIC, 2013, pp 43–47

Rothnie, Susan. 'Mikala Dwyer in conversation with Susan Rothnie', *eyeline*, no 55, spring 2004, pp 30–33

Rowell, Amanda. 'Mikala Dwyer', *Mikala Dwyer: an Australian artist's project*, City Gallery Wellington, Wellington, 2002, pp 4–8

Schubert, Robert. 'Restaging abstraction', *Art + Text*, no 49, September 1994, pp 35–37

Schwarz, Katrina, Michael Fitzgerald and Margaret Farmer, with Marni Williams and Jesse Stein. 'Mikala Dwyer', *Current: contemporary art from Australia and New Zealand*, Dott Publishing, Paddington, NSW, 2008, p 108

Stanhope, Zara and John Stringer. *This was the future ... Australia sculpture of the 1950s, 60s, 70s + today*, Heide Museum of Modern Art, Bulleen, VIC, 2003

Storer, Russell. 'Play things: some contemporary artists and their objects', *Artlink*, vol 21, no 2, June 2001, pp 37–40

Sullivan, Eve. 'Mikala Dwyer', *Australian perspecta 1993*, Art Gallery of New South Wales, Sydney, 1993, pp 32–33

Taussig, Michael. 'Art and magic and real magic', *Mikala Dwyer: drawing down the moon*, Institute of Modern Art, Brisbane, 2012, pp 25–30

Tunnicliffe, Wayne. *Still life: the inaugural Balnaves Foundation Sculpture Project: James Angus, Mikala Dwyer, Emily Floyd, Ronnie van Hout, Ricky Swallow*, Art Gallery of New South Wales, Sydney, 2003, np

Ward, Lucina. *Soft sculpture*, National Gallery of Australia, Canberra, 2009

Williams, Linda. 'Little theatre of excess: spatial theory and site-specific sculpture', *Fifth Australian Sculpture Triennial*, Australian Sculpture Triennial, North Melbourne, 1993, pp 29–44

Williams, Linda. 'The aberrant object', *Art + Text*, no 48, May 1994, p 74

Wolfe, Ross. *Samstag: the 2005 Anne & Gordon Samstag International Visual Arts Scholarships*, University of South Australia, Adelaide, 2004

Wolff, Sharne. 'One crowded hour?', *The Art Life* (blog), 26 April 2012, theartlife.com.au/2012/ one-crowded-hour/ (accessed 31 August 2017)

Notes

**Inheritance: jewellery and
the sculpture of Mikala Dwyer**
Helen Hughes

1_ Many thanks to Wayne Tunnicliffe
and Nick Yelverton for compiling
research materials for this essay, and
to Mikala Dwyer for our extended
conversations.

2_ Robert Leonard, 'Mikala Dwyer
interviewed by Robert Leonard', in
*Mikala Dwyer: drawing down the
moon*, exh cat, Institute of Modern
Art, Brisbane, 2014, p 61.

3_ See Dwyer's installation *A shape
of thought* 2007, which includes
video footage of her father's eyes.

4_ See Leonard, p 60.

5_ In *A shape of thought*, this
channelling process is evidenced by
the series of sculptural collaborations
that Dwyer undertook with other
artists to form the individual objects
in her circular installation *The
divisions and subtractions* 2017. The
collaborating artists include Stevie
Fieldsend, Andre Bremer, Nick Dorey,
Matthys Gerber and Hany Armanious.

6_ See, for instance, *19th Biennale
of Sydney: you imagine what you
desire*, exh cat, Biennale of Sydney,
Woolloomooloo, NSW, 2014, p 133:
'The body is everywhere in [Dwyer's]
art, which reasserts the relationship
of sculpture to the human form, even
when it is not figurative.'

7_ See Simon Bliss, 'Charlotte
Perriand, ball-bearings, and modernist
jewellery', *Modernism/Modernity*,
vol 20, no 2, April 2013, pp 169–88.

8_ Kevin Murray and Damian Skinner,
*Place and adornment: a history of
contemporary jewellery in Australia
and New Zealand*, David Bateman
Ltd, Auckland, 2014, p 7.

9_ Murray and Skinner, p 47.

10_ Mikala Dwyer in conversation
with the author, 1 June 2017.

11_ In 2016 Dwyer titled a new
work accordingly. *Charm for wall* was
exhibited at Hopkinson Mossman,
Auckland.

12_ Susan Rothnie, 'Mikala Dwyer
in conversation with Susan Rothnie',
eyeline, no 55, spring 2004, p 32.

13_ Mikala Dwyer, artist statement in
'History of practice', in *Mikala Dwyer:
goldene bend'er*, exh cat, Australian
Centre for Contemporary Art,
Melbourne, 2013, p 68.

14_ Linda Michael, 'The real thing',
in *Goldene bend'er*, p 6.

15_ Several of these neck cuffs were
displayed in Dwyer's 2016 exhibition
GRLZ at the Sydney artspace 55
Sydenham Rd, where she presented
a selection of her mother's jewellery
inside an acrylic vitrine.

**Marys, Lindas and
other spirited vessels**
Susan Best

1_ Marina Warner, *Alone of all her
sex: the myth and cult of the Virgin
Mary*, Oxford University Press, Oxford,
1976, p 24.

2_ 'Mikala Dwyer interviewed by
Robert Leonard', in *Mikala Dwyer:
drawing down the moon*, exh cat,
Institute of Modern Art, Brisbane,
2014, p 57.

3_ Wassily Kandinsky cited in
Rose-Carol Washton Long, *Kandinsky:
the development of an abstract style*,
Clarendon Press, Oxford, 1980, p 67.

4_ Frank Stella cited in Carel Blotkamp,
'Annunciation of the New Mysticism:
Dutch symbolism and early
abstraction', *The spiritual in art:
abstract painting 1890–1985*,
exh cat, Los Angeles County
Museum, Los Angeles and Abbeville
Press, New York, 1986, p 89.

Select bibliography

Back, Helen. 'Everybody's in the house
of love', *Mikala Dwyer: Henle's loop*,
Institute of Modern Art, Brisbane, 1993

Badham, Van. 'Who's afraid of the
art boogie monster?', *The Guardian*
(Australia),13 June 2013,
theguardian.com/commentisfree/
2013/jun/13/chris-berg-art-theatre
-australia (accessed 18 July 2017)

Barker, Victoria. 'Seeing a world
through the eyes of a child on a
mountaintop', *Mikala Dwyer: black
sun blue moon*, Spielhaus Morrison
Galerie, Berlin, 2007, pp 1–6

Best, Susan. 'Purl and plane geometry',
Fifth Australian Sculpture Triennial,
Australian Sculpture Triennial, North
Melbourne, 1993, pp 57–60

Best, Susan. 'Mineral nature: Mikala
Dwyer rocks', *Mikala Dwyer: the
garden of half-life*, University Art
Gallery, University of Sydney, Sydney,
2014, pp 13–20

Butler, Rex. 'To express the object',
Monster field, BARBERism, Newtown,
NSW, 1993, np

Butler, Sally. 'Mikala Dwyer's occult
constructivism', *eyeline*, no 77,
summer 2014, pp 46–51

Byrt, Anthony. 'Frontier spirits', *Frieze*,
issue 139, May 2011, pp 104–07

Byrt, Anthony. 'Prism break', *Mikala
Dwyer: drawing down the moon*,
Institute of Modern Art, Brisbane,
2012, pp 7–14

Chapman, Christopher. 'Conceptual
vertigo: new object art from Australia',
Midwest, no 6, 1994, pp 31–35

Clark-Coolee, Bronwyn. 'Holy hell!',
*Brainland: the believers: Maria Cruz,
Mikala Dwyer, Anne Ooms*, Art
Gallery of New South Wales, Sydney,
1999, np

Clemens, Justin. 'Charming an upside-
down brown snake', *Mikala Dwyer:
goldene bend'er*, Australian Centre
for Contemporary Art, Southbank,
VIC, 2013, pp 54–57

Colless, Edward. 'White', *Art + Text*,
no 48, May 1994, pp 67–68

Colless, Edward. 'Undone', *Mikala
Dwyer*, Museum of Contemporary
Art, Sydney, 2000, pp 12–13

Colless, Edward. 'On Mikala Dwyer',
*Face up: contemporary art from
Australia*, Nationalgalerie im
Hamburger Bahnhof, Museum for
the Present Berlin*, Hatje Cantz Verlag,
Berlin, 2003, p 72

Colless, Edward. 'Divine shit', *Mikala
Dwyer: goldene bend'er*, Australian
Centre for Contemporary Art,
Southbank, VIC, 2013, pp 38–42

Collins, Judith. *Sculpture today*,
Phaidon Press, London, 2007

Couacaud, Sally (ed). *Frames of
reference: aspects of feminism and
art*, Artspace Visual Arts Centre Ltd,
Surry Hills, NSW, 1991

Couderc, Sylvie and Victoria Lynn.
*Bonheur des antipodes, regards sur
l'art contemporain Australien: Mikala
Dwyer, Fiona Foley, Joe Furlonger,
James Houston, Guo Jian, Patricia
Piccinini, William Robinson, Harry
Wedge*, Musée de Picardie, Amiens,
2000

Craw, Janita and Robert Leonard.
'Inventing childhood', *Mixed-up
childhood*, Auckland Art Gallery Toi o
Tāmaki, Auckland, 2005, pp 127–67

Duncan, Michael. 'Mikala Dwyer at
Sarah Cottier', *Art in America*, vol 90,
no 2, December 2002, p 121

Dwyer, Mikala. 'Twinkle twinkle little
star: *Midwest* talks to Mikala Dwyer',
Midwest, no 8, 1995, pp 50–51

Dwyer, Mikala. Master of Fine Arts
thesis, College of Fine Arts, University
of New South Wales, Sydney, 1999,
np

Dwyer, Mikala. 'Mikala Dwyer:
500 words (as told to Anthony Byrt)',
Artforum, 15 March 2012, artforum.
com/words/id=30502 (accessed
31 August 2017)

Dwyer, Mikala, Linda Michael,
Rex Butler, et al. *Mikala Dwyer:
hollow-ware and a few solids*,
Australian Centre for Contemporary
Art, Melbourne and BARBERism,
South Yarra, VIC, 1995

Eagle, Mary. 'Discrete entity', *Art +
Text*, no 41, January 1992, pp 97–98

Engberg, Juliana. 'Mikala Dwyer',
*Home and away: contemporary
Australian and New Zealand art from
the Chartwell Collection*, Auckland
Art Gallery Toi o Tāmaki, Auckland in
association with David Bateman Ltd,
Auckland, 1999, pp 124–25

Engberg, Juliana, Annika Kristensen,
Talia Linz, Chantelle Woods. 'Mikala
Dwyer', *19th Biennale of Sydney: you
imagine what you desire*, Biennale of
Sydney, Woolloomooloo, NSW, 2014,
pp 132–33

Fenner, Felicity. 'Lowly grunge meets
high pop', *Sydney Morning Herald*,
8 May 1993, p 50

Fenner, Felicity. 'Coming up: the
lowdown art of Mikala Dwyer', *Art &
Australia*, vol 31, no 2, summer 1993,
pp 227–31

Forsyth, Graham. 'Monster field', *Art
+ Text*, no 46, September 1993, p 74

Gawronski, Alex. 'Mikala Dwyer',
Like, no 9, winter 1999, pp 58–59

Genocchio, Benjamin. 'Mikala Dwyer:
woops', *eyeline*, no 25, spring 1994,
p 41

Giblin, Tessa. *Mikala Dwyer: panto
collapsar*, Project Arts Centre, Dublin,
2012, np

Giblin, Tessa (ed). *Hall of half-life*,
Steirischer herbst, Graz, Austria 2015

Gibson, Jeff. 'Avant-grunge', *Art +
Text*, no 45, May 1993, pp 23–25

Hansford, Pamela. 'Enigma machines',
Mikala Dwyer: goldene bend'er,
Australian Centre for Contemporary
Art, Southbank, VIC, 2013, pp 48–53

Notes

Mikala Dwyer:
A shape of thought
Wayne Tunnicliffe

1_ Mikala Dwyer wrote this in the catalogue for the *Primavera* exhibition she curated in 2014 at the Museum of Contemporary Art Australia, describing the 'filters' that are important to her when looking at art; *Primavera 2014: young Australian artists*, exh cat, Museum of Contemporary Art Australia, Sydney, 2014, p 5.

2_ Susan Rothnie, 'Mikala Dwyer in conversation with Susan Rothnie', *eyeline*, no 55, spring 2004, p 30.

3_ In the late 1980s and early 1990s a recession occurred in many economies closely linked to the United States of America, including Australia; the latter was famously referred to by then prime minister Paul Keating in 1990 as 'the recession that Australia had to have'.

4_ Mikala Dwyer, Master of Fine Arts thesis, College of Fine Arts, University of New South Wales, Sydney, 2000, p 2, np. The 1992 *Primavera* exhibition (2 September – 13 December 1992) was curated by Linda Michael and initiated a long-term engagement between the curator and artist; Dwyer's *Primavera* installation, *Untitled* 1992, was the first of her works to enter a museum collection when the Museum of Contemporary Art Australia purchased it in 1995.

5_ Mikala Dwyer, *Untitled* 1993, exhibited in *Australian perspecta 1993*, Art Gallery of New South Wales, Sydney, 6 October – 28 November 1993; Christo and Jeanne-Claude, *Wrapped vestibule, Christo*, Kaldor Public Art Project, Art Gallery of New South Wales, Sydney, 12 September – 25 November 1990.

6_ Dwyer, Master of Fine Arts thesis, p 3.

7_ These exhibitions were all artist-curated: *Rad scunge*, Karyn Lovegrove Gallery, Melbourne, 3–26 March 1993, curated by Dale Frank; *Shirthead*, Mori Annexe, Sydney, 7–21 May 1993, curated by Hany Armanious (and described by critic Jane Rankin-Reid as 'a show that may herald a much needed generational defilement of the establishment, let alone the avant-garde of this town', in 'Shirthead', *Art + Text*, no 46, September 1993, p 78); and *Monster field*, Ivan Dougherty Gallery, Sydney, 6–29 May 1993, curated by ADS Donaldson.

8_ Jeff Gibson, 'Avant-grunge', *Art + Text*, no 45, May 1993, pp 23–25; Douglas Coupland, *Generation X: tales for an accelerated culture*, St Martin's Griffin, New York, 1991.

9_ Other artists exhibiting in the 1980s using everyday materials include John Nixon and Robert MacPherson, who painted onto materials such as fabric and masonite, and Maria Kozic, who made installations from diverse materials including found pop-culture objects. The Annandale Imitation Realists were Mike Brown, Ross Crothall and Colin Lanceley. In their individual and collaborative works they used found urban detritus gathered from the streets of Sydney's inner west during the years 1961–64. There is a much longer history in Australia of everyday materials used by painters, and in collage and assemblage works, stretching back to the 1930s and paralleling developments in international modernism.

10_ While many commentators cite Hesse and Bourgeois, Toni Ross gives a more expansive and useful list of other sculptors with whose works Dwyer's can be associated: 'Eva Hesse, Louise Bourgeois, Robert Smithson, Claes Oldenburg with Coosje van Bruggen, Franz West, and Joseph Beuys.' Toni Ross, 'Embodied reason, functionalist magic, animate objects', in *Mikala Dwyer: drawing down the moon*, exh cat, Institute of Modern Art, Brisbane, 2014, p 85.

11_ 'Considerations of gravity become as important as those of space. The focus on matter and gravity as means results in forms that were not projected in advance. Considerations of ordering are necessarily casual and imprecise and unemphasized. Random piling, loose stacking, hanging, give passing form to the material. Chance is accepted and indeterminacy is implied, since replacing will result in another configuration.' Robert Morris, 'Anti form', *Artforum*, April 1968, p 35.

12_ Examples of this aesthetic include fashion designer Pierre Cardin's silver suits for men in 1968 and the camp futurism of Paco Rabanne's costumes for Jane Fonda in the film *Barbarella* (1968).

13_ *The silvering* was exhibited in the exhibition *Square cloud compound*, Hamish Morrison Galerie, Berlin, 10 September – 23 October 2010; *The silvering*, Anna Schwartz Gallery, Melbourne, 8 July – 13 August 2011; *Panto collapsar*, Project Arts Centre, Dublin, 27 January – 31 March 2012; *Mikala Dwyer: drawing down the moon*, Institute of Modern Art, Brisbane, 18 February – 14 April 2012; *The end of the 20th century. The best is yet to come. A dialogue with the Marx Collection*, Hamburger Bahnhof, Berlin, 14 September 2013 – 27 April 2014 (on display in a room of Andy Warhol paintings); and *Triple point of matter*, Fondation Fiminco, Paris, 25–26 February 2017.

14_ *Primavera 1992*, Museum of Contemporary Art Australia, Sydney, 2 September – 13 December 1992; *woops*, Sarah Cottier Gallery, Sydney, 8 June – 12 July 1994; *Aerphost*, Debtors' Prison, Dublin, June–July 1996; *Recent old work*, Sarah Cottier Gallery, Sydney, 30 October – 23 November 1996; *Olloodoo*, collaboration with Olive Corben Dwyer, in *Beauty 2000*, Institute of Modern Art, Brisbane, 2 July – 1 August 1998; *Iffytown* 1999 and *Hanging eyes* 1999, first exhibited in *Uniform*, Sarah Cottier Gallery, Sydney, 14 April – 15 May 1999 and now in the collection of the Art Gallery of New South Wales; *Hanging eyes 2* 2000, in the collection of the National Gallery of Victoria, Melbourne; and *The additions and the subtractions* series (see footnote 21 for the exhibitions that comprise this series).

15_ Dwyer's excessive gathering of O's has an eerie quality, enhanced by the title of the work which echoes Stephen King's psychological horror book *The shining* (1977), made into a film of the same name in 1980.

16_ *Square cloud compound* was previously at Hamish Morrison Galerie, Berlin, 10 September – 23 October 2010; *Encounters*, Art Basel Hong Kong, 13–17 March 2015; *Magnetism*, Hazelwood, Sligo, Ireland, 28 June – 27 September 2015; and the Museum of Contemporary Art Australia, Sydney, 21 December 2015 – 21 February 2016.

17_ The targets recall the mid-twentieth-century paintings of Jasper Johns and Kenneth Noland, among other American painters. *Untitled* 1995 is now in the collection of the Museum of Contemporary Art Australia and was originally exhibited in *Hollow-ware and a few solids*, Sarah Cottier Gallery, Sydney, 14 October – 18 November 1995.

18_ Mikala Dwyer, 2004, quoted on the Museum of Contemporary Art Australia website, mca.com.au/collection/work/1997.13/ (accessed 17 July 2017).

19_ *woops*, Sarah Cottier Gallery, Sydney, 8 June – 12 July 1994; *Hollow-ware and a few solids*, Sarah Cottier Gallery, Sydney, 14 October – 18 November 1995.

20_ Dwyer collaborated with Justene Williams on two video works filmed on Cockatoo Island: *Captain Thunderbolt's sisters* 2010 and *Red rockers* 2010. The former addressed a specific legend about an imprisoned bushranger who escaped from the island in 1863. Dwyer also made the large circle work, *An apparition of a subtraction* 2010, for the Biennale of Sydney on Cockatoo Island, 12 May – 10 August 2010.

21_ *Black sun, blue moon*, Hamish Morrison Galerie, Berlin, 3 February – 3 March 2007; *Monoclinic*, Hamish McKay Gallery, Wellington, New Zealand, 2 February – 2 March 2008; *Outfield*, Roslyn Oxley9 Gallery, Sydney, 17 September – 10 October 2009; *An apparition of a subtraction*, 17th Biennale of Sydney, 12 May – 10 August 2010; *Panto collapsar*, Project Arts Centre, Dublin, 27 January – 31 March 2012.

22_ Mikala Dwyer, '500 words' (as told to Anthony Byrt), *Artforum*, 15 March 2012, artforum.com/words/id=30502 (accessed 31 August 2017).

23_ Dwyer has held lecturer positions at the University of Western Sydney (1995–99) and Sydney College of the Arts, University of Sydney (1999 – continuing). She cites as influences Fröbel's theories on childhood education, Jiddu Krishnamurti's ideas on world education, and various innovative teaching programs at the Bauhaus, Black Mountain College, North Carolina and Open School East, Margate, and well as her own experience of working in art schools for twenty-five years.

24_ The reduced geometric sculptural forms of these playing blocks are thought to have influenced early modernist artists and architects, including Frank Lloyd Wright and the Bauhaus movement. For a fruitful discussion of Dwyer's work in relation to the theories of children's play and object relations developed by psychoanalyst DW Winnicott, see Ross 2014 and Victoria Barker, 'Seeing a world through the eyes of a child on a mountaintop', *Mikala Dwyer: black sun blue moon*, Spielhaus Morrison Galerie, Berlin, 2007, pp 1–6.

25_ *Goldene bend'er*, Australian Centre for Contemporary Art, Melbourne, 25 May – 28 July 2013, with opening night performance on Friday 24 May 2013. The setting for the performance – including the somewhat cursorily cleaned seats – remained on display throughout the exhibition, with a video of the performance projected in the room.

26_ The negative reaction included Liberal Party senator Eric Abetz raising questions about 'decency' and 'common sense' at a Senate Budget Estimates hearing. For an account of the reaction to Dwyer's performance, see Brad Haylock, 'Goldene bend'er: Mikala Dwyer', *Vault Magazine*, issue 4, August 2013, pp 10–11; and Van Badham, 'Who's afraid of the art boogie monster?', *The Guardian* (Australia), 13 June 2013, theguardian.com/commentisfree/2013/jun/13/chris-berg-art-theatre-australia (accessed 18 July 2017).

27_ 'Mikala Dwyer walks Robert Leonard through *Drawing down the moon*', in *Mikala Dwyer: drawing down the moon*, p 57.

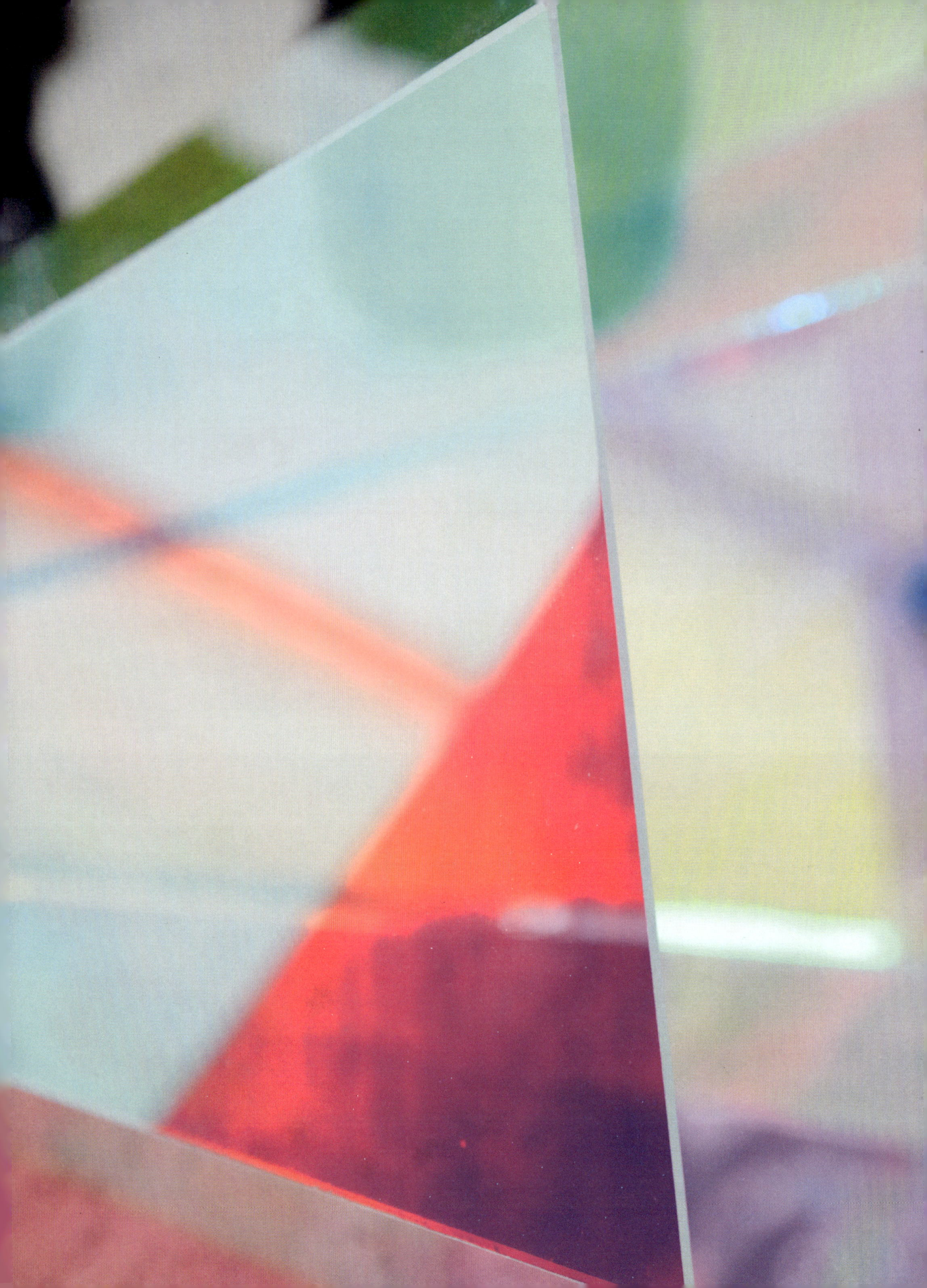

Photo credits
All photos are courtesy of
the Mikala Dwyer Studio unless
otherwise attributed.

pp 11, 62–63: Ivan Buljan
pp 12, 36–37: Ray Woodbury
pp 13, 38–39, 40–45: Ashley Barber
p 16: Shaun Waugh
p 18 above: Erling Lykke Jeppesen,
Teksas; below: Andrew Curtis
pp 27, 29, 30, 69, 81, 86–89:
Jessica Maurer
pp 19–25, 28, 32, 104, 108–43:
Art Gallery of New South Wales,
Mim Stirling
pp 34–35: Marco del Grande
pp 46–47: Ann Collins
pp 48–49: Art Gallery of New South
Wales, Diana Panuccio
pp 54–55, 66–67: Jens Sehr
pp 60–61: Nick Banks
pp 64–65: Ivan Buljan; performance:
Kelly Doley
pp 70–71: Carl Warner and Richard
Stringer
pp 72–73: courtesy Projects Arts
Centre
pp 76–77: Andrew Curtis;
performance: Alejandra Canales
p 79: Erling Lykke Jeppesen, Teksas
pp 82–83: Alejandra Canales
pp 84–85: courtesy of Mikala Dwyer
and Graz Museum
p 91: Ruth E Lyons
p 91: Charles Duprat
p 92: Sofia Freeman
p 107: Art Gallery of New South
Wales, Jenni Carter; artwork in
background: Georg Baselitz *Oven soot*
2015, oil on canvas. On loan to Art
Gallery of New South Wales from
Geoff Ainsworth AM

cover detail:
Sigil for heaven and earth 2015,
**Puzzle (after Piet Hein / Kumbel
Kumbell)** 2015, **Posession** 2015
see pages 130, 132–33, 135

page 143:
Square cloud compound 2010
(detail) see pages 113–16

endpapers:
The divisions and subtractions
2017 (detail) see pages 125–29

Published by Art Gallery of
New South Wales
Art Gallery Road, The Domain
Sydney 2000, Australia
artgallery.nsw.gov.au

© 2018 Art Gallery of
New South Wales

The Art Gallery of New South Wales
is a statutory body of the NSW State
Government

A catalogue record for this book
is available from the
National Library of Australia
ISBN 97874174360

Publishing manager: Julie Donaldson*
Text editor: Claire Armstrong
Rights and permissions: Michelle
Andringa*
Select bibliography: Nick Yelverton*
Exhibition photography: Mim Stirling*
Design: Analiese Cairis*
Production: Cara Hickman*
Prepress: Spitting Image, Sydney
Printed in Hong Kong by
Australian Book Connection
* AGNSW

Mikala Dwyer is supported by a
Visual Arts Fellowship administered
by the National Association for the
Visual Arts (NAVA) and funded
through the Copyright Agency's
Cultural Fund; the Australian
government through the Australia
Council, its arts funding and advisory
body; and Carriageworks and
Urbangrowth NSW through The
Clothing Store Artist Studio program.

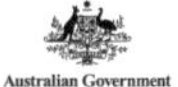 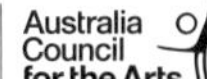
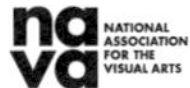 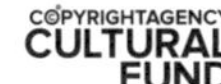

Mikala Dywer: A shape of thought
exhibition sponsor

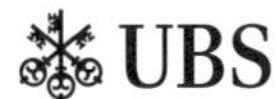

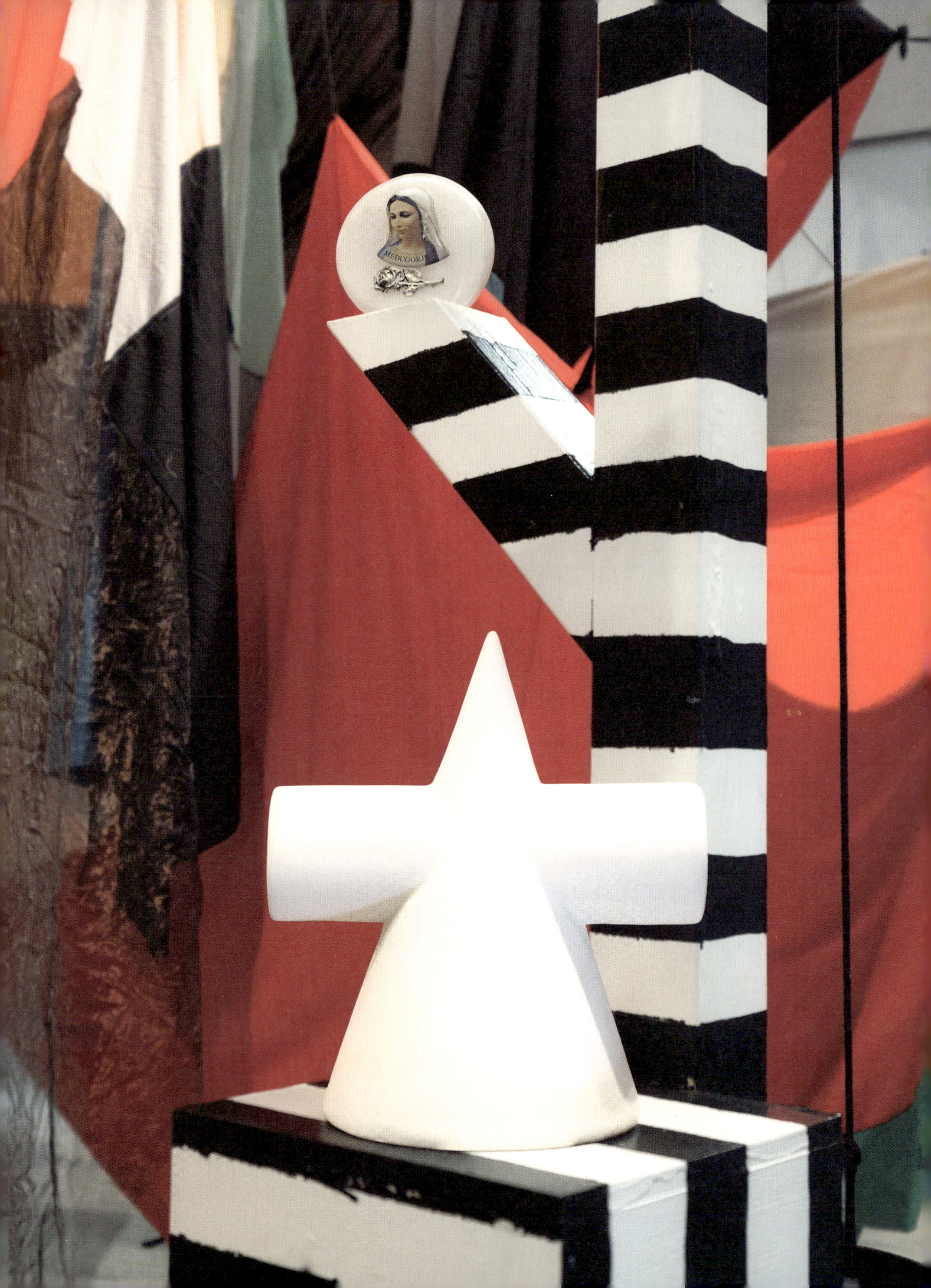
MEĐUGORJE

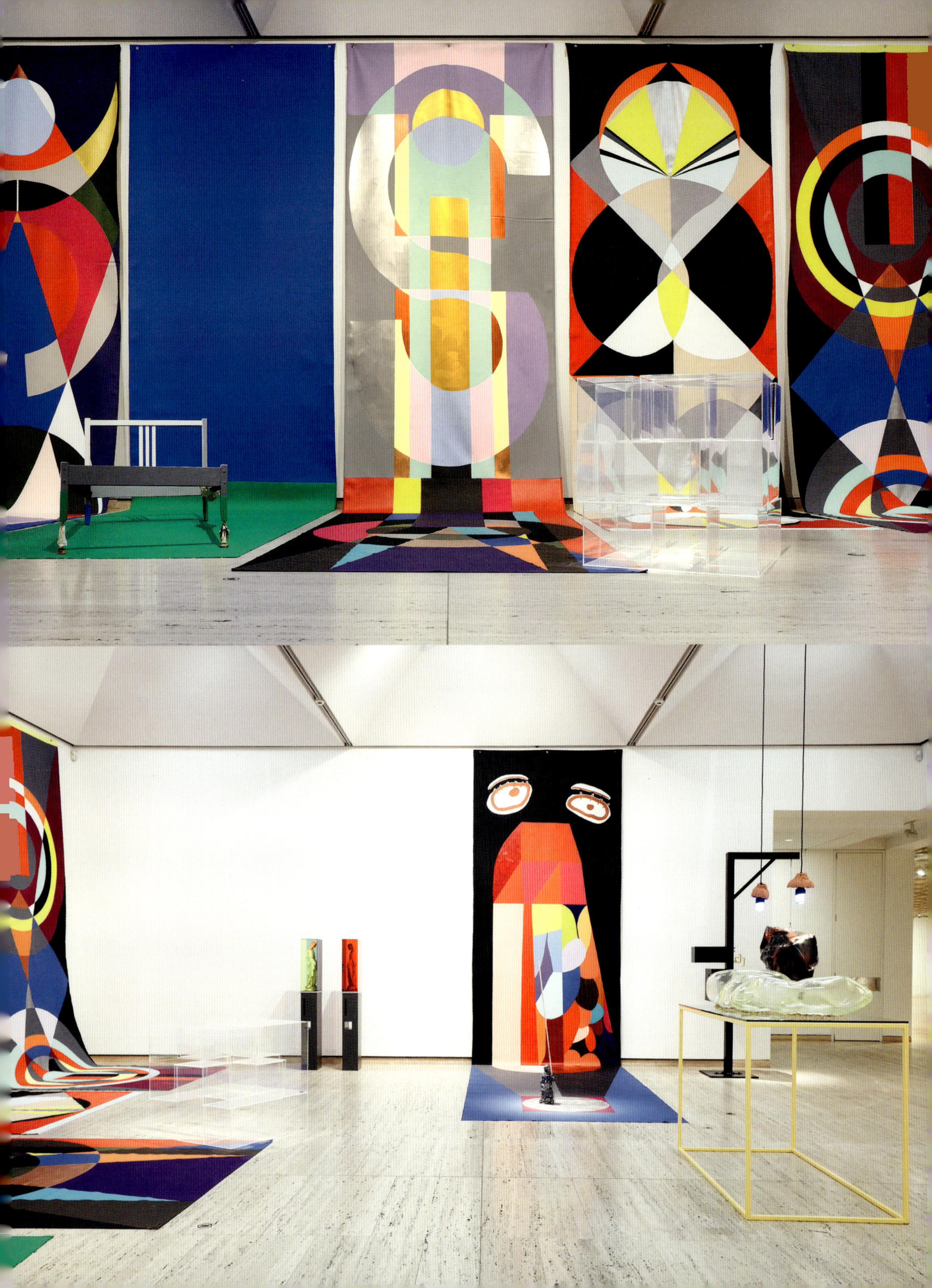

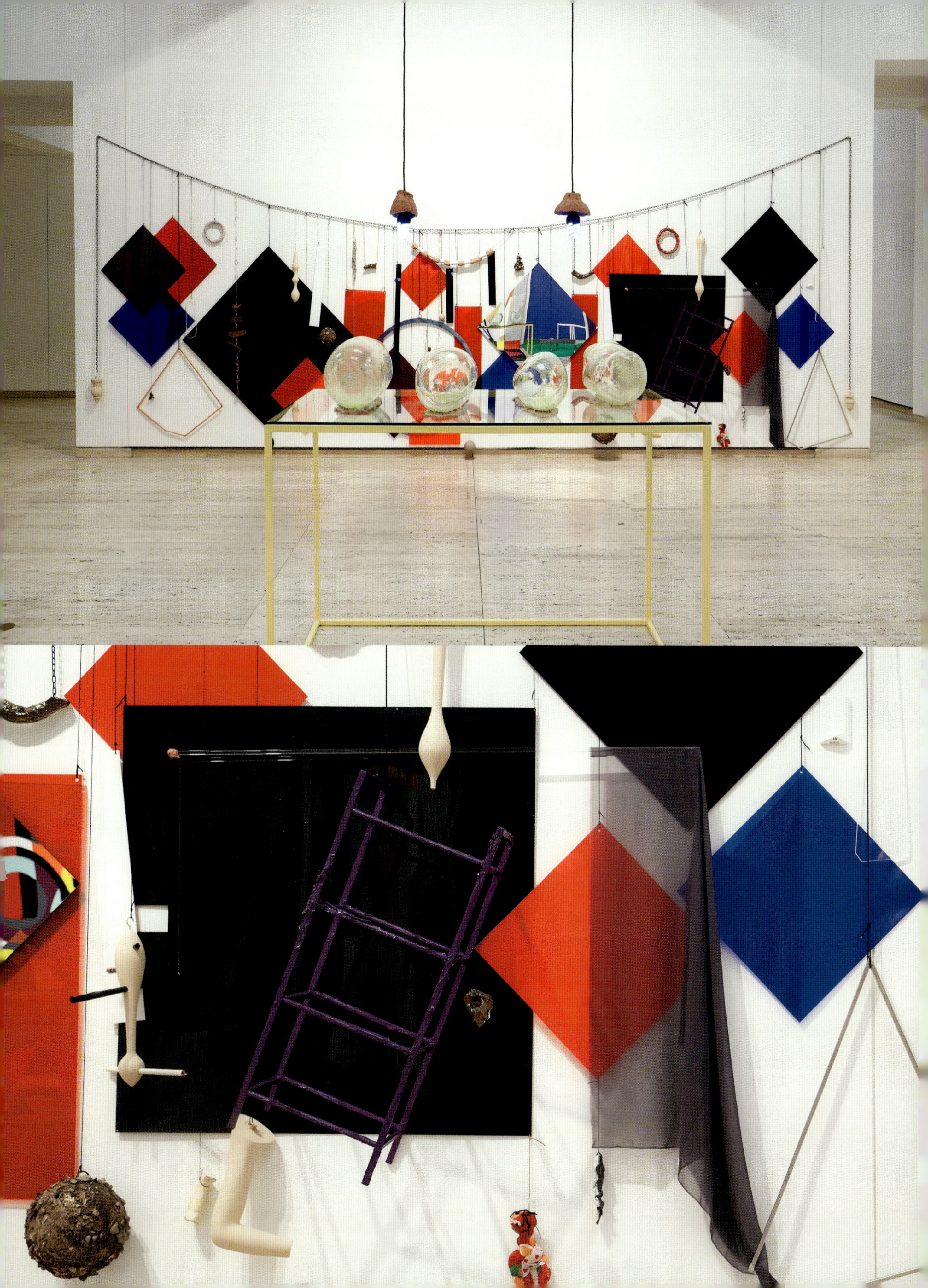

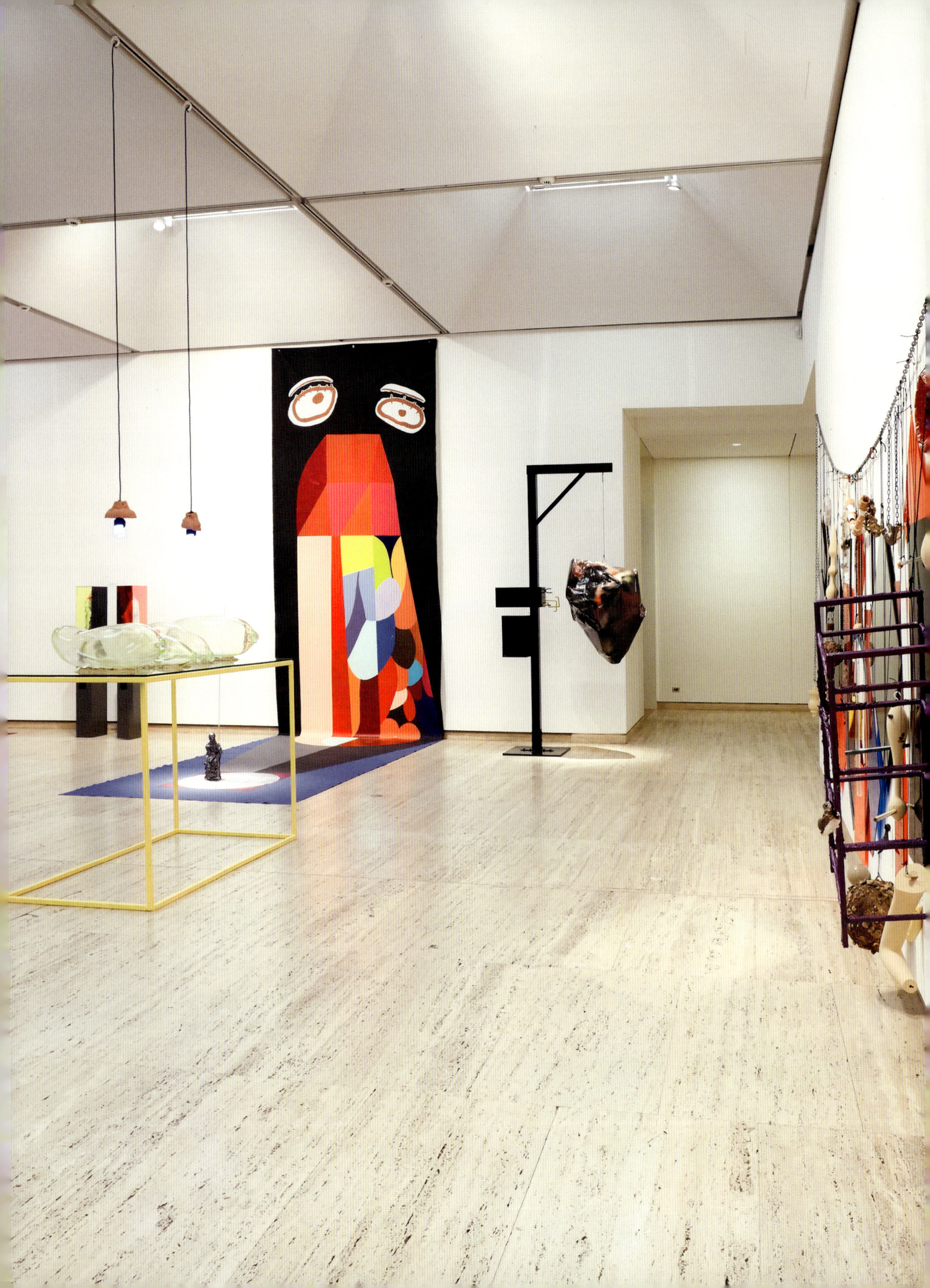